The Apollo M

Hiding a Hoax in Plain Sight

Part II

First Edition
Copyright © 2021 by Randy Walsh
ISBN#9781792117718

No part of this publication may be reproduced, broadcast, transmitted, distributed or displayed; except for brief quotations in reviews without prior written permission

Note: The author has made every effort to make sure that the quotations from literary and artistic works of other authors made in this work are within limits of fair practice as defined by Article 10 of the Berne Convention for the protection of Literary and Artistic Work.

All quotes and pictures used to the extent allowed by fair use. Should any copyright issues arise, or you just want to make a comment, please connect with the author, Randy Walsh at:

authorrandywalsh.com

authorrandy@hotmail.com

@authorrandywalsh

- Cover Page: The images have been cropped and edited digitally to fit the book layout.
- Photo Credits: NASA, Wikipedia, Wikimedia & Aulis.com

Table Of Contents

Introduction	7
Chapter One - Strange Detour: Jack Parsons, His World Of Rockets, The Occult, And His Influence On NASA	12
Welcome To The World Of Jack Parsons	13
History	16
Jack Parsons' World By Day	19
The Suicide Squad	23
Jack Parsons' World By Night	30
Aleister Crowley, The Great Beast	31
Ordo Templi Orientis	34
Jack Parsons' Worlds Collide	35
His Final Act And Demise	38
Jack Parsons' Legacy	39
An Intriguing Connection	43
In Conclusion	44
Chapter Two - The Pre-Apollo Moon Missions	51
The Manned Missions	53
The X-15 Program	54
Project Mercury	55
Project Gemini	58

The Unmanned Missions	63
The Ranger Program	63
The Lunar Orbiter Program	65
Comparison Of Photos For Ranger, Lunar Orbiter, And Lunar Reconnaissance Orbiter	70
The Surveyor Program	74
The Pegasus Program	76
Determining Success For The Apollo Moon Missions	76
Failures And Successes Of The Manned Mercury And Gemini Missions	77
Failures And Successes Of The Unmanned Missions	78
A Realistic Outcome Of The Apollo Moon Missions	79
Aviation, You Say	81
Chapter Three - Options For Manned Lunar Landing Methods - Preposterous, Irrational, And Bizarre Ideas	87
A Preposterous Idea	87
An Irrational Idea	90
Bizarre Ideas NASA Considered Viable	91
Direct Ascent	95
Earth Orbit Rendezvous	97
Lunar Orbit Rendezvous	101
The Lunar Module	106

Chapter Four - The Apollo Moon Landings   122
Lunar Training Vehicles, Fiction, And Reality

Lunar Landing Research Vehicle (LLRV)   126
     Total Number Of Flights And Flight   130
     Times For The LLRV
     Flight Times For The Astronauts In The   131
     LLRV

Lunar Landing Training Vehicle (LLTV)   132
     Total Number Of Flights And Flight   133
     Times For The LLTV
     Flight Times For The Astronauts In The   134
     LLTV

Problems With The LLRV And LLTV   134
     LLRV And LLTV Accidents   136
     Glaring Differences Between LLRV,   138
     LLTV, And The LM

Inadequate Astronaut Training In The LLRV,   140
LLTV, And The Lunar Module Simulator

Apollo 11 Lunar Landing And Liftoff - The   143
Official Version
     The LM Descent   143
     Descent Orbit Insertion   144
     The LM Liftoff   149

Apollo 11 Lunar Landing And Liftoff - The   150
Reality
     Analysis Of The LM Descent To Landing   153
     Intentional Errors   159
     Analysis Of The LM Liftoff   161

The Film Footage Of The LM Liftoff   162

Missing LM Documents	169
Two Businessmen And A Fake Lunar Module	170
Chapter Five - Re-entry Into Earth's Atmosphere, The Final Phase	**177**
History Of Spacecraft Re-entry Methods	179
The Apollo Command Module Re-entry Heatshield and Test Missions	184
Re-entry, The Official Version	187
Parachutes, The Only Solution	188
Re-entry, The Reality	191
Skip Re-entry Versus Direct Entry	194
To Skip, Or Not To Skip, That Is The Question	195
Passengers And Crew Onboard Aircraft Witness Apollo CM Re-entries	199
Passengers And Crew Describe What They Saw	200
Taking Apart The Official Witness Narrative	205
Tactics Used For Deception	208
Comparing The Official Re-entry Data, To What The Passengers And Crew Saw	209
What The Passengers And Crew Actually Saw	212
The Apollo CM Re-entry Hoax Revealed	214
In Conclusion	217

Chapter Six - The Odyssey Of It All   220
The Russians and Apollo 13's Real Journey, The JFK Assassination Connection, And Simulation - The Only Way

The Russians Capture An Apollo Command Module	221
The Russian Submarine Connection	224
Rendezvous With The Russians	229
The Real Agenda, Rendezvous In Space	237
Apollo 13 Versus Apollo 13	240
The JFK Assassination Connection	242
An Analysis Of The Official Version	246
Assassination Teams	254
Those Pesky Freemasons	261
Cold War Politics	264
The Psychological Factor	270
Simulation And The Apollo Missions	278
Conclusion	285
Appendix A - Marcus Allen	290
Appendix B - Robert Williams	294
Appendix C - TJ Hegland	299
Appendix D - Scott Henderson	304
Appendix E - Phil Kouts, PhD	317
Appendix F - Emanuel E. Garcia, M.D.	321
Glossary	326
Bibliography - Books	328
Bibliography - Internet Sources	331

Introduction

In Part I of this series, we discussed Operation Paperclip, which involved recruiting NAZI scientists at the end of World War II including Wernher von Braun, who was apparently a brilliant rocket scientist and the first director of the Marshall Space Flight Center, and chief architect of the design and construction of the Saturn rocket. Along with von Braun, a lot of these NAZI scientists were recruited to work for the National Aeronautics and Space Administration (NASA) on the Apollo space program.

However, the main focus of Part 1 was the Apollo 11 Mission, which included an analysis of the technology used in which it was determined that this technology was not adequate for any Apollo mission, especially beyond Low Earth Orbit (LEO). Further, it was shown that NASA's data regarding the space environment beyond LEO was either incomplete or in conflict with scientific institutions. Precise data would have been vital if there was to be any chance of success with the Apollo Moon missions. It was also determined that many of the documents related to the Apollo Moon program are missing and/or destroyed.

In Part II of this series, we will start with an intriguing and rather strange history in the aerospace industry, by introducing a brilliant rocket scientist, Jack Parsons. He was not directly involved with NASA given that it was formed years after his demise. However, Parsons' work paved the road to technology that was used in the Apollo Moon missions, the Space Shuttle, and the aerospace industry in general, which is still in use today. But as already established in Part I of this series, the Apollo Moon landings did not happen, and the technology for manned missions in LEO had its limitations, which does not diminish the accomplishments of Jack Parsons. But what is obvious, is that the aerospace industry hasn't been able to build on this technology and move forward, over the last 5 decades.

For the last decade, NASA has relied on Russia and its manned space program to launch its astronauts to the International Space Station, while it constantly tried to catch up as to where it left off, let alone build on technologies they claim to have once perfected. However, NASA has since contracted Space Exploration Technology Corp. (SpaceX), which is a private company founded by Elon Musk, to supply its manned launch capabilities. SpaceX launched its first manned mission with two NASA astronauts onboard the Falcon 9 rocket and Dragon spacecraft to LEO on May 30, 2020, which then docked with the International Space Station. So, it took a private company to catch up to where NASA left off after the Space Shuttle was retired in 2011.

We then continued on in Part I with the general theme of analysing the technology of the Apollo 11 mission, to show that this technology was in no way capable of sending manned missions to the Moon and back.

In Part II, we'll continue with our analysis of the Apollo 11 mission as well as some other rather interesting aspects of NASA, and its manned space program in general. This will include the many methods discussed and considered in sending manned missions to the Moon, including simulation and the training aspects of the Apollo missions.

In **Chapter 1**, we discuss the brilliant and eccentric rocket scientist, Jack Parsons. He actually had three first names, some of which may appear in quotes. But aside from the quotes, we'll stay with his more commonly known name, Jack Parsons. In many ways, Jack Parsons was a mystery to some and a compassionate and brilliant scientist to others. But regardless of what impression others may have had, Parson's importance to the aerospace industry is obvious, given that his methods are still used in rockets today. We'll discuss his involvement in the world of the occult, which may explain why NASA is hesitant in talking about this man. We'll also learn of some interesting facts that show Parsons may have had some involvement with American intelligence agencies, including a very intriguing connection to a well-known individual, who became prominent two decades later in the Apollo program.

In **Chapter 2**, we'll discuss the pre-Apollo missions, which had more to do with gathering data to fake the Apollo missions, rather than any preparations for an actual manned lunar landing. These included unmanned as well as manned missions to LEO. But the emphasis will be on the unmanned missions, which are interesting for several reasons, including their involvement in surveying and photographing the lunar surface. We can then use both the unmanned and manned missions to make an approximate determination of failure or success with the Apollo missions, especially as it applies to a hostile environment in which scientists knew little about back then. Further, we'll make comparisons of photos of the lunar surface from unmanned missions in the 1960s, to photos of the alleged Apollo Moon landing sites from the Lunar Reconnaissance Orbiter in 2009. The comparisons of the photos will raise questions as to why NASA seemingly couldn't produce the same photo detail in the 1960s, to that of the photos produced in 2009 of the alleged Apollo lunar landing sites.

In **Chapter 3**, we'll discuss some of the ideas that NASA had considered for manned missions to the Moon. Some of these ideas were grandiose and others, were just downright comical. We'll learn too of the competition and conflicts over some of these ideas, and how this was less to do with any real exploration and research, and more to do with politics. But as you'll learn, politics may have had less to do with obstructing progress in manned missions to the Moon as some proponents have contended, and more to do with the realization that the technology needed would have required decades of research.

Further, we'll discuss the design of the Lunar Module (LM) and the shoddy work and poor-quality control in its construction. Given this fact alone, few would need convincing that the only environment in which this spacecraft performed admirably, was in a film studio.

In **Chapter 4**, we discuss in great detail the training aspect of the Apollo astronauts for the actual landing on the Moon. We'll start with the training flying vehicle that was designed to simulate lunar surface gravity during portions of its flight. As we'll learn, this vehicle was plagued with problems which required more time and effort just to keep it flying in Earth's atmosphere, let alone in the $1/6^{th}$ gravity of the lunar surface it was designed to simulate. And included in this chapter, is a detailed analysis of the purported landing of the Apollo 11 LM on the lunar surface. We'll learn that any attempt to land the LM, would have been impossible or better put, a complete disaster and that's if it even managed to stay in one piece during launch, and the many elements both the LM and Command Module (CM) would have encountered beyond low Earth orbit. Further, we'll discuss a very comical business venture that involved the LM, which could have inadvertently revealed the hoax if these businessmen had their way, but did reveal some very interesting facts about the contractor that designed and built the LM.

In **Chapter 5**, we discuss some history of re-entry methods into Earth's atmosphere, and then continues with a discussion on the Apollo CM re-entry heatshield and test missions. We then look at the official version versus the reality of re-entry procedures, including the various methods NASA claims were used. However, what becomes revealing in this chapter, is the deception that NASA employed in selling the official narrative, which involved simulating an Apollo CM re-entry. This in turn, involved setting up witnesses and using the media to further the deception. The research on this alone, proved to be very enlightening as to some of the tactics used to manipulate people into either believing the official narrative and/or complying with any government policy or edict.

In **Chapter 6**, we discuss more of the tactics used by NASA to deceive the American people and the world. This involves some very interesting Cold War tactics or at least, that is what was presented in the media. But the real story may be something else entirely. From here, we discuss a controversial subject, one that many researchers have avoided as having any connection at all to the Apollo Moon missions and that is, President John F. Kennedy and his assassination. And finally, we'll briefly discuss the simulation aspect to the Apollo Moon missions and show how sophisticated the Apollo simulators were, which were used to help manipulate the public into believing that these missions were real.

While researching the Apollo missions, I learned of several researchers who have made an enormous contribution to exposing the Apollo Moon mission hoax. I was so impressed with their work, that I've added an appendix to introduce these individuals who have researched other aspects of the Apollo missions, including the anomalies in the photographic and film record. The Apollo missions have been called, "Man's greatest scientific accomplishment." However, these researchers use their expertise and skills from a variety of academic disciplines and/or professions, to offer their perspective on what is now becoming, "Man's greatest scientific deception."

In this book, I continue to expose NASA's deception with the Apollo Moon Missions.

Enjoy the ride!

Chapter One

Strange Detour:

Jack Parsons, His World Of Rockets, The Occult, And His Influence On NASA

By day Parsons' unorthodox genius created a solid rocket fuel that helped the Allies win World War II and NASA send spacecraft to the Moon.

By night, Parsons called himself the Antichrist when he performed Aleister Crowley's Thelemic rituals to create a new sort of human being that would finally destroy Christianity.

Author, John Carter

I found some very interesting information on Jack Parsons, who was purported to have been a brilliant rocket scientist. I wrote this chapter according to the two sources I cite in this book, giving them the benefit of the doubt that their information is correct, since it's difficult to verify a lot of it. However, while you're reading this chapter, you'll see more than a few hints that the full story about Parsons may not as of yet, been written. Therefore, I leave it up to the readers to decide for themselves as to whether they see the need to go beyond the official narrative of this rather, interesting and colorful character. However, the official narrative for Jack Parsons makes for some very interesting reading on its own, given his influence on rocket science.

Further, this chapter does not go into details on the occult and masonic aspect of NASA, which has been written about by numerous authors. However, it does mention Parsons' connection to the strange world of the occult, which may in part, explain why this man's name is nowhere near the forefront of the aerospace industry, given that his theories contributed to the success of unmanned as well as manned space missions, including that of the Space Shuttle program.

Welcome To The World Of Jack Parsons

A little-known history among the general public is that of the brilliant rocket scientist, Jack Parsons. And as per the quote under the chapter title, there were two sides to Parsons, his world of rockets by day and his world of the occult by night. In addition, these very same people will be surprised to learn that Parsons' passion for rocketry practically paved the road to rocket technology that is still in use today. This is all the more amazing, given that Parson's formal education was no more than a high school diploma.

His theories were incorporated into the overall design of rocket technology in general, which included the Apollo Moon missions (all of which went no further than Low Earth Orbit, if even that, as has been established in Part I of this series), and the Space Shuttle, which was retired in 2011. And in his spare time, Parsons, with an equal amount of passion, studied the world of the occult and the works of the well-known Satanist, Aleister Crowley with whom he maintained a close correspondence. His world of the occult eventually becomes his driving force which is apparent later on in his career, with many coincidences along the way that seem beyond belief.

Author John Carter:

> In an ominous coincidence, Charles Taze Russell, whose "Russellites" now call themselves the Jehovah's Witnesses, predicted the end of the world would happen on October 2, 1914, the day of John Parsons' birth, and just a couple of months after the start of World War I. When Russell announced to his congregation in Brooklyn, New York, that the end had begun, he meant the finale was not an instantaneous end to all things, but rather the beginning of the end as outlined in the Book of Revelation – the appearance of the Antichrist and the harlot, Babylon the Great, being two of the key events. It is ironic that John Parsons, who would later attempt to incarnate Babylon and who would also sign an oath stating that he was the Antichrist, was born the very day of Russell's eschatological event.[1]

NASA tends to be hesitant in its recognition of Jack Parsons, presumably due to his unorthodox background and the fact that he wasn't the usual academic or trained scientist. But there is some information about Parsons on NASA's website, though very little, given his contribution to the aerospace industry.

Parsons had the look of a man who could easily have been mistaken for a Hollywood actor, rather than the usual look of the studious scientist deep in thought in a classroom or lecture hall writing down equations on a blackboard. Further, it's not often that a man who not only lacked the recognized academic credentials but was also a passionate pursuer of the occult, would have the influence that he did on the whole area of rocket propulsion systems. This included the fact that he not only co-founded the Aerojet Corporation, later named the Jet Propulsion Laboratory, but also had a lunar crater named after him.

Figure 1.1- Jack Parsons
Source: Wikimedia

However, as will be discussed, Jack Parsons' world by day, would eventually come in contact with his world by night. He would slowly move away from the industry he so passionately devoted most of his career to and immerse himself in the world of the occult with equal passion. Ironically, he would eventually find himself working in the film industry, not as an actor, but in the area of special effects. But as you'll learn, both his worlds would inevitably collide, bringing an instant and early end to the world of Jack Parsons.

This is a man who is just now being revered for his contribution to an industry dominated by the appearance of the stereotypical looking, suited, dark rimmed glasses academics.

History

Jack Parsons was born in Los Angeles on October 2, 1914. Soon afterwards in 1915, Jack's parents, Marvel and Ruth Parsons divorced. He saw little of his father in years to come. This would haunt Jack for the rest of his life, compounded by the fact that he always strived to find that father figure he so longed for. It has often been said that brilliance and genius go hand in hand with emotional turmoil, leading to a complicated, insecure, sometimes insensitive and eccentric human being, which aptly describes the brilliant Jack Parsons.

After Jack's parents divorced, his mother Ruth had agreed with her wealthy parents Walter and Carrie Whiteside that they should live together for the sake of young Jack. The Whiteside's moved to Los Angeles and bought a home in the posh town of Pasadena. Jack was fortunate enough to grow up in a wealthy environment with servants, which gave him plenty of time for his wild and young imagination to flourish. It wasn't long before he came across Jules Verne and his classic book *'From the Earth to the Moon.'* This is a story about a group of

American soldiers who designed a plan to send themselves into Low Earth Orbit (LEO) and beyond on a journey to orbit the Moon. Then, the young Jack Parsons eventually found the popular magazine series *Amazing Stories,* which was the first magazine that concentrated solely on space-age fiction. Here, we see more than a hint of how this young Jack Parsons' passion for rocket technology stood out from most children his age.

There was little inspiration in the 1920s and 30s for a child fascinated by rockets, to pursue this as a career. In fact, rockets were comic book lore and although they were written about in some nonfiction articles, they were not considered part of the scientific literature and therefore, were not to be taken seriously. Further, that meant that there were no courses on rocket science in the education system available at that time, so there was no guidance for anyone wanting to pursue a path to what is now known as the aerospace industry. But that didn't deter Parsons with his passion for rockets as he was already dreaming of interplanetary travel, when most children his age were off chasing each other in hide and seek games and/or acting out their favorite movie idols.

Individuals like Jack stand out from the rest us, although to be fair, without the rest of us, there wouldn't be a society for these exceptional people to flourish. More often than not, men and women like Parsons usually defy conventional thinking and walk a path to greatness that then leads people to ponder their greatness for centuries to come. We've seen many examples of this in history in areas such as mathematics, physics, philosophy, medicine (both conventional and alternative) and music, including classical, jazz, right up to contemporary genres. You occasionally see it in politics although not so much these days, as the message to anyone who dares to have a mind of their own is usually offered a fact-based report, other than the fictional *Warren Commission Report,* for their 'reading entertainment.'

To add to Parsons' mystic, he was not exactly a stellar student. In fact, he was considered to have been below average by an education system that more often than not, misses the real intelligence and potential in students such as Parsons. The education system tends to judge intelligence on how well students memorize and regurgitate their answers on paper. It makes one wonder how many seemingly and wrongfully labelled 'unintelligent' students, have been deprived of their rightful place in history and how society has been cheated out of their brilliance and genius. And to further compound the mystic about Parsons, he was considered to have had a learning disorder. It is now called dyslexia, a disorder that causes the individual to read words in sentences in different orders or to misspell them.

Author George Pendle writes:

> Throughout his life he would misspell words, and his handwriting in particular -the words usually printed in capitals rather than written in cursive -indicates a learning disorder. At the time dyslexia was not considered a legitimate complaint and children who suffered from it were generally considered to be backward or stupid. For anyone, let alone such an avid reader as Parsons, the variable grades that resulted

from this learning disorder would have only fueled a dislike for establishment education.²

Thankfully, society is now recognizing that dyslexia is no determination of intelligence. In fact, in some cases, people with dyslexia have above average intelligence and creativity, as was apparent with Jack Parsons.

How ironic then that Jack, who was constantly being harassed and bullied in school, would be rescued on one such occasion by a fellow student who himself had dyslexia, Edward Forman. The two students would soon become lifelong friends and future collaborators in the pursuit of rocket science, producing work that would reverberate for decades to come.

If the idea of two people with dyslexia accidently meeting and then going on to make a major contribution to the aerospace industry seems coincidental, it gets even better.

Jack Parson's World By Day

A well-known rocket scientist by the name of Robert Goddard had started writing his theories down long before Jack Parsons arrived on the scene, notwithstanding the Russians. It would take another book to discuss Goddard's contribution to the world of rocketry. But where Goddard retreated into obscurity after being constantly ridiculed by the media for his theories on rocket science, Parsons was the opposite, who was much more confident, not caring all that much what people or the media had to say about it.

Parsons enrolled at Pasadena Junior College, but because of the great depression of the 1930s, their family's fortune dwindled and he was forced to drop out after one term and find work. However, 18-year-old Parsons turned this unfortunate situation into an asset when he found work at the Hercules Powder Company in Los Angeles, which was known as the largest TNT production company for the United States during World War I. It was here that Parsons began to hone his skills in the mixing of propellants that he would incorporate into his theories on rocket propulsion systems in the future. It was here too that he became an expert on chemicals and explosives, two very important aspects of rocket technology.

Parsons' friend Ed Forman also worked at the Hercules Powder Company as an apprentice and they eventually collaborated on developing rocket technology to the point where their trial-and-error approach to solving problems, now required the type of mathematical calculations that they both lacked. Even though Parsons was by no means devoid of mathematical abilities, as his papers with numerous algebraic calculations show, he lacked the necessary skills of differential calculus necessary for the complex calculations needed in rocket technology.

By chance, a set of circumstances that could only apply to Parsons and Forman, led to a direct connection to the California Institute of Technology (Caltech). Caltech needs no introduction and a quick google search will show the many famous scientists who were either students and/or employees there.

What's even more amazing is Caltech's acceptance of two seemingly uneducated individuals, Parsons and Forman, when they casually walked into this preeminent university in 1935, looking for the author of an article on *'Rocket Technology'* published in the *Los Angeles Times*. It's another example of Parsons' confidence and refusal to be intimidated by the appearance of what many would consider, academic men beyond reproach. The author's name of the article was William Bollay.

> A graduate student in aeronautics (the study of motion in air) named William Bollay had presented a paper at Caltech on the recent work of a member of the amateur Austrian Society for Rocket Technology, Eugen Sanger. Sanger, who had conducted most of his work apart from the scientific establishment and without any outside funding, spoke in strongly optimistic terms about the possibility of rockets being used to power aircraft. What the newspapers were most excited about was the mention of maximum velocities and breaching of the stratosphere.[3]

Parsons and Forman walked right into Bollay's office and introduced themselves, expressing interest in his work. But what Parsons and Forman really saw in this article, was the potential for rockets to be used other than in aircraft. For them, they saw an obvious means of leaving Earth's atmosphere for LEO. It's an example of how Parsons envisioned a future for rockets as compared to his academic contemporaries who lacked the insight of a man like Parsons, going as far as to mock those who even suggested the use of rockets in any other capacity, besides aircraft. However, some of that mocking behavior from his peers would turn out to be justified, given the present state of NASA's nonexistent manned launched capabilities to LEO, which is no fault of the brilliant Parsons.

Bollay was busy with his own research unrelated to rockets, but was impressed enough upon meeting Parsons and Forman for the first time, to recommend them to a graduate student named Frank Malina. It was this introduction that formed the team of Parsons, Forman, and Malina.

Frank Malina had studied mechanical engineering and had an interest in interplanetary spaceflight. However, at the time he met Parsons and Forman at Caltech, he was working at the Guggenheim Aeronautical Laboratory at the California Institute of Technology (GALCIT), specifically in the wind tunnel experimenting with scale model designs of aircraft submitted by several aviation companies. But he was so impressed with Parsons and Forman's work that he immediately saw the possibilities, which rekindled his own passion for rockets.

Since the 1930s was a time when rockets were not a part of any academic curriculum, this meant of course there were no scientists trained in any aspects of rocketry, or better put, there were no rocket scientists as of yet. Rockets were only taken seriously when seen on the big screen alongside Buck Rogers. This is all the more remarkable when considering the future achievement of Parsons, who had little more than a high school education, whose work would be credited with solving problems that eventually contributed to the success of the Space Shuttle program.

But at the time, Frank Malina clearly saw Parsons' potential, regardless of his lack of academic credentials.

Pendle, quotes Frank Malina:

> It seems to me that at most he had finished high school. When I met him, he already had a certain amount of experience with the manufacture of explosives…but I think what was outstanding about him was that he was not of any fixed view on which way to go…He had a very flexible sort of attitude.[4]

Soon, Parsons and Forman would be working alongside the university educated Malina at GALCIT and in the process, the team acquired its skill for differential calculus. And this "flexible sort of attitude" would soon lead Parsons and his new-found team aptly called the Suicide Squad, due to their experiments and the occasional explosions that would reverberate throughout Caltech, on a path that would bring innovative technologies for the future of the aerospace industry. These technologies were then incorporated by an industry that would benefit most from Parson's brilliance, even more so than the manned space program, that of the military industrial complex. Parsons, Forman, and Malina, would go on to influence the aerospace industry for decades to come.

The Suicide Squad

Although the Suicide Squad would add other members, Parsons, Forman, and Malina would be the foundation of this team. And now Parsons and Forman had access to GALCIT, a remarkable and unheard-of achievement despite the fact that these two seemingly uneducated members literally walked into

Caltech from the street. This meant that they had access to the laboratory's equipment regardless of the fact that Parsons and Forman were not even students, let alone formal employees of one of the most revered academic institutions in the United States. However, they soon developed a not so flattering reputation through their laboratory work which was compounded by their lack of formal education. They would never be fully accepted as equals into the 'perfect' world of Caltech, despite their obvious brilliance and their eventual acceptance by the scientific community in general.

Note: This is one of several red flags as to the official narrative regarding Jack Parsons. There are many examples of formally uneducated but very intelligent individuals, who have been written about in history. But few of these individuals have literally walked into a prestigious academic institution such as Caltech, only then to be accepted as faculty members.

Figure 1.2 - Jack Parsons and The Suicide Squad
Source: Wikimedia

However, in another of many ironies with Parsons, it wasn't his achievement in rocket technology that gave him the much-needed acceptance and recognition he deserved. It was his participation as an explosive's expert at a car bombing trial reported in the media at that time, in which his testimony won the prosecution its case against the defendant, Los Angeles Police Department Captain Earl Kynette who was eventually sentenced to San Quentin prison. It was considered a sensational news story at the time, with Parsons as the prosecution's star witness impressing everyone in the courtroom with both his brilliance and charm as reported by the media.

Parsons, Forman, and Malina went on to continue their research apparently impressing almost anyone they came in contact with. But what eluded them was a means of getting their work the wide attention and recognition it so deserved. They finally found their path, not in terms of launching rockets, but in how useful rockets would be in military aircraft.

Frank Malina had travelled to Washington D.C. to meet with the National Academy of Sciences (NAS) Committee on Army Air Corps Research to make a proposal to study Jet-Assisted Take-Off (JATO) for aircraft. As you no doubt noticed, 'Jet' had now replaced Rockets, given the mocking behavior of the scientific community when the mention of the word rocket was used. He explained to the NAS the potential for jets to boost overall aircraft performance in takeoffs, speed, and range. The NAS was impressed enough to give Parsons' Suicide Squad $1,000 to prepare a proposal. After they submitted their paper to the NAS, they were impressed enough to increase their budget to $10,000.

However, there were serious problems with the combustion of solid fuels or more specifically, the black powder used in rockets which proved to be unstable, somewhat different to what was discussed in Part 1 of this series with the liquid fueled F-1 engines. In that case, it was the ineffective cooling system which caused combustion chamber instabilities. The propellant itself was apparently stable. And there's no comparison in metal rockets with a length of two feet, with the complexity of the 9-ton F-1 rocket engine in the Saturn V, in which its combustion chamber instability problems were never solved, and was therefore discontinued after the fake Apollo Moon program which ended in 1972.

Parsons consulted with some of the best minds in the business, but to no avail. However, a renowned scientist at Caltech Dr. Theodore von Karman devised four differential equations to determine if the process of restricted burning powder was stable in solid fuel rockets. He then gave the equations to Malina who studied them and made the determination that the process was indeed, stable.

Pendle:

> Malina eventually emerged triumphant. Karman's equations had proved that the process was inherently stable. Parsons just needed to find the right combination of ingredients to create a fuel of suitable strength capable of uniform burning.[5]

After Karman's equations proved solid fuel rockets were possible, Parsons continued with his work even more motivated than before. By this time, they had moved their work to a more secure area away from Caltech, leasing six acres of land in Arroyo Seco, from the city of Pasadena. Parsons spent the next several months laboring over powder formulations and numerous testing of rockets, to find a solid fuel mixture that would sustain a controlled burn. Parsons eventually solved the problem when he devised his own black powder propellent. With this new powder propellent, Parsons was able to accomplish for the first time, a controlled and steady burn in a rocket.

With the success of experimenting with rockets and boosting the overall power output of aircraft, NAS increased their funding to $22,000, which then increased to $125,000 dollars the following year. Clearly, NASA was impressed with the potential possibilities of Parsons and his team's work.

All of this work by the Suicide Squad led to their first contract which was to produce 60 JATOs for the army air corps. This meant that these jets had to perform to near perfection with the expected reliability to go with it. Further, World War II had broken out, so the air force was now requesting even more powerful JATOs to assist heavily loaded aircraft in takeoffs from aircraft carriers. In order to help fulfill this military contract, Parsons and Malina decided to form a company in 1942 called Aerojet Engineering Corporation.

This eventually led to a three-million-dollar contract (an impressive amount of money for that era) to produce guided missiles with a range of 150 miles and a payload of around 1000 pounds of explosives. And given the significance of the work Parsons and his Suicide Squad were doing, along with the fear of NAZI involvement in their own rocket program, this now required all of the members to undergo FBI security checks.

Given the increased demands of military contracts, Aerojet Engineering Corporation was reorganized and became the Jet Propulsion Laboratory (JPL). Again, the use of the word 'rocket' was avoided for fear that the company wouldn't have been taken seriously.

But before JPL could fulfill their new multi-million-dollar military contract, it was necessary for them to solve one more problem with these rockets, a problem that would be solved by the only member of the team who had the inspiration and ingenuity to do so, Jack Parsons.

Because of the ammonium nitrate used in the propellant mixtures, black powder rockets were prone to unexpected explosions, brought on by temperature changes. So, Parsons had to devise a method to prevent these unexpected explosions from happening.

He then came up with a brilliant idea!

The consensus of how Parsons solved the problem was that he was inspired when he happened to observe workmen pouring asphalt on a roof. This caused him to remember a method first used 1,500 years ago but was famously used in 648-685 A.D. by the Byzantine Empire and their use of a liquid flaming weapon. Theories of its ingredients included asphalt. Parsons' idea in solving the problem of using black powder, was not to use it at all.

Pendle:

> He made up for his lack of theoretical and mathematical schooling with his prodigious memory, broad experimental knowledge, and, most importantly, his ability not to be dissuaded by conventional thought. Black powder would never be a suitable rocket fuel. But the armed forces wanted a solid-fueled JATO. When is a solid fuel not a fuel? It was a question that Parsons answered with an Archimedean "Eureka!" As Malina affirmed, it seemed that suddenly, as if by the addition of some ingenious ingredient, "all the various stuff that was in the back of Jack's mind, jelled." [6]

Parsons replaced black powder with asphalt after hundreds of years of an established method, making them stable and reliable. In essence, Parsons rewrote the book on solid fuel rockets and is a method that is still in use today. Once again, Jack Parsons refused to allow himself to be restricted by any preconceived notions including an education system that more often than not promotes a consensus, and there's nothing wrong with that. However, there are occasions when the consensus has been proven wrong by individuals who have had the insight and have refused to allow themselves to be governed by a set of rules. Thanks to Parsons' work, solid fuel boosters were used to successfully launch the Space Shuttle for thirty years.

Parsons and his team now concentrated on the area of liquid fueled rockets and were faced with similar instability problems experienced with solid fuel rockets. They needed to find a stable liquid fuel. There were pros and cons to using both solid fuel and liquid fuel rockets. When solid fuel rockets are ignited, they cannot be shut down so they burn until their fuel runs out. But liquid fuel rockets were considered more practical since unlike solid fuel rockets, they can be shut down at any time.

Parsons' work had proved essential in the design and engineering of future weapons systems and rocket technology in general. Most notably, his inventions included the solid fuel boosters used to help launch the Space Shuttle to LEO. These accomplishments to the aerospace industry are all the more amazing when you consider Parsons' passion for a darker and more sinister world. This will be discussed next.

Jack Parson's World By Night

For many people, the attraction to the occult by a rocket scientist is contrary to the logical and studious academic, whose only interest should be reading, researching, and doing scientific experiments. It is a community of trained scientists who present themselves as society's sober second thought, logic being their only trait or at least, that is how they like to be portrayed. Yet, how disturbing it is for many people, especially among scientists from all backgrounds, to find out that one of the most innovative and revered rocket scientists of the 20th century, whose theories have been instrumental in the Space Shuttle program and military ballistic missiles, would also be a devout occultist going so far as to practice the very Satanic rituals most people would be horrified by. But that is exactly who Jack Parsons was, filled with as much passion for the occult as he was with his work in the field of rocket science.

But to gain some understanding of Parsons' attraction to the occult, it's necessary to at least briefly discuss one of the occult's revered and infamous leaders, Aleister Crowley, to whom Parsons corresponded with on a regular basis.

Aleister Crowley, The Great Beast

For many people, Aleister Crowley was a man who needed no introduction. He was revered, despised, and/or feared, depending on your opinion of him. He was also one of the world's most infamous Satanists whose admirers and followers included celebrities, top rock musicians including The Beatles and Led Zeppelin, the power elite of British society, and of course one very innovative rocket scientist, Jack Parsons. Several books and online sources elaborate more on this and I leave it up to the reader to pursue more details from other sources if they so choose, as this book will focus mainly on Parsons' connection to Crowley.

It is intriguing to see the world from Parsons' perspective while appreciating his enormous contribution to the world of rocket science and the influence he had with the aerospace industry. He is an example of how scientists and aerospace engineers are subject to the same kind of influence as anyone else, whether that is religion, culture, books, movies, the occult…the list is long, including an admiration for Aleister Crowley aka, 'The Great Beast.'

As peculiar as it may seem, the influence Aleister Crowley had on Parsons may have influenced his push for more powerful rocket systems. It's also not surprising that Parsons wasn't all that concerned about the fact that his work was being used in propulsion methods on weapons systems, which are now standard in the military industrial complex. In part, the military industrial complex is the area where Parsons' true legacy lies. That is not to say that Parsons deliberately set out to harm humanity and in fact, he may have thought he was doing a noble service, or one can assume. But nonetheless, most would agree that his desire to follow a man who called himself Baphomet, Frater Perdurabo, The Master Therion, 666, and The Great Beast, definitely had some influence on his work.

Pendle:

> A novelist, poet, philosopher, mountaineer, chess master, painter, big game hunter, but above all, magician, Crowley was born in England in 1875, into a wealthy but austere religious family. As a child he was allowed to read only the Bible; it did not convince him. He grew up to rail furiously against both the British prudery and the strictures of orthodox religion, proudly positioning himself in direct opposition to God and the established Christian church. To this end he identified himself with the "The Great Beast" from the book of Revelation.[7]

After Crowley had joined several occult societies, he found a way to separate himself from the hierarchy found in any religious and satanic order, when his wife, Rose Kelly, who was in a hashish-induced trance at the time, ordered him to go to a temple he had constructed in his apartment while they were visiting Cairo, Egypt in 1904. Here, he heard a man's voice, which dictated to him. Crowley has claimed to have written down every word this voice said, which then became a book,

The Book of the Law. This book became the central text of Thelema, a spiritual philosophy followed by all members of the Ordo Templi Orientis (OTO).

Figure 1.3 - Aleister Crowley
Source: Wikimedia

It is this book that is the basis of an occult ritual that Parsons saw for the first time and would influence him for the rest of his life; a book that would create two worlds for Jack Parsons that would inevitably lead these two worlds to collide.

As for Rose Kelly's hashish-induced trance at the time, drugs would play a prominent role with Crowley and it is said with Parsons too, which eventually led to Crowley having a serious addiction to both drugs and alcohol later in life. However, there appears to be no evidence of Parsons using drugs when involved in the serious issue of rocket science which indicates that he limited his use of any drugs to occult rituals.

Ordo Templi Orientis

Parsons was soon to be introduced to Wilfred Talbot Smith by another scientist, whose identify is unknown. But it would seem Parsons was not the only scientist at Caltech with some connection to Crowley's Ordo Templi Orientis (OTO). Smith was Crowley's representative in Los Angeles who introduced Parsons to Crowley's mystical order, the OTO. This was the only OTO order in Los Angeles and in another of many coincidences, it was located only a few miles from Parson's own house.

There are many aspects to Satanic rituals which people find disturbing, which were now a routine part of Parsons' life. This author will not indulge in writing about it here, however, as author John Carter says:

> This enigmatic fusion of "sex and rockets" was to prove a fascinating development in the history of the aerospace industry in America.[8]

In yet another interesting coincidence, Parsons happened to meet L. Ron Hubbard, the founder of the Church of Scientology which needs no introduction considering its connection to Hollywood and the numerous stories that are so often sensationalized in the media. And as is typical of Parsons' apparent vulnerability, Hubbard too had a major influence on him. And in one of many letters Parsons had written to Crowley, whom he referred to as 'Most Beloved Father,' he explained his friendship with Hubbard saying that he is the most Thelemic (explained below) person he had ever met.

Wikipedia:

> Within the modern system of **Thelema**, developed by occultist Aleister Crowley in the first half of the 20th century, **Thelemic** mysticism is a complex mystical path designed to do two interrelated things: to learn one's unique True Will and to achieve union with the All.

Aleister Crowley's work is now being taken seriously by historians, so there is plenty of literature in books and online for those of you interested in Aleister Crowley's influence on celebrities and the power elite.

Jack Parsons' Worlds Collide

In 1944, both Parsons and Forman were forced to sell their stock in JPL. This eventually led to Parsons being ostracized by the scientific community, even though the rocket industry was now being taken seriously and more so by the military industrial complex. In their world, there was just no room for the unorthodox style of a scientist who lacked the formal education of an academic, despite the fact that Parsons' innovation and insightfulness brought solutions which are still in use today.

Pendle:

> At the age of 30, Parsons was cut adrift from the world of rocketry for the first time in his adult life. It was

plain to see that, like Goddard before him, he was left behind as the very science he had helped to create soared up and away from him.[9]

This led to Parsons' deeper involvement into the occult and his increased use of black magic. This greatly disturbed Crowley, who saw black magic as nonsensical. Instead, Crowley preferred his own form of magic to be used for mental and mystical development. Parsons however saw it differently who preferred the version put forward by the media, that of evil rather than good. This shows another aspect to Parsons where he seems to have chosen a deliberate path to evil, which could be interpreted by many as a disdain for humanity. However, given the complexity of a man like Parsons, one can never be too sure as to what the path he chose meant for him.

The path that Parsons was on would lead those closest to him to worry as to what his real motivations were, and how far he was prepared to go in many of the rituals in which he immersed himself. His trusted friend and colleague Ed Forman was always there to support him in any endeavor, including the many magic spells and rituals Parsons was working on. However, it seems Forman too had his limits when one of these magic spells went horribly wrong, at least for the shaken and frightened Forman.

The story, as has been described, is that after one of these rituals with Parsons late one night, Forman claims to have felt the whole house shake. He then heard screams and a number of entities outside his window, which he claimed were banshees. He ran downstairs and asked if anyone else had felt the house shake and if they saw any of the entities, but no one did. Whether all of this was in Forman's imagination or not, is a matter for debate among those in the Fortean world. But the fact is, something happened that night which would have a profound psychological effect on Forman for the rest of his life.

To add to Parson's despair of being ostracized by the scientific community, he was now being investigated by the FBI for allegedly having a connection to a Communist Party. With this investigation, the FBI would inevitably come across his occult background as well. To make matters worse, Parsons was also being investigated for the more serious offence of espionage.

This was around the early 1950s when the country was in an era of paranoia over the fear of communist infiltration in government, the military industrial complex, educational institutions, Hollywood, and just about any other facet of society, as named by The House Committee on Un-American Activities. This led to Parsons' security clearance being revoked as he was a member of the scientific community that was under close scrutiny given the importance of their work, especially in the military industrial complex.

As a result of no security clearance, Parsons could no longer be employed in the aerospace industry. However, due to insufficient evidence of any espionage activity, Parsons' security clearance was renewed by the Industrial Employment Review Board (IERB). But that didn't last long, as the IERB revoked his security clearance yet again, this time permanently, due to his connections to the occult, which they used to judge his character.

Parsons was no longer involved in the OTO and now without a security clearance, he was no longer allowed to work within the military industrial complex. In essence, Parsons' two worlds collided, which in a twist of fate, would annihilate one another and as we'll soon see, Parsons along with them.

His Final Act And Demise

The early 1950s was an era of change for Parsons. He had taken on other projects for example, working in the film industry as a special effects expert on explosives. It was during the period, that he and his wife Cameron had already made plans to relocate to Mexico for at least several months.

It was on the very day that he and Cameron had planned on leaving for their trip, that he received a call from the Special Effects Corporation for a quick project they needed done before he left. In fact, he had been storing his highly volatile chemicals in their warehouse at the time since he was on contract with them. But because someone had rented some space from the Special Effects Corporation, Parsons was forced to move his highly volatile chemicals and stored them in the laundry room of his house.

Parsons had agreed to the Special Effects Corporation's request. It was around 5 pm while Parsons was alone mixing various chemicals for their project, when the house shook from an explosion. When people rushed to Parsons's makeshift laboratory, he was found seriously injured but conscious. His injuries included multiple fractures and serve burns. He lingered on in obvious shock for an estimated 37 minutes.

Jack Whiteside Parsons died at Huntington Memorial Hospital at the young age of 37. After hearing of her son's death, Ruth Parsons had gotten a prescription for Nembutal to help her cope with her understandable and obvious grief. However, in an obvious moment of intense grief, Ruth Parsons, who is alleged to have overdosed at the young age of 61, joined her son hours after hearing the tragic news.

There has been speculation over the years as to what led to the explosion that killed Jack Parsons. Some say that Parsons was careless and sloppy with his work, but that seems out of character for a man who was meticulous and organized about the work he did. Others say that there was something more nefarious going on which is intriguing given his background both personally and professionally. The more likely scenario is, it was an unfortunate accident, although we will most likely never know for sure.

Jack Parsons' Legacy

It's obvious to anyone with a basic background knowledge of Jack Parsons, why NASA is reluctant to discuss this man although even they can't deny his proven methods, which as mentioned above, were included in the launch of the Space Shuttle. Further, his place in history has in part, been solidified by others including JPL. In an open house to the public once a year, JPL recreates a scene that depicts its founders Rudolph Schott, Amo Smith, Frank Malina, Ed Forman, and Jack Parsons relaxing after their first test of a liquid fueled rocket on October 31st, 1936, which is the very day of JPL's foundation. Halloween day seems a fitting choice to officially start a company by a self-taught scientist who had as much passion for the occult as he did for rockets. And it was the International Astronomical Union in France, not NASA, who honored Parsons in 1972, by naming a lunar crater after him called "Parsons Crater." The crater is appropriately located on the 'dark side of the Moon.'

Figure 1.4 - Jack Parsons on the lower right, and The Suicide Squad, Founders of JPL
Source: *Wikimedia*

Parsons and Forman are a great example of how insightful people can be even when they lack an academic background, but nonetheless inspire academics like Malina and others, to form working relationships that lead to inventions of new technologies and methods. But as we will learn in this book, this was but one step in technology on a road to discovery for future generations to build on, in expanding an industry that should have flourished, regardless of the cost. Instead, this has led to a roadblock in the aerospace industry that has been felt for decades and will most likely continue for decades more; an industry that has not progressed much further in technologies in terms of its rocket propulsion systems since the early 20th century for military and commercial use. It's akin to the aviation industry going no further than single pilot, propeller driven aircraft. As with the unmanned and manned space programs, the continuous use of early 20th century propulsion systems are still in use for example, Russia, which at least has managed to maintain a consistent capability of launching manned missions to LEO.

The claim of limited funding is often used as an excuse by proponents for the lack of progress in the manned space program. However, all anyone has to do is follow NASA's funding to see that billions of dollars could easily have been prioritized for its manned space program. Yet from 2011 and on, NASA has spent billions of dollars funding unmanned missions and maintaining the International Space Station (ISS), while they neglected their own means of getting their astronauts to it, relying instead on the Russian manned space program to do it for them. Given NASA's claims of superiority in the manned space program, one would expect that they would have had a workable manned spacecraft ready for launch, after the Space Shuttle was retired.

Jack Parsons' theories and work is credited with those propulsion systems still in use, a first step that has now been forever assigned its proper place in history, regardless of the fact that today, NASA has not been able to build on this technology. This is apparent not only with its decision to fake the Apollo Moon missions, but for the fact that for thirty years, their manned space program i.e., the Space Shuttle, went no further than LEO. Yet, from 1961 to 1969, NASA claims to have designed and engineered spacecraft and accomplished six manned lunar landings. In the same time period from 2011, NASA managed to launch only one manned mission to the ISS with the SpaceX Falcon 9 and Dragon spacecraft, on November 15, 2020.

A counter argument to this is that previous to NASA the National Advisory Committee for Aeronautics (NACA) founded in 1915 leading up to NASA, which was established in 1958, had actually been gathering data that was then incorporated into the relatively new aerospace industry and of course for the Apollo Moon mission program. So, the proponents say NASA had decades of data to access, so the timeline of eight years to land men on the Moon is misleading.

However, the goal of the NACA was to collect data for the aeronautical industry that already existed for an environment that mankind was more than familiar with. The manned space program required data for an environment never before experienced by mankind. So, in essence, NASA had little or no data for the hostile environment in which they planned on sending manned missions through. Therefore, the real timeline was closer to eight years for which they needed to collect data for a hostile environment, to design and engineer spacecraft capable of sending manned missions to LEO, landing and liftoff from the lunar surface, travelling safely back to Earth, and for re-entry and splashdown in the Pacific Ocean. NASA has never been able to duplicate its own claim of technological prowess, in such a short timeline since.

As for writing about Parsons' world of the occult, the point is to once and for all, break the myth that somehow scientists are immune to some of the influences of our respective societies when in actuality, they are subject to the same desires, competitiveness, spiritual beliefs, likes, dislikes, jealousies, egos, and many of the other human traits that make us who we are. And in the aerospace industry, these traits are more common than most people know, Parsons being but one example. This along with Parsons' deep involvement in the occult, is the foundation in which JPL was formed, which leads a straight path to NASA.

An Intriguing Connection

Although this has been reported in other sources, I gained more insight from my research into Parsons' and Forman's numerous contacts with Wernher von Braun, before World War II.

Pendle quotes from Ed Forman's third wife:

> Both of the boys had talked to von Braun many times by telephone, way before he ever came to the U.S.... They were crazy about von Braun and he was crazy about them, because they were out horsing around with the same stuff.[10]

Jack Parsons' contact with Wernher von Braun before and possibly even during World War II, makes one wonder what else has been left out of the history books regarding von Braun and any other contacts he may have had with American officials, before he surrendered to America military forces in 1945. This raises serious questions as to how the FBI either missed this correspondence with a known NAZI before and possibly during World War II, or they knew about it and for some reason they weren't overly concerned. Further, it is now rumored that Parsons may even have met von Braun after he was brought to the United States under Operation Paperclip.

Parsons' ongoing contact with von Braun before and possibly during World War II, is yet another of many coincidences we've seen with Parsons in both his world by day and his world by night. And although Parsons' contact with von Braun may appear to have been innocent, it's a stretch to believe that American intelligence agencies didn't know about this. A more likely scenario is that American intelligence agencies did know and were collecting intel, possibly through others along with Parsons. This more than indicates that Parsons was in some capacity, an intelligence agent. Either way, it seems von Braun had at least indirect connections to American intelligence agencies before and during World War II, which have not yet have been fully disclosed.

However, one undeniable fact is clear: Jack Whiteside Parsons' legacy in the aerospace industry, has now secured its proper place in history.

In Conclusion

It's obvious that NASA and people in general are reserved in their recognition and praise of such a controversial man like Jack Parsons. He was a mysterious and insightful man not bound by a set of rules that were forced on scientists by academia, and he refused to allow the academic community to influence him in any way. When there was a problem which no one could solve, Parsons stepped out from the established norms and solved the problem with an insight that very few scientists had. In a sense, he rewrote the rules and then told the academic community to make their equations fit those new rules, as we saw with his brilliant insight that solved the problem of combustion instabilities with solid fuel rocket boosters.

Aside from Jack Parsons belief in the occult, other scientists obviously had and have a belief in something far more esoteric including intuition, than what established conventional science is willing to admit even exists.

After the Apollo 1 tragedy, NASA engineers and scientists were clearly spooked to the point of demanding an unmanned mission for the first Saturn IB launch with Apollo 5.

Charles R. Pellegrino and Joshua Stoff:

> No crew? Well, of course, no crew. That was clearly understood through unspoken law: No men were to fly in the Saturn 1-B 204. Ever. This is not to say that NASA was acknowledging a belief in ghosts or spirits or anything else supernatural, but the space organization did believe that there was something basically wrong about sending a crew up in a rocket with so many bad memories attached to it.
>
> And there was something else, probably nothing more than a trick of the imagination. Still, if you touched the vehicle – those memories – a touch would bring them out
>
> *-get us out-*
>
> bubbling up out of the subconscious.[11]

As we've seen in Part I of this series, logic is not exactly emblematic of NASA's overall philosophy when it comes to their manned space program. The absence of proper and rigorous flight-testing standards needed to certify spacecraft for human travel, has been well documented. Yet here we see NASA adopt a far more esoteric reason for unmanned flight testing for Apollo 5, contrary to the established laws of logic and common sense, as is prevalent in the scientific community. This is an intriguing area with many examples that needs to be taken more seriously by the scientific community. Maybe if they allow themselves to explore more esoteric themes, it will bring enlightenment in ways no equations can bring on their own.

Here are some good examples of scientists who allow their esoteric beliefs and intuitions to rule:

Pellegrino and Joshua:

> No, scientists really don't believe in these things, not really. Then again, on a one-to-one basis, very rarely and in secret, some will admit to the possibility of a whole new science yet to be explored, and they dare not risk their reputations and their careers to explore it.
>
> We know of a paleontologist who can pick up a rock and tell you where that rock has been. Suddenly the desert we are standing is no longer a desert but a forest that grew here one hundred years ago. He holds the rock – a timegate – and looks ahead (through the trees?). "Come," he says. "Follow me. I'll show you

where the lake was, where the stream deposited the amber, and … oh, Charlie, there's something else near the stream. A Tyrannosaur died there." We walk. We dig. We find the lake and the amber. The expedition that arrives after us finds the Tyrannosaur.

We know of a geneticist who, like the paleontologist, explores nature through … through what? supernature? "When I was really working with chromosomes, I wasn't outside the microscope. I was right down there with them and everything got big. I saw things nobody else did. I was even able to see the internal parts of the chromosomes – actually everything was there. It surprised me because I actually felt as if I were right there and these were my friends." And this approach to discovery, laughable as it may seem, led Barbara McClintock to a Nobel Price.

We know of a rocket that had no crew.[12]

Replace paleontologist and geneticist with rocket scientist in the above quote, and you have Jack Parsons. This is the best analysis of how Parsons was able to see such details without any formal education, unlike his highly educated colleagues. This may also explain Parsons' fascination with the occult, given that he saw more and experienced more than most people. Like the paleontologist and the geneticist, Parsons became one with his work, a gift that can never be learned in a classroom. However, we must give credit to his colleagues who worked with him, and had the wisdom and foresight to follow Parsons, even though they didn't fully understand his methods; a cooperation among professionals who unlike some of their contemporaries, cared more for finding real answers, while refusing to allow their egos and their competitive nature to rule the day. Unfortunately, scientists like Jack Parsons and his colleagues, are lacking in today's academic institutions.

Scientists for the most part, are no longer allowed independent thought or research. Their research has become influenced by government and corporate funding. Corporations use their power to influence science, which is turn is then used to influence people. This is usually done with corporations and the corporate controlled scientific community, lobbying governments to pass legislation forcing people into submission in so many facets of our society. Science has taken on a whole new meaning and it is not so much about serious research anymore. It is research that is so often influenced by corporations and politics, with profits and power as its real goal. The new unwritten policy is:

Questions and concerns will no longer be tolerated by the general public.

However, there are some scientists who do pursue research for the betterment of mankind. I know of a few who refuse to be dictated by fiduciary obligations. Their only goal is to go wherever their research leads them. These are very dedicated individuals whose work is free of any outside influence that usually has an agenda, so they are free to pursue real science first.

As for the manned space program today, NASA could definitely benefit from the likes of Jack Parsons to take propulsion systems to the next level. Parsons knew the limitations of the propulsion systems used today, which is probably why he sold his shares in JPL. This is supported by NASA's inability to send manned missions beyond LEO using this technology, and it doesn't seem they'll do so in the foreseeable future.

The following chapters in this book will now show the limitations of this technology, which is the real reason why there hasn't been a manned mission beyond LEO, at least with technology that the public is aware of.

Chapter One – Endnotes

[1] John Carter, *sex and rockets:* THE OCCULT WORLD OF JACK PARSONS, p. 2.

[2] GEORGE PENDLE, *STRANGE ANGEL:* THE OTHER WORLD LIFE OF ROCKET SCEINTIST JOHN WHITESIDE PARSONS, p.44.

[3] Ibid., p. 74.

[4] Ibid., p. 77.

[5] Ibid., p. 164.

[6] Ibid., p. 199.

[7] Ibid., p. 136.

[8] John Carter, *sex and rockets:* THE OCCULT WORLD OF JACK PARSONS, p. 45.

[9] Op Cit., p. 241.

[10] Ibid., p. 55.

[11] Charles R. Pellegrino and Joshua Stoff, CHARIOTS FOR APOLLO: THE UNTOLD STORY BEHIND THE RACE TO THE MOON, p. 151.

[12] Ibid., p. 152.

Chapter Two

The Pre-Apollo Moon Missions

Part I of this series described and analyzed the Apollo 11 mission that supposedly journeyed to the Moon and back. It described how 1960s technology would have been inadequate for a manned Moon mission, for example, the inability of the F-1 engines of the Saturn V to use their full power capacity because of combustion chamber instabilities. And without the F-1 engines in the first stage of the Saturn V working at full power capacity, Apollo 11 could not have reached its optimum altitude two minutes after launch, where the first stage would have been jettisoned. After the jettison of the first stage, and regardless of the fact that the Saturn V's J-2 engines in the second stage apparently ignited and worked perfectly, Apollo 11 was still lower in altitude two minutes after launch. This means that Apollo 11 could not have reached optimum orbit necessary for its eventual translunar insertion, no matter how perfectly the J-2 engines worked.

If a contingency was worked out to have the J-2 engines burn longer to compensate for a lower than planned altitude after launch, then more propellent would have been needed. But because of weight restrictions, propellent was limited to what was originally planned for in terms of the Saturn V trajectory on launch. This would have prevented any contingency for a further burn duration of the J-2 engines in the Saturn V.

Further, since the F-1 engines were not capable of using their full power capacity, or they weren't even used at all, Apollo 11 and subsequent Apollo missions could not have launched the necessary payloads into LEO necessary for manned lunar landings.

We also described in Part 1, the impossibility of a mission like Apollo 11 to have safely travelled through the Van Allen belts due to intense radiation, as well as other hazardous elements like solar particle events, galactic cosmic rays, the problem of thermal control, and micrometeoroid impacts. As has been established, any one of these elements would have ended an Apollo mission. However, the more aspects of the Apollo 11 mission that are analyzed, and by inference that includes all of the Apollo missions, the more we counter NASA's claims that six of these missions landed safely on the lunar surface.

In the early 1960s, NASA had to choose between competing companies who would bid on contracts to design and engineer manned and unmanned spacecraft, for the pre-Apollo missions. Specifically, the unmanned missions included taking detailed photos of the lunar surface to help NASA decide which landing sites to choose from as well as soft landing unmanned spacecraft on the lunar surface. But first, we will look at the first two manned space programs that were used to collect data as well as the practicing of techniques in LEO, specifically rendezvous, docking, and manual versus automated maneuvers.

Near the end of this chapter, we will determine the failures and successes of the pre-Apollo missions. We will then use this information to make an estimate of the chances for success with the Apollo Moon missions, had they really taken place. NASA itself would have done this, but we'll use an arbitrary method to arrive at our own estimation based on existing technologies for that era, while giving NASA the benefit of the doubt.

The Manned Missions

In the last section, I mentioned NASA had two manned space programs leading up to the Apollo missions. But some say there were actually three manned space programs leading up to the Apollo missions. So, it's worth clarifying the discrepancy as to the number of manned space programs during the early 1960s.

Since the United States defines the boundary of space as being over 50 miles, the first American to have technically reached space was Airforce test pilot Robert Michael White when he reached an altitude of 59.6 miles with the X-15, which was a rocket powered aircraft. However, the internationally accepted boundary of space is the Karman line at 62 miles, which means White is only recognized as the first American astronaut within the United States.

Since the X-15 reached just beyond the boundary layer to space, which means the pilots would have experienced weightlessness, then technically it is considered one of the three manned space mission programs whose objectives were to collect data for future manned space missions. But the international community only recognizes Project Mercury and Project Gemini as the first two manned space missions. This is what has caused the discrepancy in manned space missions.

We will not include the X-15 as a manned space program, since this was a rocket powered aircraft, not a spacecraft. So, when referring specifically to the pre-Apollo manned missions, we will only involve the Mercury and Gemini missions. But it is worth mentioning the X-15 program for its contribution to the data it collected for the overall space program, which is still being evaluated decades later.

The X-15 Program

The X-15 flew from 1959 to 1968. It was launched from under the wing of a B-52 at 45,000 ft., which then fired its rocket engine and flew to an altitude of over 50 miles, i.e., the boundary layer of space. Each mission would last approximately 10 minutes and then land at Edwards Airforce Base. The main purpose of these missions was to gain data on re-entry into Earth's atmosphere for the American space program. Re-entry procedures will be discussed in detail in Chapter Five.

Figure 2.1 - The X-15
Source: NASA

However, another aspect gained from the X-15 program and its most enduring legacy, was the importance of designing more sophisticated simulators capable of duplicating flight conditions for the aviation and aerospace industries. This too would greatly enhance training for both pilots and astronauts. This also started the debate regarding manual versus automation which as we'll soon learn, was an ongoing debate within the manned space program.

The X-15 made a substantial contribution to re-entry procedures. This involved corrective control during re-entry using a vehicle with the aerodynamic design of an aircraft. However, NASA had decided on the capsule concept for its manned space missions in the 1960s. So, we will focus instead on that concept and design in Chapter Five when discussing re-entry into Earth's atmosphere, which had little or no corrective control abilities.

Project Mercury

There were six manned missions for Project Mercury from 1961 to 1963. These were one manned spacecraft which were the first American spacecraft to reach LEO. These missions had an apogee of no more than 176 miles and a perigee of 100 miles.

Figure 2.2 –The Mercury Launch
Source: Wikimedia

The goal of the Mercury program was straight forward:

1. To send astronauts into LEO, and
2. Practice re-entry into Earth's atmosphere and eventual splashdown in the Atlantic or Pacific oceans.

Therefore, the Mercury Program had met its objectives. However, the issue of manual versus automation was brought to the forefront of the discussion, which had caused a fierce debate among many at the astronauts who objected to just being "passengers" in Mercury spacecraft.

Figure 2.3 – Mercury capsule Splashdown
Source: *Wikimedia*

Author David A. Mindell

> As John Glenn told a press conference soon after his selection to the Mercury team, "We don't want to just sit there and be just like a passenger aboard this thing. We will be working the controls." Nevertheless, the automatic-as-primary approach would survive through Apollo.[1]

It's interesting to note that Buzz Aldrin has been heard to repeat a similar theme when he was questioned decades later about the validity of the Apollo missions, saying that they were just "passengers." Although given what we know now, this definitely has more than one meaning.

Project Gemini

Project Gemini consisted of 10 manned missions which were regarded as being a step forward in progress in terms of astronaut participation, as supposed to just being monitors or "passengers" of the spacecraft. However, the issue of manual versus automation would continue, even more so, when it came to accomplishing the objectives of these missions.

Figure 2.4 – Gemini Launch
Source: Wikimedia

The objectives of the Gemini missions were designed specifically to practice maneuvers in LEO for the upcoming Apollo Moon missions. These objectives included long duration missions, rendezvous and docking, extra vehicular activity (EVA), and precision landings. It was planned that after the Gemini spacecraft re-entered the atmosphere, it would then deploy a parachute on the last several thousand feet of its descent, and the astronauts would hand fly their spacecraft with skids deployed to a precision landing on a runway. However, because of technical and funding issues, it was decided instead to continue with the method of splashdown in the ocean, which was used for all manned missions in the 1960s and 1970s.

Figure 2.5 – Gemini Landing On Runway
Source: Wikimedia

Figure 2.6 – Gemini Splashdown
Source: NASA

Note: Lack of funding issues is an overall theme regarding the manned space program. However, a more realistic reason for the claim that there was a 'lack of funding,' may have more to do with the realization that Congress knew much more about the impracticality of manned missions to LEO. Further, Congress may have known too of the impossibility of manned missions beyond LEO, using present technologies. However, NASA still gets on average of about 20 billion dollars per year. Therefore, they could easily prioritize its funding for a manned spacecraft launch capability to LEO, if they choose to. As to why they don't, has little or nothing to do with the claim of not being provided adequate funding.

One major component of both the Gemini and Apollo missions was that of rendezvous and docking, where the need for automation was made even more apparent. Although NASA claims that Gemini III demonstrated manual maneuvers quite successfully, astronaut Jim McDivitt tried unsuccessfully to rendezvous with a spent booster during the Gemini IV mission. He realized that piloting skills alone were inadequate for rendezvous. In fact, there were those within NASA who would go as far as to question any need for flying skills at all, as a requirement for astronauts.

Mindell

> Afterward McDivitt attributed the problem to poor lighting, but he was facing something new. Orbital dynamics created a strange brew of velocity, speed, and range between two objects and called for a new kind of piloting. Catching up to a spacecraft ahead, for example, might actually require flying slower, to change orbit. "It's a hard thing to learn," observed Deke Slayton, "since it's kind of backward from anything you know as a pilot." A NASA investigation concluded that training had been inadequate, and that the entire program had underestimated the subtlety of the rendezvous task. Gemini IV taught an important lesson: pilots could not rendezvous by eye.[2]

Note: Deke Slayton was a World War II pilot and aeronautical engineer. He was also a test pilot who was selected as an astronaut for the Mercury program but was disqualified due to a medical problem. He was then made Chief of the Astronaut Office and Director of Flight Crew Operations, responsible for NASA crew assignments for both the Gemini and Apollo missions. By 1972, Slayton had resolved his health problems and returned to flight status. He was one of the astronauts on the Apollo – Soyuz mission.

One would assume that NASA was fully aware of these new orbital dynamics and would have known about the problems of using manual techniques for rendezvous, before attempting any manned mission. And aside from any claims from some of the Mercury and Gemini astronauts, piloting skills were increasingly becoming less of a prerequisite, while the need for a fully automated and autonomous computer would become a necessity. And as we see in the above quote, astronauts could not rendezvous manually. The issue of manual versus automation will figure prominently when discussing the lunar landing in chapter 3.

However, with the Gemini program, NASA claimed to have found a way to appease both the astronauts and engineers by adopting more of a hybrid method, i.e., having the astronauts participate by interfacing with the onboard computer for many of the programs involved in manned missions. Manual and automation would coexist, for now that is. Or put another way, astronauts' piloting skills were to be seen more as a necessary component that would enhance any success for manned missions, especially when landing on the lunar surface; in essence, NASA needed to build on the heroic fighter pilot image, to sell the official narrative to the public, which in turn, would solicit the necessary emotional response. This was apparent in the official narrative of the Apollo 11 lunar landing.

The Unmanned Missions

In 1961, NASA implemented a program to use unmanned spacecraft to collect data for the Apollo Moon landings. There were four different types of spacecrafts designed and built called, Ranger, Lunar Orbiter, Surveyor, and Pegasus. The Pegasus missions were designed to record micrometeoroid impacts, which posed a very real threat to any of the Apollo missions. However, these missions went no further than Earth orbit. The Pegasus missions were discussed in Part I of this series.

The Ranger Program

The Ranger program took place between 1961 to 1964. The purpose of these missions was to take the first ever up-close images of the surface of the Moon, then impact the lunar surface after each mission had met their objective. However, there were serious problems encountered with these missions so NASA did not achieve the overall objective of the program.

There were nine missions in all, which are detailed here:

- **Ranger 1** experienced numerous problems after launch. Among them, radio interference prevented ground-based tracking systems from properly tracking the mission. Further, it did not enter an elliptical orbit after the Agena rocket engine failed to reignite its engine for its mission. Ranger 1 re-entered Earth's atmosphere several days later.
- **Ranger 2** had similar problems after launch when its Agena rocket engine failed to reignite for its mission

and, it too entered Earth's atmosphere several days later.
- **Ranger 3** actually made it out of LEO and was on course to impact the lunar surface until its downlink to ground based tracking systems failed, causing the vehicle to enter solar orbit, which meant a loss of the mission.
- **Ranger 4** was on its way to impact the lunar surface, when it tumbled out of control during separation from its spent stage and impacted the far side of the Moon, therefore it never accomplished its objective.
- **Ranger 5** lost its downlink to ground-based tracking stations apparently to loss of battery power. It then entered solar orbit therefore ending the mission.
- **Ranger 6** had managed to successfully impact the lunar surface, but it failed to take any photos. So, it too did not meet its objective.
- **Rangers 7, 8, and 9** had met their objectives in sending back photos of the lunar surface before impact, classifying these three missions as a success.

Figure 2.7 – Ranger Mission Launch
Source: NASA

The images taken by Rangers 7, 8, and 9 enabled the U.S. Geological Survey to make plaster models of the lunar surface for study. This is an important point to remember when discussing the simulation aspect, and how NASA used these lunar surface models in simulators which were a necessary component in faking the Apollo Moon missions.

The simulations will be discussed further on.

The Lunar Orbiter Program

There were five Lunar Orbiter missions launched between 1966 and 1967.

- o Lunar Orbiters 1, 2, and 3 photographed potential landing sites for the Apollo missions.
- o Lunar Orbiters 4 and 5 photographed the entire lunar surface.

These landing sites were chosen using Earth based observatories. But the Lunar Orbiters were used to get more detailed photos of the areas selected. Considerations of the landing sites included, smoothness of the terrain, number of craters, hills, and cliffs in the surrounding areas, the amount of propellant needed for the LM aspect of the mission, and a free-return trajectory for any of the Apollo missions, should it be required due to a failure of the service propulsion system.

Note: A free-return trajectory meant that if any of the Apollo missions experienced engine failure on the way to the Moon, they would have been able to coast around the Moon and back to Earth, in theory, that is. However, that was changed after Apollo 11 in favor of a hybrid trajectory supposedly due to

NASA's increased confidence in the CSM propulsion system. This meant that the missions would start out on a free-return trajectory and then would perform a mid-course maneuver for more precision in their approach to the landing site, giving up the free-return trajectory. For those who believe the official version of the Apollo missions, one should wonder why this confidence was maintained after the near alleged disaster of the Apollo 13 mission.

Micrometeoroid experiments were done on each of the five unmanned spacecraft. Each of them carried 20 detectors to record micrometeoroid impacts. The spacecraft flew both equatorial and polar orbits around the Moon. Their orbits ranged from approximately 20 to 3,900 miles. Micrometeoroid data was collected for seventeen months.

> The five Orbiters recorded 22 punctures during a time-area exposure of 139.0 square meters per day. These figures gave an average rate of 0.16 puncture per square meter per day (m2 x day-2) in the near lunar environment, or about one half the average rate of flux recorded by the Earth-orbiting satellites Explorer XVI and Explorer XXIII.[3]

The five Lunar Orbiters recorded approximately 22 micrometeoroid impacts per day according to what is documented, and the impacts were greater near the lunar surface. However, there is no mention of any damage to the detectors themselves on these unmanned missions, which leaves one to guess as to how many detectors were actually working during that seventeen-month period. Hence, the number of micrometeoroid impacts recorded per day has to be considered a conservative estimate, to say the least.

Micrometeoroids would have posed a serious risk to any Apollo mission, especially the LM. As documented in Part 1, the LM walls had a thickness equivalent to three layers of kitchen foil, which needs no explanation as to the lack of protection for the astronauts. Either a micrometeoroid impact, or an astronaut putting his foot through one of the LM's walls, would have ended a mission instantly. And given some of the carelessness of these astronauts while allegedly walking on the lunar surface, causing them to fall several times and risk tearing their spacesuits, accidently putting one's foot through the LM wall was not out of the realm of possibilities.

Radiation experiments were done by each of the Lunar Orbiters too. Each Lunar Orbiter had two cesium iodide detectors on board.

> The data obtained from the radiation experiments on board the five Lunar Orbiter spacecraft had significant implications for the Apollo Program. What would be the approximate doses of radiation experienced by astronauts in space suits? In the Lunar Module? In the Apollo Command Module? To obtain an answer, the primary investigator, Dr. Trutz Foelsche, analyzed the data recorded by the two-cesium iodide (CsI) detectors in each of the five Orbiters. One of the two was shielded by 0.2 gram of aluminum per square centimeter, the other by 2.0 grams aluminum per square centimeter. Because of the higher absorption of protons and alpha-particles per gram per square

> centimeter in soft tissue or water, the doses recorded by the Lunar Orbiter dosimeters had to be multiplied by two. The analysis showed that all events recorded were of significance to a man in space only where shielding was light, specifically in a space suit or in the Lunar Module.[4]

This is a very interesting and revealing quote from NASA given the lack of shielding for the Apollo missions, especially the LM, which this quote makes very clear. It substantiates researchers' claims that radiation in space would be a hazard to any Apollo manned mission outside of LEO, given the level of protection they had or lack thereof.

NASA then compared data from Pioneer 5 launched in 1960 to the data from Pioneer 6 launched in 1965, with that of the Lunar Orbiter. Both Pioneer missions recorded data from SPEs and after they reviewed the data from the Pioneer and Lunar Orbiter missions, their conclusion was very revealing and clear:

> From these data the inference could be made that in rare cases of large event groups, such as those of 1959 and 1960, the Apollo astronauts might experience skin doses greater than 1,800 to 5,000 rads in one week, if no precautions were taken.[5]

Doses of 200 to 1000 rads in a few hours will cause serious illness. Any dosage beyond 1000, means a quick end to a manned mission outside of the relative protection of Earth's magnetic field. Further, as was explained in Part 1, NASA did not have the capability of recording the true radiation flux. So, this data supplied by NASA, must be taken with caution. NASA says that the astronauts could experience up to 5,000 rads in one week. On average, that's at least over 700 rads per day. The yearly average dosage per person is less than 1 rad.

However, given the inconsistencies over the years in the data as reported by scientists (directly or indirectly involved with NASA), one thing is for sure: NASA should have a much better understanding of the radiation intensity within both the Van Allen belts and solar particle events (SPEs). But given NASA and its contractors' propensity for destroying its own data related to the alleged Apollo missions, this data must be looked on with caution. And it seems that NASA has put itself in a very untenable situation since to reveal the real data for the Van Allen belts and SPEs, would surely be akin to admitting that even if the Apollo missions reached LEO, they definitely went no further confirming what many researchers have been saying for years and that is, the real missions were recorded in a film studio.

There is a phase in where the Moon is protected by Earth's magnetic field, which would have given the astronauts some protection in the event of an SPE. But the alleged Apollo missions took place while the Moon was outside of Earth's magnetic field. And the "precautions" that the Apollo astronauts would have taken beyond LEO should they have encountered a solar storm, involved orienting the CSM so that the rear of the spaceship would take the brunt of it. And aside from the obvious intense radiation that would have enveloped the spacecraft regardless of its orientation, no one seemed too concerned about the effect kinetic energy would have had on the highly volatile propellants. As for the LM, no explanation is needed to comprehend the level of protection (or lack thereof) with walls equivalent to three layers of kitchen foil.

Further, a lot of the data collected by the unmanned missions was recorded on magnetic tapes, which are commonly referred to as, telemetry tapes. But as we learned in Part I of this series, NASA tends to 'lose' these telemetry tapes. And in fact, the evidence in Part I, shows that NASA destroyed 14,000 reels of telemetry tapes for Apollo 11. And we now know that all of the telemetry tapes for all of the Apollo missions have been destroyed. That's an estimated 140,000 reels of telemetry tapes with valuable information that is gone forever, meaning there is nothing to back up any paper records showing the alleged data.

There is one more interesting note to make about both the Ranger missions between 1964 and 1965, and the Lunar Orbiter missions between 1966 and 1967. Both of these missions had taken photos of the lunar surface. And more recently, NASA had launched the Lunar Reconnaissance Orbiter (LRO) in 2009 to map the lunar surface in more detail. And aside from its mission, the LRO also took photos of the alleged Apollo landing sites. However, when comparing the photos from the Ranger and Lunar Orbiter missions to the LRO photos, something is very noticeable about them, and you don't have to be an expert to see it. That is discussed next.

Comparison Of Photos For Ranger, Lunar Orbiter, And Lunar Reconnaissance Orbiter (LRO)

We'll first take a look at a couple of photos from the Ranger and Lunar Orbiter missions.

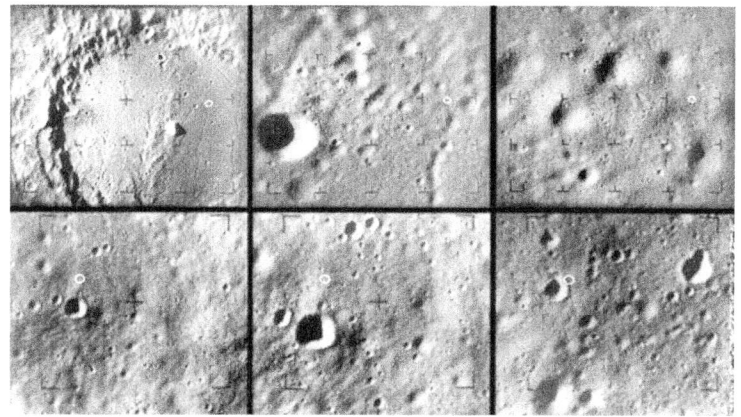

Figure 2.8 – Photos From Ranger Mission
Source: NASA

Figure 2.9 – Photo From Lunar Orbiter
Source: NASA

Now we will look at a photo from the LRO.

Figure 2.10 – Photos Of The Alleged Apollo Moon Landing Site From Lunar Reconnaissance Orbiter
Source: NASA

What's interesting about the photos taken in 1964 to 1965 by the Rangers missions, and the photos taken in 1966 to 1967 by the Lunar Orbiter missions, is they are comparable to photos of the alleged Apollo Moon landing sites taken by the LRO mission in 2009. Yet, we see little difference in the quality and resolution of the photos after more than four decades, when comparing the photos from each mission. However, the LRO photos of 2009 taken of other areas of the lunar surface outside of the alleged Apollo landing sites, show remarkable detail which would be expected with 21st century photographic technology.

Figure 2.11 – Photo Of The Lunar Surface outside of the alleged Apollo landing sites, from the LRO
Source: NASA

Proponents have gone through great lengths to explain the reasons for the poor quality of the photos of the alleged Apollo landing sites, to the superior quality of photos taken of other areas of the lunar surface from the same LRO in 2009, but to no avail, since it defies basic common sense.

The conclusion is clear: The LRO photos of the alleged Apollo landing sites, were photoshopped with as little detail as possible. To show up-close detail of the alleged Apollo Moon landing sites, would require these photos to give a realistic scenario of what the Apollo equipment supposedly left on the lunar surface would look like, after decades of bombardment by SPEs, galactic cosmic rays, and micrometeoroids. To estimate the erosion of the equipment left on the lunar surface, would be quite difficult to do. So, the obvious way out of this, would have been to avoid doing it, much like the reasoning for not including the stars in photos allegedly taken from the lunar surface by the Apollo astronauts.

Before we leave the subject of lunar photos, there's one more interesting anomaly I would like to point out. I've noticed that in most of the photos of Earth taken during the Apollo missions, or at least the ones allegedly taken from the lunar surface, the Earth appears to be smaller than it should be. It appears even smaller than the Moon does when viewed from Earth. This is peculiar since the Earth is almost four times the size of the Moon, so it should at least appear larger than that of the Moon when viewed from Earth, yet it doesn't. It's quite the opposite.

There is more discussion on this peculiarity as well as other anomalies in the photographic record in the Appendices.

The Surveyor Program

The objective of the Surveyor program was to soft land unmanned spacecraft on the lunar surface, and these were the first American spacecraft to do so. There were seven missions in all between May 1966 to January 1968 as follows:

- **Surveyor 1** landed on the lunar surface and transmitted 11,237 TV photos.
- **Surveyor 2** crashed into the lunar surface.
- **Surveyor 3** landed on the lunar surface and took some soil samples as well as photo experiments.

- o **Surveyor 4** was presumed to have crashed into the lunar surface after its signal was lost 2.5 minutes before landing.
- o **Surveyor 5** landed on the lunar surface and took over 19,000 photos and did some soil analysis.
- o **Surveyor 6** landed on the lunar surface and performed a liftoff and travelled 2.5 miles before landing again. It transmitted 30,065 TV photos and analyzed soil.
- o **Surveyor 7** landed on the lunar surface and took 21,000 TV photos. It analyzed soil and dug a trench. It also took a photo of the Earth and Jupiter.

At this point, NASA seems to have gained some proficiency in landing unmanned missions on the lunar surface, but as is apparent not without risks.

Figure 2.12 – Surveyor 7 on the Lunar Surface
Source: Wikipedia

The Pegasus Program

The Pegasus missions went no higher than 500 miles in Earth orbit. They were designed to record micrometeoroid impacts, which posed a very real threat to any of the Apollo missions. The Pegasus missions were discussed in Part I of this series.

Determining Success For The Apollo Moon Missions

Researching the pre-Apollo missions reiterated the point about the numerous problems that would have been encountered and the inevitable failures, before any success of both unmanned and manned missions were to take place on a consistent basis, especially for a hostile environment in which scientists knew very little about at that time. This would have been perfectly understandable when designing and engineering new technologies for missions in space, which is why static testing along with test flights in actual conditions would have been required, especially for manned missions. And although static testing seemed adequate, comparable testing standards in actual flight conditions were anything but the norm in certain aspects of NASA's manned space program, especially the Saturn V and the LM.

We'll now make an estimate as to any chance for success with the Apollo missions, by analyzing the failures and successes of the pre-Apollo missions. This is purely arbitrary and not what most people would consider scientific. But this can be used as an indicator to estimate the probability of success for any of the Apollo Moon missions to have met their objectives. This in turn, would help to determine any need to improve on technologies for these missions. Further, this estimate can be used to improve on many of the aspects of preparing for manned lunar missions, for example testing of the hardware, software, and training. To be as fair as possible, we will give NASA the benefit of the doubt when making this determination.

Failures And Successes Of The Manned Mercury And Gemini Missions

The **Mercury missions** seemed to have met their objectives. So, we'll classify these missions as a **100% success rate**.

Gemini met most of its objectives, but had a near catastrophic mission with Gemini 8 that nearly killed the crew due to a thruster malfunction, and was forced to make an emergency re-entry and splashdown in the Pacific Ocean. So, the Gemini 8 mission has to be considered a failure, given the potential seriousness of the outcome, especially since there was never a definitive answer as to the cause of the thruster malfunction. There was also a launch failure of the Agena Target Vehicle, which was needed for rendezvous and docking practice with the Gemini spacecraft. The Agena rocket was supposed to have been proven to be relatively reliable, yet one of them failed, unlike the new and most powerful rockets ever launched, the Saturn V, which seemingly had a perfect record, according to NASA. However, since the Gemini 8 mission was considered a failure, that would give the manned **Gemini missions an overall 90% success rate**.

Missions	Number of failed missions	Success %
Mercury	All 6 succeeded	100%
Gemini	1 out of 10 missions ended in failure	90%

We already see a hint that the more complex manned missions became, the higher the probability of failure, especially given the minimal testing of these spacecraft. This will be factored into the overall chances of success with the more complex manned Apollo Moon missions.

Failures And Successes Of The Unmanned Missions

1. Although the **Ranger** program had met some of its objectives, six of the nine missions ended in failure.
2. The **Lunar Orbiter** program appears to have been an overwhelming success, since all five of its missions had met their objectives.
3. The **Surveyor Program** had met most of its objectives, however two of the seven missions ended in failure.

Missions	Number of failed missions	Success %
Ranger	6 out of 9 missions ended in failure	33%
Lunar Orbiter	All missions succeeded – no failure	100%
Surveyor Program	2 out of 7 missions ended in failure	71%

The Ranger program led to much better success with the Lunar Orbiter program. But the trend with the Mercury and Gemini programs, versus the Lunar Orbiter and Surveyor programs, is clear. Since manned missions are more complex, the more likely the chances of encountering problems and/or failures, which factors into the overall success rate of these missions.

So far, by combining both the manned and unmanned pre-Apollo missions, we see a potential of an **overall success rate of 79%** for the Apollo missions.

A Realistic Outcome Of The Apollo Moon Missions

As mentioned earlier, for now, we'll exclude the information in Part I of this series. Instead, we'll use the failures and successes of the pre-Apollo missions as discussed in this chapter, to determine the probability of success with the Apollo missions. The Apollo 1 tragedy is not included since this occurred during a simulation. And although Apollo 13 had an explosion in one of its oxygen tanks ending its objective of landing on the Moon, it is not considered part of the failure rate. Unlike Gemini 8, which made an emergency re-entry into Earth's atmosphere for splashdown into the Pacific Ocean, Apollo 13 apparently continued on and circumnavigated the Moon, that is, the objective of the mission changed to getting the astronauts safely back to Earth. And because their trajectory took them around the Moon for the sling shot maneuver, better known as a gravity assist, the astronauts didn't seem to be in imminent danger and as NASA claims, they even managed to take photos of the lunar surface before making it safely back to Earth. Therefore, the new objective for Apollo 13 was met, which qualifies as a success.

Further, there are three additional facts that now need to be taken into consideration from the first two manned missions to LEO. They are as follows:

1. The Mercury and Gemini manned missions never left LEO.
2. The Mercury missions were nowhere near the endurance of an Apollo mission. And only two of the Gemini missions met that endurance.
3. Further, these manned missions were far less complex in technology than the Apollo missions, and didn't involve the complex navigation required for circumnavigating the Moon and landing on the lunar surface.

To give NASA the benefit of the doubt, we'll deduct only 5% for each of these three points, from the overall success rate of 79%.

This now gives a **64% probability of success** (79%-15%) for the manned Apollo Moon missions, based on existing technologies for that era.

In addition, we must also factor in the data regarding micrometeoroids and radiation collected from the Lunar Orbiter missions, showing that cislunar space is a hostile environment. Micrometeoroids and/or radiation, could have instantly ended an Apollo mission. But again, giving NASA the benefit of the doubt, we'll deduct only 5% for each of these two elements which now gives a **success rate of 54%.**

Information from Part I of this series, including chapters 3, 4, and 5 of this book, will be added at the end of Chapter Five to determine the real probability of success with the Apollo Moon missions, had they even been attempted with pre-existing technologies, NASA's flight-testing standards, and training methods. But it doesn't take a mathematician or rocket scientist to know where the percentage of this success rate is going.

Aviation, You Say

To put these percentages into perspective, we'll use an analogy. We'll pretend for the moment that the aviation industry had adopted the same flight-testing standards as NASA. We'll then use the same percentages in determining the success rate of the Apollo missions and apply it to the aviation industry. We'll leave out the percentages for LEO, duration of unmanned or manned missions, as well as the environmental elements that would have been encountered in LEO and beyond, since we are now talking about the performance of technology in a terrestrial environment.

Instead, we'll only use the percentage for the actual performance of this technology used as has been determined in this chapter. This of course worked out to be approximately 79% for the technology used in unmanned and manned missions combined, leading up to the Apollo Moon program. There was no further testing of unmanned and manned missions to try and improve on this percentage. The primary contractors and subcontractors for NASA built more complex spacecraft for the Apollo Moon landings without improving on existing technologies for that era, and with very little testing of this new technology in the actual conditions of spaceflight, which was discussed in Part I of this series. So now, we'll apply a similar approach to aviation, and factor- in the probability of success for aircraft in general.

Today we know there are approximately 40 million commercial flights per year in the United States alone. We'll apply the percentage of a 79% success rate to the technology leading up to the manufacture and certification of commercial airliners. To reiterate, we're applying this percentage on the basis of NASA's flight-testing standards.

- There are an estimated 110,000 flights per day in the United States. That's approximately 40 million flights per year. Using NASA's flight-testing standards and applying a 79% success rate for the technology used in the aviation industry leading up to more complex modern airliners, would mean that there would be a serious of incidents or crashes involving approximately 22,000 flights per day.
- On a yearly basis, that would mean approximately 8.4 million flights out of the estimated 40 million flights per year would likely have being involved in a serious incident and/or crash. This is based on the kind of flight-testing standards that was so prevalent with NASA during the Apollo Moon program, which is really nothing more than a hit and miss approach to solving problems with devasting outcomes.

This is not exactly what one would call, *a good marketing strategy* for the aviation industry. Not to mention the enormous loss of lives that would occur due to downright negligence on the part of the manufactures which in reality, would been considered criminal in a court of law. Of course, the testing and training standards used by NASA and its subcontractors, would never even be considered in the aviation industry. We're just using this analogy to make a point. For example, we witnessed the tragic consequences of what happens when one aspect of testing and training was neglected, when two Boeing 737 Max-8 series aircraft crashed in 2019, killing all onboard, which resulted in several lawsuits against Boeing and the grounding of these planes around the world. There was nothing wrong with the aircraft design itself, since it was based on a design that has had a very good safety record for decades. It was a new software program that was added to its flight management system which was the problem. But even though the aircraft itself was basically a new version of the successful B737 series, it would have had to go through a certification process. But the certification process is costly, so Boeing basically called it an updated version therefore avoided any certification costs. But there were problems with the new software, which was never detected until the planes were approved for commercial use. Further, pilots should have had hours of training on this new software. Instead, they got about fifteen minutes on an iPad. But if a full certification process was done, these accidents would not have happened. That is what was so tragic about this.

Thankfully, the aviation industry in general chooses to follow a more rigorous flight-testing standard that increases the safety of aviation, which is almost unmatched by any other industry. NASA should take note, considering that it has up to a 50% failure rate in the last several decades with its unmanned missions.

Proponents of the Apollo missions have countered that the reason for minimal testing in actual flight conditions, is because of the enormous cost involved, that there was a space race between the Americans and Russians to get to the Moon, and that the F-1 engines in the Saturn V were for one time use only. Further, unlike aircraft, rockets would not be put into commercial service and carrying millions of passengers. This appears to be a valid point, except for the fact that safety for anyone, whether it be for pilots, passengers, or astronauts, should always be a first priority. And even though these rockets were for one time use, there still needs to be a reasonable consistency in data performance in actual flight conditions, which didn't exist for the F-1 engines of the Saturn V.

There's always going to be an element of risk. But space agencies can limit that risk through adequate testing of its equipment in actual flight conditions. Astronauts are not going to be volunteering for missions, with the chances of every third or fourth rocket blowing up on the launch pad. I'm not suggesting that NASA adopt the same standard of testing for each of its rockets for hundreds of hours in actual conditions of flight, as the aviation industry does with its new aircraft. The cost alone would be enormous and overall, it just isn't practical or even necessary. Instead, NASA needs to establish its own flight test standards, comparable to its static testing, much like the aviation industry has done. This wasn't done with the F-1 engines of the Saturn V. In fact, NASA's contractor Rocketdyne flight tested the precursor to the F-1 engines, the H-1 engines in the Saturn I and the Saturn IB, with 14 unmanned launches before the first launch of a manned mission with Apollo 7. So, NASA didn't even follow its own flight-testing standards when it came to the F-1 engines in the Saturn V. And given the problems with the F-1 engines, the testing in actual flight conditions of these engines, would very likely have needed to exceed that of the H-1 engines. This can only mean one thing: As early as the 1960s, NASA knew the F-1 engines could not perform as claimed, which is why funding wasn't provided to at least match the test flight standards of the H-1 engines in both the Saturn I and Saturn IB.

Instead, NASA basically claims its hit and miss approach worked. But a hit and miss approach may explain why this hasn't led to a robust space industry involving manned launch capabilities which leads one to conclude, that decades of research and data need to be collected before anything resembling the aviation industry can take place. And given the lack of interest from other countries around the world, anything resembling a robust space industry for manned missions is definitely decades in the future, if at all. Except for manned launch capabilities to the ISS, NASA and the rest of the space agencies around the world seem to have distanced themselves from either seeking or investing a substantial amount of funding for manned missions to LEO and beyond, nor do they seem to be making any plans to do so. As I've said before, static testing is one thing, but it requires a comparable amount of flight testing to go with it.

In the next chapter, we will discuss some early and rather insane ideas that were actually considered for manned missions to the Moon, as well as a detailed analysis of the Lunar Module.

Chapter Two – Endnotes

[1] David A. Mindell, *Digital Apollo: Human and Machine in Spaceflight*, p. 75.

[2] Ibid., p. 86.

[3] U.S. Government, National Aeronautics and Space Administration (NASA), *Destination Moon: A History of the Lunar Orbiter Program: NASA Apollo Moon Landing Preparations, Boeing and Kodak Photo System, Problems with the Spacecraft, Greater Lunar Exploration Achievements*, p. 120.

[4] Ibid., p. 121.

[5] Ibid., p. 122.

Chapter Three

Ideas For Manned Lunar Landing Methods

Preposterous, Irrational, And Bizarre

There are two rather bizarre ideas that were actually considered for landing astronauts on the Moon which are worth mentioning, before we discuss what option was considered to be the most practical way of accomplishing a manned lunar landing.

A Preposterous Idea

The first idea involved launching the components of a spacecraft that was to be assembled in LEO. Wernher von Braun, Director of the Marshall Space Flight Center, which designed and built the Saturn V, had actually been advocating for a manned lunar landing for years before the decision was made to fund the Apollo Moon missions. He had grandiose ideas of a space station in LEO, as well as manned missions to the Moon and other planets. But as you'll see in this chapter, grandiose would be better replaced with the word, insane.

Authors Charles R. Pellegrino and Joshua Stoff:

> One thing President Kennedy had failed to mention was *how to get there*. Von Braun favored a multiple-rocket approach, in which as many as fifteen rockets would be put in orbit around the earth, there to rendezvous and be assembled to produce a 420,000-pound spacecraft.

This giant could then push off to the moon, dropping empty fuel tanks along the way. The whole thing would then arrive directly on the moon's surface. Von Braun viewed plans for orbiting the moon before landing as an unnecessary maneuver. William Pickering, of the Jet Propulsion Laboratory (JPL), agreed. "You don't have to go into orbit; you just aim at the moon and come straight in." Maxime Faget, chief assistant to the Space Task Group and one of the prime designers of Project Mercury, said quickly, "That would be a pretty unhappy day if when you lit up the rockets they didn't light." [1]

Assembling a spacecraft of any size in LEO, requires a lot of resources and technological means. To launch the necessary hardware into LEO and to assemble a spacecraft, especially one that was supposed to have been 210 tons, was no easy task and would have required very innovative ideas, to put it mildly. To put this into perspective, the Apollo CSM and LM combined, was approximately 47 tons. For NASA to have the capability of assembling a spacecraft in LEO, they would have needed a working manned space program already in place. At a minimum, this would have involved the following:

1) A program for the recruitment of engineers from other industries (like the aircraft industry), to train them in the new concepts of rocket technology, launch procedures into LEO and re-entry into Earth's atmosphere, and the study of a whole new and hostile environment and its effects of short-term and long-term missions on astronauts.

2) A program for designing and building rockets to launch astronauts into LEO.

3) A program for the recruitment and training of astronauts.

4) A program to build rockets powerful enough to launch the components of the spacecraft to be assembled in LEO.

5) And finally, a program for training astronauts in how to assemble this spacecraft, in such an unfamiliar and hostile environment.

In addition to all of the above five programs, there would have to have been numerous static and flight-testing standards established for the spacecraft to be launched, as well as the spacecraft to be assembled in LEO. The resources for this new manned space program, would have been enormous. For a comparison, NASA spent approximately 150 billion dollars on the Apollo program (in today's value), which included 12 Saturn V launches specifically for the Apollo Moon landing program, including 6 lunar landings.

To design, build, and implement a space program needed just to assemble spacecraft in LEO for manned lunar landings, and then implement the manned lunar landing program, would easily have increased the necessary funding upwards of a trillion dollars or more (in today's value), and that is a conservative figure depending on how many manned lunar missions NASA planned on. And considering the magnitude of this manned space program, the timeframe for its implementation would have taken decades.

At the time this idea was considered, the United States was also dealing with some serious domestic problems and was on the road to miring itself in a decade long war in Vietnam. Thus, another method was required to keep costs down for manned lunar landings as well as to meet the schedule set for NASA by the Kennedy administration, while coming up with a viable option that would convince the public. Hence, NASA came up with another 'genius' idea, which is discussed next.

An Irrational *Idea*

If the idea of assembling a 210-ton spacecraft in LEO sounds crazy, then this next idea was even crazier. This called for one spacecraft, with one astronaut onboard, to land on the lunar surface and conduct some scientific work. But there was one slight problem. Because of the technological challenges, there was no way for the astronaut to liftoff from the lunar surface. Instead, it was planned for the astronaut to reside on the lunar surface, to bask in the brilliant sunshine (at 250 degrees Fahrenheit). The idea was to send supply rockets to the Moon and land them on the lunar surface for the astronaut now stranded there. This would supposedly give NASA time to figure out how to build and launch a spacecraft capable of landing and liftoff from the lunar surface, in order to bring the stranded astronaut back. And as we've established, designing, building, and flight testing of spacecraft would have taken years. The main goal for America was to land a manned mission on the lunar surface before the Soviets did and at virtually any cost, even if that meant potentially sacrificing an astronaut to do it.

The reality is, it would not have only been a one-way trip to insanity, but a recipe for disaster not only for the astronaut, but for the entire space program. It doesn't take much to fully understand the psychology involved with an entire nation for a manned mission to the Moon, which very likely involved stranding an astronaut on the lunar surface permanently. The Moon in the sky to the average observer, would have taken on a whole new meaning. The public outrage alone, would have prevented any funding for decades to come, as well as the embarrassment and humiliation of a nation, at the stupidity of such a mission.

There was actually a variation of this irrational idea. This involved landing components of a return spacecraft on the lunar surface. The astronauts themselves would then land on the lunar surface and while on their mission, they would assemble the components of the spacecraft to launch them from the lunar surface and bring them back to Earth.

Both these methods were finally put where they belonged and that is, in a folder filed under the name, *NASA's insane Moon landing ideas.*

Bizarre Ideas NASA Considered Viable

Soon after President Kennedy's announcement in 1961 to send a manned mission to the Moon by the end of that decade, NASA went into a frenzy at the mere thought of it. Robert C. Gilruth, leader of the Space Task Group (STG), was dismayed when he heard Kennedy's announcement.

James R. Hansen and Anne M. Platoff:

> The message stunned him. "An accelerated program, yes," he wanted that. "A lunar landing, yes, in orderly fashion, with time to work through all the difficulties that such an enterprise was bound to encounter," he wanted that, too. "But not this," he thought to himself. This was too much, too fast. Talk about overconfidence – the first piloted Mercury flight by Alan Shepard had taken place only three weeks ago, on 5 May; NASA had made this one brief fifteen-minute suborbital flight – not even a complete orbit yet – and the president announced that the nation is going to the Moon and on a very ambitious schedule. Suddenly, the STG really had more than it could handle. It already was busy preparing for another suborbital flight (Virgil I. "Gus" Grissom's, on 21 July 1961) and for the first orbital flight sometime early next year (John Glenn's on 20 February 1962). The group's top talent was still "involved almost exclusively" preparing for the first manned orbital flight, and Gilruth himself, before the president's announcement, "had spent almost no time at all" on lunar studies, so demanding were the activities of Project Mercury.[2]

Note: This was at a time when astrophysicists were not taken too seriously by the public and officials alike, and there were no accredited academic aerospace industry programs as of yet. Most of the engineers back then were aeronautical engineers, who needed to educate themselves on orbital mechanics first. The term aerospace engineer was barely known and they were definitely in the minority. So, it was left up to these engineers to educate themselves, eventually earning the title aerospace engineers.

To prepare for a manned lunar landing, NASA needed to contract companies to design and build the spacecraft to be used for both the translunar phase and landing phase of the mission. It is only then, could NASA design a training program for the astronauts to practice procedures, which included simulators. NASA also decided that it was prudent to give the astronauts practical experience outside of simulator training, but that really depended on which method was to be used. This meant that they also needed to design and build a training vehicle that would simulate $1/6^{th}$ gravity for the astronauts to practice in. However, it may not have been practical or even possible to have designed and built a training vehicle capable of simulating lunar gravity, considering which method was to be chosen for the lunar mission. So, NASA first needed to determine which method was the most practical for landing men on the Moon, and then proceed from there.

The methods to be considered would have involved many possible scenarios. For example:

- Was the spacecraft to be launched from Earth and sent direct to the lunar surface, with the same spacecraft used for liftoff and return to Earth?
- Or, was this spacecraft to be assembled in LEO, then sent direct to the lunar surface, with the same spacecraft again used for liftoff?
- Or was the design to involve two spacecraft, the main spacecraft for transporting the crew to the Moon, and

of course the spacecraft for landing on the lunar surface?

- And if it's two spacecraft, were they to be assembled on Earth or in LEO?
- And if assembled on Earth, were they to be launched separately or together?
- And what were the design specifications for both the main spacecraft and lunar lander, as well as how many crew members were to be onboard?
- And where would be the most effective and safest way for rendezvous and docking procedures in space?
  - In Earth orbit?
  - In Lunar orbit?

Several methods of accomplishing a manned lunar landing were considered and a decision had to be made quickly in order to pave the way for a spacecraft to be designed, built, and flight tested, and all of this had to be done in a matter of eight years.

NASA had finally considered three methods that involved all of the possible scenarios mentioned above. These three methods became known as:

1. Direct Ascent,
2. Earth Orbit Rendezvous (EOR), and
3. Lunar Orbit Rendezvous (LOR)

And all of them had serious risks with the consensus being, LOR involved the most risks. These three methods will be discussed next.

Direct Ascent

The details of Direct Ascent, EOR, and LOR would take a whole chapter just to explain. But it's not important to get into all of the details of Direct Ascent and EOR, since these two methods were never used. But for the purposes of this book, we'll discuss the basics of both Direct Ascent and EOR methods, to show how NASA reluctantly decided on the LOR method for the Apollo Moon missions, although there's still some controversy as to how that decision was made, will be explained later in this chapter. And the method that was chosen is explained in Part I of this series and will continue to be discussed in this book.

Wernher von Braun had first considered two methods that he believed were more practical in accomplishing a manned lunar landing; Direct Ascent, and Earth Orbit Rendezvous.

The idea was to launch one spaceship on a direct trajectory to the Moon, with a landing on the lunar surface, called Direct Ascent.

Author and historian Michael J. Neufeld:

> In fall of 1958 and spring of 1959, the Sunday newspaper supplement *This Week* published his novella, *First Men to the Moon,* in four parts, detailing a two-man expedition to that body using a huge rocket and a direct launch from Earth. Turning around as it

approached the Moon, his spacecraft ignited a landing stage to alight on the lunar surface without going into orbit; that stage provided the launch platform for the two astronauts in their winged reentry vehicle to propel themselves back to Earth.[3]

But von Braun's Direct Ascent method required an enormous rocket with incredible power, larger and more powerful than the Saturn V that was eventually used for the Apollo missions. This rocket, the Nova, would require eight engines in the first stage each producing 1.5 million pounds of thrust for a combined total of 12 million pounds of thrust. But a rocket of this size and power was beyond the technical capabilities for that time (and still is). Then a technical director by the name of Milton Rosen, who was a proponent of the Direct Ascent method, proposed a smaller version of the Nova rocket with six F-1 engines. Each of the six F-1 engines would produce 1.5 million pounds of thrust for a combined total of 9 million pounds of thrust. However, it was determined that this version of the rocket wasn't powerful enough for the Direct Ascent method. So, for now, the direct ascent method was on hold.

Figure 3.1 – An example of a spacecraft used for launch, with the same spacecraft used for a Lunar Landing and return to Earth in the Direct Ascent method
Source: Wikipedia

Earth Orbit Rendezvous

The Nova rocket in its original concept was reconsidered for the EOR method. However, aside from the technical challenges involved, the sheer size and power of the Nova rocket presented all sorts of problems.

Michael J. Neufeld:

> The Nova, if it had the eight F-1 first stage, would not only be about 50 ft (15 m) in diameter, it would be around 400 ft (122 m) tall, and would create so much noise during static testing and launching, and such a blast danger if it blew up, it was dubious if it could even be tested at Cape Canaveral. Perhaps they would have to go to some uninhabited island or off-shore platform. [4]
>
> The main idea of EOR was to launch two pieces into space independently using advanced Saturn rockets that were then in development; have the two pieces rendezvous and dock in Earth orbit; assemble, fuel, and detach a lunar mission from the modules that had joined up; and then proceed with that bolstered ship, exactly as in the direct flight mode, to the moon and back to Earth orbit. The advantage of EOR was that it required a pair of less powerful rockets that were already nearing the end of their development.[5]

This is a variation of what was discussed above under Direct Ascent. But instead of launching the spacecraft from Earth, components of the spacecraft were to be launched into LEO and then assembled. This would have been preferable given that the spacecraft would have been approximately 90 ft long, about the height of a 10-story building. A version of the Saturn rocket was to be used for this purpose.

Figure 3.2 – The NOVA rocket that was to be used in the Earth Orbit Rendezvous method, was to be larger and more powerful than any previous rocket, including the Saturn V
Source: Wikimedia

But once again, to assemble components of a spacecraft in LEO, required the establishment of a fully functional manned space program. But like the previous plans to assemble a 210-ton spacecraft in LEO, this too meant that NASA had to become proficient in its manned space program first, to actually have done the work necessary to prepare this spacecraft in LEO for a manned lunar landing.

It was an impossible task to accomplish in just a few years, as well as several more years that would have been needed just to test the assembled spacecraft in LEO for the EOR method, if they were going to meet the first manned lunar landing by the end of the 1960s. Even with trying to duplicate the minimal flight-testing standards in actual conditions as was done with Apollos 5, 8, 9, and 10 leading up to Apollo 11, and then learning how to assemble the components of a spacecraft in LEO, and doing it within the necessary timeframe to meet President Kennedy's goal, would have been impossible, to say the least.

And even if NASA had the means to assemble a spacecraft in LEO, the EOR method had presented some serious problems of its own.

> For many, including von Braun, it was the spacecraft design argument that finally decided the issue. Faget and his people were never able to satisfactorily solve the problem of how to land the big EOR vehicle on the Moon. Originally it was something like 90 ft long. On February 20, the Mercury team had at last succeeded in launching John Glenn on his three-orbit trip around the world, yet here they were trying to figure out how to back a vehicle the size of the entire Mercury–Atlas rocket down to the lunar surface![6]

Note: Maxime Faget mentioned in the quote above, designed the Mercury spacecraft and was involved in the Gemini and Apollo programs as well as the Space Shuttle.

Given the enormous technological challenges and costs involved in the EOR method, the LOR method was finally given serious consideration. It was then that Wernher von Braun grudgingly supported the LOR method, but only after a great deal of procrastination and consternation, which will be discussed next.

Lunar Orbit Rendezvous

After NASA seemingly came to its senses and realized that a Direct Ascent wasn't possible, and that sending a person to the Moon on a one-way trip wouldn't *fly* (pun intended) with the public, and that the EOR method proved to be impossible, the LOR method was now promoted as the most practical way for a manned lunar landing, which many still considered a very risky idea.

The LOR method has been attributed to aerospace engineer, John Houbolt.

Neufeld:

> A Langley Center aeronautical engineer, John C. Houbolt (pronounced "Ho-bolt"), had been championing the idea since at least 1960 on behalf of a small group there. He pointed out the fundamental physics. Whether you went direct or by EOR, and whether you went into lunar orbit first or not, the entire vehicle descended to the lunar surface. That meant that you had to carry a lot of propellants to get the big vehicle down, plus all the propellants needed to lift the Apollo spacecraft off the surface and back to Earth. Why not leave the propellants needed to get back to Earth in lunar orbit, and for that matter the whole main spacecraft, and descend to the Moon in a light vehicle designed simply for that job?[7]

However, Houbolt's LOR method was not popular, and he went through great lengths to convince everyone that LOR was the best method.

Equally outlandish, at least at first glance, was NASA engineer John Houbolt's plan for Lunar Orbit Rendezvous. At a May 1961 meeting held in Washington, D.C., he outlined the following scenario: Send one rocket, insert a "mother ship" in lunar orbit, and let the mother ship dispatch a lander to the surface. "A rendezvous around the moon is like been in a living room," he said. "Why take the whole damn living room down to the surface when it's easier to go down in a little tiny craft? It becomes a chain reaction of simplifications: development, testing, manufacturing, launch and flight operations. All would be simplified. Don't you see! This is it! If there is any area we should push, this is the one." [8]

Figure 3.3 – The Apollo 11 LM returns to rendezvous and dock with the CM in the Lunar Orbit Rendezvous method
Source: Wikipedia

Houbolt persisted saying that it was the only practical solution and would solve the problem of the enormous amounts of propellants needed for both the Direct Ascent and EOR methods. This involved the CM docking with the LM outside of LEO on its way to the Moon. The docked spacecraft would then enter lunar orbit and the LM would separate from the CM and navigate to its planned lunar landing site. It would then liftoff from the lunar surface to rendezvous and dock back with the CM. Houbolt called this method, simple. Yet, it was anything but simple as everything had to work perfectly in this method.

Being 240,000 miles from Earth, meant there was no assistance or rescue possible if anything went wrong during rendezvous and docking while in lunar orbit. There was absolutely no room for error. This was the main point of the controversy.

When it comes to human ingenuity, as impressive as it has been in many facets of our society, nothing works to perfection, which is why we have redundancy built into most of our technology. Today, whenever there is a catastrophic failure of technology for example the passenger ship and aviation industry, there is a whole rescue apparatus in place for the people involved. But there was no rescue apparatus in place for emergency situations with manned missions in LEO, let alone 240,000 miles away in lunar orbit. And if the Ranger, Lunar Orbiter, and Surveyor unmanned programs are to be used as examples of how *reliable* our technology was, then the LOR method used in the Apollo Moon program was another recipe for disaster. And as we've determined in Chapter 2, the Apollo missions had at best a probability of a 54% success rate, based on our analysis of the Mercury and Gemini manned missions, as well as the Ranger, Lunar Orbiter, and Surveyor unmanned missions. This is definitely a generous success rate percentage, without factoring in the complex technological challenges of manned missions using the LOR method, as well as all the many variables involved including the environment. This, along with any number of other scenarios that could easily have led to disaster, will be discussed further in Chapter 5 where we'll conclude by determining a more realistic chance of success for the Apollo missions, if they had actually been attempted.

It's interesting to note too that Wernher von Braun still favored the EOR method and had spoken out against LOR. No doubt, he seems to have had an intuitive sense of the dangers involved in the LOR method. But clearly both the Direct Ascent and EOR methods were not practical either and as has been established, were technically impossible. So, it was much later, around May 1962, when von Braun reluctantly decided on the LOR method, which he publicly endorsed on June 7th, 1962, much to the surprise of his inner group of colleagues. That narrowed the timeline for designing, building, and testing of the Apollo spacecraft to less than 7 years; realistically, given the amount of testing that should have been done on the CM, LM, and Saturn V, this would have far exceeded the time frame of 7 years.

But the question is, why did Wernher von Braun hold out so long to endorse the LOR method? And what explains his strange behavior in not telling his closet colleagues? There is only speculation, according to historians.

Neufeld:

> We are left with one mystery: why should he have withheld his change-of-heart from key associates in Huntsville, especially in view of his general management practice of making all technical decisions through long-drawn-out discussions with his German dominated Development Board? Part of the answer has long been obvious from his prepared remarks: he was worried that the mode decision had already gone on too long and that the President's timetable was under threat. He decided he had to lead. But that still does not explain why, during the previous week, he never informed Ernst Geissler and the other MSFC lecturers of his decision. He let them stand up on June 7 and give pro-EOR arguments for 6 h before his surprise summary. Ultimately, that question is unanswerable on the basis of the surviving documents, so any historian or biographer is left to speculate. Perhaps he had decided to wait till the next Board meeting to discuss it with his staff, but then changed his mind when the Shea briefing was held. Perhaps he did not want to undercut his presenters' enthusiasm by telling them in advance that their hard work was perhaps irrelevant. Or perhaps the week prior to June 7 had been so hectic he had no time to properly think through how and when he was going to declare his pro-LOR sentiments.[9]

Note: The mode decision in the quote above, refers to connecting the modules of the spacecraft in LEO for the EOR method. And MSFC is for Marshall Spacecraft Flight Center.

Speculating and "perhaps," are necessary when it comes to analyzing historical decisions. But, from the above quote, it's obvious that there is no need for speculation at all. It is clear from Wernher von Braun's behavior towards his colleagues on June 7th, 1962, that he and NASA knew as early as then, that manned missions to the Moon were impossible in the foreseeable future, and that it would most likely be decades before a manned mission could even be attempted. So, the LOR method was the best option to manipulate the public into believing in the validity of these missions.

In the LOR method, absolutely nothing could go wrong while in lunar orbit including lunar landing, liftoff, rendezvous, and docking. And docking presents an even greater risk of disaster, because if anything went wrong, both spacecraft would have been severely damaged and/or destroyed. Everything had to work to perfection. Anything short of perfection, meant disaster. Having no redundancy and no means of rescue was a fundamental flaw in the planning of all of the Apollo Moon missions. However, the decision to use the LOR method led to the design and construction of the LM, which will be discussed in the next section.

The Lunar Module

The contract for the LM was awarded to Grumman Aircraft Corporation in November, 1962. The contract was worth 1.61 billion dollars and they were to build 15 LMs, 10 test vehicles, and 2 simulators. Tom Kelly who worked for Grumman, is credited with the original concept and design of the LM.

The LM was to be used specifically for the space environment. It was never meant to be used in Earth's atmosphere, hence it didn't need to be aerodynamically designed. This is what gave the LM it's ungainly look.

Figure 3.4 – Buzz Aldrin descends on the Lunar Module ladder
Source: Wikimedia

The LM consisted of two main stages:

<u>The Ascent stage:</u>

- Height: 9.284777 feet

- Width: 14.0748 feet
- Crew capacity: 2
- Total Mass: 10,361.73 pounds

The Descent stage:

- Height: 10.59711 feet
- Width: 12.23753 feet
- Width, with landing gear extended: 31.00394 feet
- Total Mass: 22,784.775 pounds

As you can see, propellant makes up for the majority of the mass, which was needed for landing and liftoff from the lunar surface. The need for this amount of propellant added considerable weight, which is why every effort was taken to keep the overall weight of both the CM and LM to a minimum. But as we learned in Part I of this series, even that effort made no difference since the F-1 engines did not perform to its full potential capacity, which meant these engines could not have launched a fully loaded 3,000-ton Saturn V.

The crew area in the LM ascent stage sounds fairly large according to the specifications, but those specifications represent the overall dimensions of the structure. The pressurized area in the LM was approximately 235 cubic feet. The actual habitable area for the astronauts was approximately 160 cubic feet, or 7 feet wide, by 3 feet deep, by 9 feet in height. There were no seats for the astronauts, so restraints were added to hold them in place. 160 cubic feet is not much room by anyone's standards and when you factor in their bulky spacesuits, you

get a good idea of the little maneuvering room they actually had.

Note: When you look at photos of the interior of the LM, or you see the interior of an actual LM at a space museum, you really don't get a sense of just how small the habitable crew compartment really was. This is because your position is from several feet back looking forward towards where the two astronauts would have stood. This gives the illusion that the astronauts have plenty of room to maneuver, which is not the case. The crew compartment is actually quite cramped. To get a better idea of the size of the interior, you need to picture yourself standing three feet from the control panel. And it would be interesting to see an actual mockup of this crew cabin in its original form, that is, in an enclosed environment like that of an actual LM ascent stage, with cameras inside showing two people demonstrating changing into and out of their Apollo spacesuits.

The ascent stage was cylindrical in shape and had two propellant tanks. It was made of aluminum alloy skins and had three sections: the front face, the midsection, and the aft section. To protect the astronauts from the temperature extremes of up to 500 degrees Fahrenheit as well as the dangers of micrometeoroid impacts, the ascent stage was covered with a thermal blanket and aluminum shield. This consisted of 25 layers of aluminized sheets (Mylar or H-film), covered by a sheet of aluminum between 0.004 to 0.008 inches. We'll discuss this outer shielding a little more, shortly.

The descent stage was cruciform in shape and included four large propellant tanks, one pressurant tank, one water tank, all of which were made of the same basic materials. Its thermal blanket was heavier for added protection because of the exhaust from the reaction control thrusters on the ascent stage, which is why it was on the outside of the structure.

Both the ascent stage and descent stage had their own rocket engine with an additional 16 reaction control thrusters (RCS) on the ascent stage. The RCS were grouped in four and each group had four RCS thrusters. Each thruster produced 100 pounds of thrust to control pitch, roll, and yaw. The ascent stage rocket engine produced 3,500 pounds of thrust, while the descent stage rocket engine produced 10,125 pounds of thrust. The descent stage rocket engine was used for the lunar landing, and was also used as a launch platform by the ascent stage for liftoff from the lunar surface.

Figure 3.5 – The Apollo 17 LM launch shows how the descent stage was used as a launch platform to liftoff from the lunar surface
Source: Wikipedia

Note: Apollos 15, 16, and 17 were supposed to have carried the lunar rover onboard the descent stage. The lunar rover is a subject for another book, but it's interesting how NASA claims to have solved the problem of the limited space within the descent stage, which included 4 large propellant tanks, one pressurant tank and one water tank. This would have made for some very interesting weight and balance calculations for the proper distribution of weight. It also would have required the onboard computer to determine whether the extra distribution of weight was moving aft or forward of the center of gravity, due to the reduction in the onboard propellant while approaching to land on the lunar surface. This in turn, would then have needed to be calculated for the RCS thrusters to compensate for aft or forward distribution in weight. And although the onboard computer supposedly would have proven itself in its ability to do this with previous Apollo missions, there was no further testing of a LM in actual flight conditions with the lunar rover onboard. And yet, Apollos 15, 16, and 17 were supposed to have worked perfectly.

But there were even more troubling aspects to the design and building of the LM, for example, it's fuel system. Because of weight restrictions, there was no fuel pump. It was a pressure feed system that used hypergolic fuels, which would ignite on contact, thus producing thrust. But a pressure feed system wouldn't work very well in the vacuum of space. Therefore, supercooled liquid helium was sent in from a separate tank. This would build up pressure in the propellant tanks, which could then be released to come into contact for the controlled explosion to produce thrust.

> "It was something that had never been done before," recalls rocket expert Manning Dandrige. "The idea was resisted by Max Faget, a leading spacecraft designer at the Space Task Group who hated the smell of anything having to do with cryogenics. We had a good deal of difficulty getting the helium-pressure system in, but it was bound to save us eight or nine hundred pounds in pistons and pumps at the top of the rocket stack, which is where weight really counted, because it was going to cost something like twenty thousand dollars to lift each pound from the top of that stack to the moon." [10]

This propellent is a highly volatile mixture. Nothing could be left to chance as there were concerns about the efficacy and safety of using hypergolic fuels. This also meant that the LM's engine had to ignite on its first try because of the corrosive nature of these propellants, which had the potential to severely damage the engine, not to mention the real possibility of an explosion. And as was mentioned earlier, there was little or no redundancy and any means of rescue in LEO, let alone 240,000 miles from Earth on the lunar surface. So, everything had to work perfectly at all times. This of course would make for an interesting few seconds leading up to ignition of the LM ascent engine, for liftoff from the lunar surface.

Note: As the reader no doubt remembers, there were many examples of how vulnerable our technology can be, as with the unmanned space missions discussed in chapter 2. Having no redundancy or any means of rescue for a manned mission in LEO or beyond, is a disaster waiting to happen.

The LM had its own Primary Guidance and Navigation System (PGNS), very similar to the Apollo Guidance Computer (AGC) in the CM. It also had a back-up computer called the Abort Guidance System in the event of a PGNS failure, which they could have used to rendezvous with the CM (in theory, that is). The basic design of the LM PGNS involved the inertial measurement unit, a DSKY (an acronym for display and keyboard) that was used for the astronauts to interface with the computer, and the optical equipment used for star sightings. It also had two radar measurement systems, one for the lunar landing, and the other for rendezvous with the CM after liftoff from the lunar surface.

Note: Refer to Part 1, Chapter 3 of this series for more details on the AGC. And for complete details of the LM specifications, please refer to the bibliography of this book, or www.nasa.gov and many other online sources.

As was mentioned above, the LM's outer protection from the thermal extremes of cislunar space and the real possibility of micrometeoroid impacts was a sheet of aluminum 0.004 to 0.008 inches thick. There was much consternation over this thickness of the outer shielding from Grumman personnel, as well as concern for the overall flimsy design of the LM itself. It was said that the actual LM was not able to support its own weight in an Earth environment with the two astronauts onboard. But once again, the restrictions on weight, necessitated the reduced thickness of this outer shielding which was a real risk to the safety of the astronauts and could not be overlooked.

> One two-thousands of an inch – roughly the thickness of two sheets of newspaper – that's what was going to hold all the air inside the LM. One hard kick and you could put your foot right through the wall of the ship and into space. The astronauts would have to be isolated from the skins with fiberglass shields and plastic covers and false floors. And Tom Kelly would worry, when men were on the moon, especially when it came to plan overnight missions, when the astronauts would come in from a full-day excursion and take off their helmets and gloves and backpacks and settle into their hammocks for a few hours' sleep. They'd be relying, then, for a long time, on the structural integrity of the skins, and this troubled Tom. It troubled him very much, because he knew that the cabin had scores of angular bends in it – very complicated geometry – and if there was a weak rivet or weld, or a crack somewhere...[11]

Considering the flimsy design of the LM, one would understandably expect that stringent and vigorous tests were done of the LM not only on the ground, but in actual flight conditions. Instead, NASA used what it called LM test articles. These were incomplete LM structures, designed to duplicate an actual LM to test components on the ground and in the space environment. They were not actual LMs, so any tests done on them would not have produced any data as to the effects on an actual LM. As Joshua Stoff, curator of the Cradle of Aviation Museum on Long Island explains:

> This LM will be dropped from varying heights to see how the landing gear and shock absorbers are

functioning. As these tests were very stressful to the vehicles, only test articles, not flight vehicles, were used.[12]

The actual LM tests in space involved:

- One LM test article on Apollo 4
- One incomplete LM test on Apollo 5
- One LM test article on Apollo 6
- The first manned mission of the LM on Apollo 9, which included separation of the ascent stage from the descent stage.
- The second manned mission of the LM on Apollo 10, which was the first LM to leave LEO to circumnavigate the Moon and descend to within 50,000 feet of the lunar surface, before aborting the descent, to rendezvous back with the CM.

As is apparent, there were only two fully functional tests of the LM in actual conditions of space before the Apollo 11 mission. No actual LM was tested on the ground. The reasoning behind this, was because of the risk of damage that could have been done to such a flimsy design.

The LM test articles that were used for testing had no aluminum outside covering, no landing gear, and no engine. This is hardly an example of rigorous testing of an actual LM, especially where it was needed most before any test trials were done in the vacuum of space, or the lunar environment with its $1/6^{th}$ gravity.

Given the complex geometric design of the LM, and the very real potential of a catastrophe with using hypergolic fuels escaping through a compromised structure, rigorous testing should have been done on a fully functional unmanned LM in all possible scenarios on the ground, then through rigorous and numerous testing involving unmanned LMs in actual flight conditions in LEO and the lunar environment, before any manned missions involving the LM were approved. Two manned tests of the LM don't come close to qualifying as rigorous testing, that is, if we are to believe NASA that these tests even took place. And given the evidence so far, this did not happen.

As an example, concerns for the safety of both the crew and passengers regarding the design specifications of aircraft in the aviation industry, would be solved through rigorous and numerous tests. When this is not done, we see the unfortunate outcome and the loss of souls, examples of which have been reported in the news. But apparently not so with the Apollo Moon mission program. Instead, we were told by NASA that the shielding of the LM, which was equivalent to the thickness of two newspapers, was enough to prevent any serious damage by micrometeoroids and any of the possible scenarios that could have exposed the crew to the vacuum of space. Never, before or after the Apollo Moon program, has there been such an example of 'perfection' in technology, without any of the rigorous flight-testing standards that have been set by other industries.

However, in subsequent years, serious concerns have been raised by the very same engineers who worked on the Apollo Moon program. These concerns were usually raised years, sometimes decades later while being interviewed by various authors e.g., Charles R. Pellegrino and Joshua Stoff, both of whom are proponents of the Apollo Moon missions. And one of the concerns raised with the Apollo Moon program, was the issue of Quality Control, which is equally important in increasing the chances of success for manned missions.

Accidents and disasters are usually caused by a chain of events, as in aviation. Far too often, the media looks to the pilots as the source or cause of the accident until a proper investigation is done, which can take months or years. And some investigations remain controversial decades after a tragedy. But many of the incidents, these investigations lead right back to quality control. And more often than not, it is the area of shoddy quality control which starts the chain of events that can lead to a disaster. This quality control can mean anything from manufacturing to crew training. A pilot can only prepare for what he or she is trained for. If there are gaps in that training process, then the potential for a disaster is there, no matter how experienced a pilot is. We saw evidence of this 25 years ago, when two brand-new Boeing 737s crashed due to a problem with the rudder system. And we saw this again, most recently and coincidently with two other brand-new Boeing 737 crashes with the Boeing 737 MAX 8, brought on by software problems. Tragically, accidents happen. But it is even more of a tragedy, when people have lost their lives due to shoddy quality control and gaps in training. And although there are many personnel involved in this process, it starts and ends with upper management.

Therefore, it's not surprising to learn that there was a lack of quality control with the Apollo Moon program. And what's more, this source happens to come from none other than NASA quality-control inspector Mel Friedman:

> It troubles me to this day, that the kind of quality control we were fighting for early in the program was not demanded by NASA until later in the program, until *after* the first men landed on the moon. You think it would have been the other way around. [13]

This quote needs no explanation, as its obvious to the reader the lack of quality control involved in NASA's claim of sending manned missions to the Moon. It is just one more statement in a long list of statements showing the many disturbing practices within NASA during the Apollo Moon program. And as in other examples of how quality control can lead to disasters, NASA management is mostly to blame. I say mostly, since the engineers and technicians also had an obligation to reveal what was going on at the time, instead of waiting decades later.

It's obvious why proponents of the Apollo Moon missions tend to chastise those who use quotes to make their point. Quotes can often reveal and literally destroy work that was once perceived to have been verified through the peer review process. And we've just seen one very good example of this, with NASA quality-control inspector Mel Friedman's quote above.

Further, the usual rebuttal from NASA's proponents for not following its static testing with a comparable amount of unmanned flight testing, is that the aviation industry follows the same pattern of flight testing with its aircraft. However, the aviation industry has had decades of data and experience from an environment in which they are more than familiar with, even up to the Apollo program. Yet the aerospace industry in the 1960s had little or no credible data or experience to build on, for a hostile environment between the Earth and Moon with which manned missions were to take place.

As for automation, the first fully automated aircraft was flown in 1947 but this still required pilots onboard, as these automated systems were still in the process of being perfected. Pilots monitored the plane and could take over the controls if necessary, and it was still years before a fully automated system without the need for pilots was perfected. Yet, by the 1960s, NASA had already shown its proficiency in automation for manned space vehicles, for example, the two unmanned launches of the Saturn V. NASA could have taken full advantage of this when flight testing its spacecraft, in an attempt to minimize the potential risks to any manned mission to LEO and beyond.

There's one other point to note here: The actual design of the LM wasn't finalized until 1965, which further narrowed the time frame for the rigorous testing that should have been done with a fully functional and unmanned LM. Further, the training vehicle that was designed based on the LM, which was supposed to have given the astronauts practical experience in simulated lunar landings, had numerous problems of its own. That is discussed next in Chapter 4, along with a detailed discussion of the Apollo 11 lunar landing and as we'll learn, NASA's 'facts,' don't fit with reality.

Chapter Three – Endnotes

[1] Charles R. Pellegrino and Joshua Stoff, *CHARIOTS FOR APOLLO: THE UNTOLD STORY BEHIND THE RACE TO THE MOON*, p. 25.

[2] National Aeronautics and Space Administration (NASA), World Spaceflight News, James R. Hansen, Anne M. Platoff, *APOLLO and AMERICA'S MOON LANDING PROGRAM, ENCHANTED RENDEZVOUS – John Houbolt and the Genesis of the Lunar-Orbit Rendezvous Concept, and POLITICAL AND TECHNICAL ASPECTS OF PLACING A FLAG ON THE MOON*, p. 4.

[3] Michael J. Neufeld, *Science Direct: von Braun and the lunar-orbit rendezvous decision: finding a way to go to the moon (article).* p.3. doi:10.1016/j.actaastro.2007.12.011 (si.edu)

[4] Ibid. p.4.

[5] *The Rendezvous That Was Almost Missed: Lunar Orbit Rendezvous and the Apollo Program, December, 1992, NF175*
https://www.nasa.gov/centers/langley/news/factsheets/Rendezvous.html

[6] Op Cit., Neufeld. p.7.

[7] Ibid. p.6.

[8] Charles R. Pellegrino and Joshua Stoff, *CHARIOTS FOR APOLLO: THE UNTOLD STORY BEHIND THE RACE TO THE MOON*, p. 26.

[9] Op Cit., Neufeld, p.10.

[10] Op Cit., Pellegrino, Stoff, p. 59.

[11] Ibid., p. 83.

[12] Joshua Stoff, *IMAGES OF AMERICA: BUILDING MOONSHIPS: THE GRUMMAN LUNAR MODULE*, p. 74.

[13] Op Cit., Pellegrino, Stoff, p. 89.

Chapter Four

The Apollo Moon Landings

Lunar Training Vehicles, Fiction, And Reality

Before we get to the lunar landing training program, we must first review some history which goes back to the year 1961, before the LOR method and LM design were finalized. NASA's Flight Research Center (FRC) on Edwards Air Force Base, California, had taken the lead role in deciding which simulation methods were to be used for a manned lunar landing. In 1961, the FRC also established the Advanced Planning Office led by Hubert M. "Jake" Drake, who formed a committee of five FRC engineers to study lunar landing simulation methods.

The committee soon realized the enormous technical challenges involved, not only in an actual manned lunar landing, but in ways to practice this lunar landing in ground-based simulators and the need to program the simulator for the many complex variables, that would be encountered while descending to the lunar surface. This was an era of analog simulations, which was not capable of the complicated factors needed to simulate manned lunar landings below 10,000 feet above the lunar surface. Adding to these complicated factors, the astronauts were asking for some form of manual control of the LM, although automation versus manual control of the lunar landing would be an ongoing debate. Eventually, simulators were built, with more sophisticated software to try and deal with all variables involved in a manned lunar landing, but other options where still needed, more specifically, to find a way to give the astronauts more practical training. This practical training is a crucial point to keep in mind, as we discuss the training and preparations for a manned lunar landing.

The committee of course had no previous data as of yet for actual unmanned, let alone manned missions designed to land on the lunar surface. However, in their research, they discovered that the Naval Ordnance Test Station (NOTS) at Inyokem, California, had been simulating unpiloted lunar landings since 1959 and had recently tested a 700-pound simulator.

> Fabricated from available hardware, the vehicle consisted of four fuel tanks, one oxidizer tank, one pressurizing tank, one variable-thrust rocket engine, four landing shock absorbers, and control hardware. The machine used a storable hypergolic fuel-unsymmetric dimethyl hydrazine-and relied on red fuming nitric acid as an oxidizer. The primary controlling device consisted of an optical altitude/velocity sensor at the top of the vehicle.
>
> During testing, the vehicle was constrained by four cables suspended from the top of a 150-foot tower. Controlled entirely from the ground, the vehicle's first test successfully demonstrated only the rocket system. The second test successfully verified that both the engine vibration and the dust created by the engine had only negligible effect on the optical scanner. The NOTS project planned more tests for demonstrating

the closed-loop operation of the optical sensor and control algorithms under a variety of conditions and surfaces. Members of the FRC committee decided to stay abreast of the NOTS research since it involved critical control parameters essential to their project.[1]

As you can see this test was done under strict conditions, was controlled from the ground, did not involve a crew, and was nowhere near the mass of a lunar lander needed to simulate the LM. And although these tests seemed promising, the committee seemed rather ambivalent as it continued to look for other viable options to simulate a lunar landing.

Drake and his committee had considered its options for a training vehicle including a vertical take-off and landing vehicle (VTOL). The obvious choice for a VTOL vehicle was the helicopter. But the thrust vector created by the rotor blades, precluded any chances for practicing the flight attitudes necessary for a LM in the lunar environment. This then led to the design of a landing vehicle without the need for any aerodynamic characteristics, since airfoils were not needed for lift in the vacuum of space.

Note: Flight attitude is the aircraft's movements around the horizontal, lateral, and vertical axes in relation to the Earth's horizon.

The concept was to design a free-flying vehicle capable of simulating $1/6^{th}$ gravity. However, there were challenges in the design and building of such a vehicle.

Bell AeroSystems was one of the companies which studied the lunar landing. An engineer from this company Ken Levin and his colleagues, came up with a solution for simulating lunar gravity:

> Levin and his associates proposed a neat solution for simulating lunar conditions: a double gimble that would allow the outer vehicle to duplicate the moon's motions while a lift-supporting propulsion device maintained vertical orientation.[2]

The training vehicle had to perform in a vacuum of space scenario and it also had to duplicate the flight characteristics of the LM, as well as having the same thrust-to-mass ratio. But most important was this training vehicle had to duplicate the gravity of the Moon, which of course is $1/6^{th}$ that of Earth, while also flying in Earth's gravity. So, in essence, they had to design a hybrid vehicle, which we'll learn, made for some very interesting and harrowing flying with some very close calls for the astronauts.

To help simulate the Moon's gravity, Kevin Levin and his team of engineers proposed the concept of having small rockets mounted on the outside of the vehicle's frame, and a ducted-fan orjet engine for the center of the vehicle. The small rockets would provide deceleration on descent, and the orjet engine would simulate lunar gravity. The orjet engine was gimballed, which allowed the training vehicle to maneuver through different attitudes around the orjet engine, similar to maneuvers expected of the LM.

After approval of Kevin Levin and his engineers' proposal, Bell AeroSystems was awarded the contract for the lunar training vehicle in January 1962. Yet, Wernher von Braun didn't endorse the LOR method until May 1962. Further, the design of the LM wasn't finalized until 1965, so there's an obvious disconnect here. However, now that NASA had awarded the contract, they concentrated on designing the training vehicle for the astronauts to practice simulated lunar landings, which was eventually called the Lunar Landing Research Vehicle.

Lunar Landing Research Vehicle

The Lunar Landing Research Vehicle (LLRV) went through several designs and cost overruns for almost two years. Further, the LLRV was a truss structure in design with no airfoil to produce lift, but was still subject to aerodynamic forces, while expected to perform the complex maneuvers necessary for lunar simulation. To accomplish these complex maneuvers as well as the increased pilot workload, it was soon realized that a conventional state-of-the-art flight control system was inadequate. This led to a seemingly innovative idea:

> The LLRV team chose analog fly-by-wire technology as its basic systems design, as there was no other way to meet the vehicle's wide range of control requirements. In the early 1960s, digital control technology still lay over the horizon. At the same time, team members opted to forego the complexities that accompanied a mechanical system approach as to avoid the weight such systems would add to the LLRV. And since weight was a critical issue, every possible weight option had to be considered in order to attain acceptable vehicle thrust-to-weight margins for both VTOL and lunar-simulation operation. Analog fly-by-wire technology also would provide the great degree of

flexibility needed to allow for design modifications that would later be required on the vehicle. Developmental testing for final verification of operation and performance would replace the usual exhaustive design analysis. This approach, accommodated by the fly-by-wire configuration, would be less costly and aligned with FRC test philosophy so long as changes could be made easily in the field.[3]

Fly-by-wire systems were already in use for several years by the military for some of its aircraft. However, the LLRV was actually the first to use a fully integrated fly-by-wire system, which is often touted as leading the way in this technology. But there's no doubt that the military would have had plans for such innovation for its aircraft with or without the LLRV. And in fact, the passenger aircraft Concorde, was designed and built during the Apollo Moon program and used a fully integrated fly-by-wire system.

The fully integrated fly-by-wire system for the LLRV was designed because of the realization that no other method would suffice, given the nature of this hybrid vehicle and the maneuvers it was expected to make in lunar simulated mode. Further, this fly-by-wire system replaced any need for cables or hydraulics, which kept the overall weight of the vehicle to a minimum. This system would also automatically make corrections for keeping the LLRV stable during flight, as well as having an automatic-throttle system which would be switched on by the pilot for lunar simulation mode.

The design of the LLRV was finalized and assembled in 1964. Its dimensions were as follows:

- o Height: 10 feet.
- o Width: 13.35 feet.
- o Length: 22.50 feet.

There were two LLRVs built for the training program which were designed for one pilot, who sat in the front of the vehicle. The controls for the pilot were set up identical to what would normally have been found in an aircraft which included rudder pedals for yaw, and a center stick for pitch and roll. It had a center thrust jet engine that was gimballed and had thrusters for attitude control. There were sixteen thrusters in all, each grouped into clusters of four on the outer corners of the vehicle.

Figure 4.1 – Lunar Landing Research Vehicle (LLRV)
Source: Wikimedia Commons

During takeoff and ascent, the jet engine provided thrust for lift, since as already mentioned, there was no airfoil for that purpose. A typical flight included an ascent to 1000 feet above ground level (AGL). The pilot then switched to the lunar-simulation system, which would activate the auto-throttle, and the jet engine would automatically be set to simulate lunar gravity.

> The basic requirement of the lunar-simulation system was to reduce the influence of aerodynamic drag forces to a level not noticeable by the pilot while at the same time maintaining the jet engine's vertical thrust at 5/6 of the vehicle's weight. This was done by using the gimbals to vector the engine's thrust and by using the auto-throttle system to vary it.[4]

Once in simulator mode the auto-throttle decreased the jet engine thrust to adjust to $5/6^{th}$ gravity. The pilot would then use the thrusters for a controlled descent from 1000 AGL, to a distance of approximately 3000 feet to its designated touch down point.

The first flight of the **LLRV No. 1** took place at Edwards Air Force Base's South Base, Kern County, California on the morning of October 30, 1964. The flight lasted 56 seconds. There were two other flights that morning, the second, again was 56 seconds in duration and the third landed after 29 seconds, due to a failure in the attitude-rocket selection relay. In all, there were 34 flights that were used to check out the vehicle leading up to the first simulated lunar landing flight. After a year of experimental flights in the LLRV, the first simulated lunar landing training flight, that is, from an altitude of approximately 1000 AGL to a designated landing point, took place on September 8, 1965.

On January 11, 1967, **LLRV No. 2** had its first flight. The first practice flight took place on March 3, 1967. Apollo 11 commander Neil Armstrong first flew the LLRV on March 23 of that same year. This now left two years to gather all of the data required, and train the Apollo 11 astronauts to land the LM on the lunar surface, which seemed adequate. But since there was no margin for error and propellent in the actual LM was limited because of weight restrictions, this training took on even more importance, meaning that the astronauts would have had to land in the designated lunar surface area with near precision on its first attempt. And once passed a certain point in the approach, an abort was risky, so they were basically committed to the landing.

Eventually, the LLRVs' center stick and pedal controls were replaced with a three-axis side-arm hand controller from the one used in the Gemini spacecraft, in an attempt to duplicate the flight controls of the LM. The LLRVs were then test flown by Manned Spacecraft Center pilots, before the Apollo astronauts logged any flight time in these modified training vehicles.

Total Number Of Flights And Flight Times For The LLRV

We'll discuss the number of flights and average out the flight times for the LLRV. And although the astronauts selected to fly the LM were required to log a required amount of flight times in the LLRV, we'll focus more on the flight times involving Apollo 11 commander Neil Armstrong, since he was purportedly the first person to have landed and walked on the lunar surface.

The number of flights and flight hours for the LLRVs are as follows:

- LLRV No. 1 had 282 flights. Each flight was on average, about 7 minutes. The total flight time was approximately 33 hours.

- LLRV No. 2 had 6 flights. The total flight time was approximately 42 minutes. None of the astronauts in training flew this particular vehicle.

The total flights for both LLRV No. 1 and LLRV No. 2, was 288 flights. The total time flight time for both LLRVs, was 33 hours and 42 minutes.

Flight Times For The Astronauts In The LLRV

For the astronauts who specifically trained in the LLRV No. 1, we further breakdown the hours as follows:

- o Of the 282 flights for LLRV No.1, NASA's Calculated Vehicle Flight Log lists 84 flights at Ellington Air Force Base.

- o Of these 84 flights, 46 of them were flown by various astronauts, which gave them a combined total flight time of approximately 5 hours.

Of the combined total flight time of 5 hours, Neil Armstrong flew a total of 21 flights in LLRV No. 1, which was approximately 2 hours and 45 minutes.

Lunar Landing Training Vehicle

The LLRV was then upgraded in a new version of the vehicle called the Lunar Landing Training Vehicle (LLTV). On the whole, the basic design stayed the same, but with these modifications:

- ⇒ New miniaturization of electronic circuitry and packaging technologies. This reduced the overall weight of the LLTV, which allowed the structure to be strengthened to compensate for previous problems with vibrations in the LLRV.

- ⇒ Gemini spacecraft side-arm hand controller used in the LLRV, which was replaced for a LM hand controller in the LLTV.

- ⇒ Instrument panel, which was reorganized to closely duplicate the LM's instrument panel.

In addition, there was also a plan to enclose the flight deck of the LLTV with triangular windows similar to those on the LM. The purpose of all this was to replicate the LM as much as possible, and to give the astronauts more familiarity with the spacecraft to be used in the actual landing on the lunar surface. However, the closed new design restricted the pilot's downward view, which was a concern for safety. Therefore, a compromise was made to eliminate the lower front part of the enclosure.

Figure 4.2 – Lunar Landing Training Vehicle (LLTV)
Source: Wikimedia Commons

The astronauts' training took place at Ellington Air Force Base, Houston, Texas. Final proficiency flights for the astronauts, took place at the Kennedy Space Center, the launch site for all the Apollo Moon missions.

Total Number Of Flights And Flight Times For The LLTV

There were three LLTV vehicles built and the number of flights and flight hours for each LLTV, are as follows:

- LLTV No. 1 had 15 flights. Each flight was on average 8.56 minutes. The combined total flight time was 2 hours, 8 minutes, and 35 seconds.

- LLTV No. 2 had 206 flights. Each flight was on average, 7 minutes. The combined total flight time was 24 hours, 2 minutes, and 26 seconds.

- LLTV No. 3 had 286 flights. Each flight was on average, 7 minutes. The combined total flight time was 33 hours, 18 minutes, and 51 seconds.

Flight Times For The Astronauts In The LLTV

According to the Calculated Vehicle Flight Log, the LLTV had a combined total of 507 flights. This amounts to a total flight time of approximately 59 hours. Of the 507 flights, 216 flights involved the Apollo astronauts, which gives them a combined total flight time of approximately 25 hours.

Of the flight time of 25 hours, Neil Armstrong flew a total of 6 flights in the LLTV No. 2, for a total flight time of approximately 42 minutes.

Problems With The LLRV And LLTV

The LLRV and LLTV looked nothing like the LM that it was supposed to duplicate. One could argue that this was because of the need to build a hybrid training vehicle to fly in Earth's atmosphere while simulating lunar gravity, and they would be partly right. However, the configuration of both the LLRV and LLTV made the vehicle difficult to fly and more effort was spent in trying to control it, while trying to fly in lunar simulated mode. This greatly affected the astronauts' perspective and concentration needed to practice simulated lunar landings.

To increase the astronauts' perspective for a lunar landing, there are several things NASA could have done:

1) They could have sent fully automated and unmanned LMs to land on the lunar surface, which was within their capability.

2) The unmanned LMs could have been equipped with cameras inside the flight deck pointing towards the lunar surface, to film the approach and landing.

3) The footage from these cameras could have then been used in LM computer simulations, to give a better perspective to the Apollo astronauts in training. This in turn, could have been used to enhance training in the LLTV.

Had this approach to training taken place, it would have greatly increased the astronaut's perspective when visually landing the LM on the lunar surface, which would have been paramount to any success.

However, none of this was done for the Apollo Moon program. Instead, NASA relied on unmanned missions that took photos (without the necessary details), to design lunar surface models which can best be described as a facsimile of the lunar landing area, which was used in simulators to train the astronauts. This is just one more example of NASA's neglect in their Apollo Moon landing training program. And it is another example of NASA's real intention, which was to fake the Apollo Moon landings from the very beginning of the program.

In addition, there are some gaps in the record regarding missing data for LLTV No. 1 and LLTV No. 2. Further, there are very few films showing the LLRVs and LLTVs in flight. Common sense dictates that each flight should have been filmed and then studied in meticulous detail. But once again, we see evidence of NASA's shoddy record keeping and missing data.

To recap, Neil Armstrong's total flight time in the:

- LLRV, was approximately 2 hours and 45 minutes.

- LLTV, was approximately 42 minutes.

That is a combined total flight time in both the LLRV and LLTV, of approximately 3 hours and 30 minutes.

Although Neil Armstrong was an experienced military pilot, 3 hours and 30 minutes of experience in a vehicle configured to simulate landing in lunar conditions, which was used to practice what was supposed to be the first ever manned lunar landing, is minimal to say the least.

LLRV And LLTV Accidents

Up to the Apollo 11 mission, there were two accidents involving the LLRV and LLTV:

- LLRV No. 1 with Neil Armstrong at the controls, crashed May 6, 1968. Armstrong successfully ejected, just before the LLRV plummeted to the ground and exploded on impact.

Figure 4.3 – Lunar Landing Research Vehicle (LLRV) Crash
Source: Wikimedia Commons

- LLTV No. 1 with NASA test pilot Joe Algranti at the controls, crashed December 8, 1968. Algranti too successfully ejected before the LLTV plummeted to the ground and exploded on impact.

Figure 4.4 – Lunar Landing Training Vehicle (LLTV) Crash
Source: Wikimedia Commons

After the Apollo 11 mission, there were two more crashes that involved the LLTV. NASA's investigation into these accidents gave various reasons as to the cause. But suffice it to say, these accidents could not have inspired any of the Apollo astronauts.

NASA admits that they could only do so much to replicate the LM, including an effort to design a triangular window to match that of the LM, which was not quite as effective for astronauts' perception as it should have been.

Glaring Differences Between LLRV, LLTV, And The LM

Here are additional observations about the LLRVs and LLTVs, that were far from duplicating the LM:

LLRV & LLTV	Lunar Module
Designed for one pilot	Designed for two astronauts
The pilot was in a sitting position	The astronauts were in a standing position
The pilot at the controls did not wear a bulky spacesuit	The astronauts at the controls wore bulky spacesuits
The pilot flew and landed in controlled conditions	The astronauts allegedly descended to the lunar surface and successfully landed in unfamiliar conditions
The pilot's visual reference from the flight deck, was approximately 8 to 10 feet above ground	The astronauts' visual reference from the flight deck, was approximately 15 to 16 feet above ground
These training vehicles were not configured to simulate a liftoff from the lunar surface	All six LM's apparently lifted off perfectly from the lunar surface

Since the LLRV and LLTV were not configured to simulate a lunar liftoff, it's interesting that the LM allegedly performed a liftoff from the lunar surface perfectly on its first attempt. And the first attempt at liftoff had to be perfect, since there were no second chances, meaning that if it failed, the astronauts would have been marooned on the lunar surface forever, that is, if the LM's hypergolic fuels hadn't exploded due to any number of reasons.

It is clear that the LLRVs and LLTVs were nowhere close to duplicating the LM in any meaningful way. Further, important aspects of a real mission were not possible to duplicate, for example, the horizon in the lunar sky and its colour, versus the horizon in the Earth's sky and its colour, further adding to the major gaps in training. Therefore, the astronauts would not have gained much if any perspective on what they could have expected in a real lunar scenario, using these vehicles for training.

Inadequate Astronaut Training In The LLRV, LLTV, And The Lunar Module Simulator

As mentioned, Neil Armstrong's combined total flight time in both the LLRV and LLTV, was approximately 3 hours and 30 minutes. And further, we noticed that Armstrong had more flight time in the LLRV. This is significant, since he should have had more flight time in the LLTV, as the flight controls were supposed to have been closer in design to that of the flight controls of the LM.

Neil Armstrong's experience in the training vehicles configured to simulate landing in lunar conditions, seemed minimal to say the least. Add to that, the glaring differences in the LLTV to the LM. Therefore, most of the Apollo astronauts' training for a lunar landing would have had to come from LM simulators and as we mentioned before, NASA did not have any actual footage from unmanned LM missions landing on the lunar surface, or more specifically, landing in the exact areas the LMs were supposed to have landed. Data from these unmanned LM landings, could have been programmed into computer simulations. It could be argued that in an era before the onset of computer simulations, that the aviation industry didn't do this either. But that is not a fair comparison, since there has never been an attempt to land a manned mission beyond LEO on another world, so every source available to NASA should have been used.

However, in reality, the film footage from the flight deck of the LM that is presented as an actual lunar landing, is instead taken from computer simulations, which of course is a facsimile of what a manned lunar landing would have looked like. The astronauts trained for hundreds of hours in the Lunar Module Simulator (LMS). Specifically, Neil Armstrong had 285 hours, and his LM pilot Buzz Aldrin, had 332 hours. But there were no motion sensors in these simulators for the astronauts to experience the LM maneuvers in $1/6^{th}$ gravity as they descended to the lunar surface. Instead, it was done through a visual system and they would use this reference to interpret the motions. This is why the LLRVs and LLTVs were considered to be one of the most important aspects for training. But as we've learned, these training vehicles were plagued with problems.

As mentioned, there was a point of no return during the descent and approach to the lunar surface. So, if there had been a problem beyond this point of no return in the approach, then they would have been committed to the landing, to be followed shortly thereafter by the launch of the LM ascent stage. Therefore, if Armstrong had become incapacitated on the approach for any number of reasons, Buzz Aldrin would have had to take control of the LM at such a critical phase of the mission. However, Aldrin had no training in the LLRV or LLTV. And now it appears that Jim Lovell, the backup commander for Apollo 11, also had little or no training in both the LLRV or LLTV, at least up to the launch of Apollo 11. It's difficult to believe that NASA would have made such an incredible blunder, since Lovell would have had to fill the position as commander of Apollo 11 at a moment's notice, if Neil Armstrong for any reason was unable to participate in the mission. This is another gap in training, as well as a serious breach in safety protocols. Again, this shows that NASA had no intentions of sending manned missions to the Moon.

However, aside from the hundreds of hours each astronaut spent in the LMS, Neil Armstrong and apparently all of the other LM commanders, credited the LLRV and LLTV with their success in manually landing the LM. But not everyone agrees with this assessment:

> As it was impossible to fly an LM on earth, NASA developed this device to simulate the final phase of a lunar landing in actual flight. It was powered by a large jet engine in the center with small gas reaction-control rockets on the sides. The astronauts found it very difficult and unstable to fly, and it was ultimately not used by the later crews.[5]

Translation: Contrary to what the Apollo astronauts have said, the LLRV and LLTV training program, was a total failure.

Everything we've discussed so far, indicates that none of the Apollo missions landed on the lunar surface. And to further reiterate the point, we will continue to discuss the reasons why a manned lunar landing was never even attempted. But first, we'll familiarize ourselves with the official version of Apollo 11's descent from lunar orbit, to its landing on the lunar surface.

Apollo 11 Lunar Landing And Liftoff

The Official Version

After entering a 50-mile lunar orbit, preparations were made for the LM to undock from the CM, with Neil Armstrong and Buzz Aldrin onboard for the descent down to the lunar surface. This section will describe the process according to the official NASA narrative.

The LM Descent

The LM descent was accomplished in two flight maneuvers:

A) The descent orbit insertion and

B) The powered descent maneuvers.

This description of the Apollo 11 LM landing phase from 50,000 feet above the lunar surface, is from the book *LANDING EAGLE: INSIDE THE COCKPIT DURING THE FIRST MOON LANDING* by Michael Engle.

After the LM undocks and separates to a safe distance from the CM, it must now begin a descent from its 50-mile lunar orbit.

Descent Orbit Insertion

The LM initiates descent orbit insertion using 10% thrust to make sure the engine thrust is through the LM's center of gravity, and 26 seconds later, the engine is now at full thrust.

The LM then begins a power descent trajectory to 50,000 feet above the lunar surface. From 50,000 feet, there are three phases:

- The Braking Phase
- The Approach Phase
- The Landing Phase

Included in the 3 phases, are High Gate and Low Gate. High Gate in the descent refers to the beginning of the approach phase, and Low Gate is the beginning of the Landing Phase. A minute-by-minute description of the powered descent trajectory is shown in the chart below.

MINUTES TO LANDING	DESCRIPTION
12	The LM computer begins its breaking phase by initiating the powered descent from an altitude of 50,000 feet from the lunar surface, and approximately 260 nautical miles from the landing site. It is now under automatic control by the computer. However, Mission Control in Houston loses communications with the LM, so Mike Collins is now relaying communications from Mission Control to the LM. Soon after, the LM

	reestablished communications with Mission Control.
11	Aldrin reports that the Primary Guidance and Navigation System (PGNS) and the Abort Guidance System (AGS) agree closely. The LM will use the PGNS to navigate to the lunar surface. In the case of a PGNS failure, the LM will switch to the AGS. However, the AGS is not capable of navigating to the lunar surface, therefore the function of the AGS is to abort the landing and bring the LM back to orbit, for the eventual rendezvous and docking with the CM.
10	The LM rendezvous radar is now switched to the SLEW position, to track the CM if such an abort back to orbit is necessary. At approximately 45,000 feet, Armstrong rolls the LM so the windows are facing the lunar surface and is now using the Landing Point Designator (LPD), which is a grid pattern on the LM window. The grid lines are spaced 2 degrees apart and is used to estimate how fast the LM is moving over the lunar surface. The computer provides an angle and Aldrin would then provide that angle to Armstrong, who would then look for the corresponding line on the LM window grid that corresponds to that angle. The point directly under the LPD line, is the landing site.
9	The LM now has a velocity of 3,600 miles per hour. However, this apparently translates into landing about 3 miles long. At this time, a check is done of the explosive device batteries. This is the method used to separate the LM ascent stage from the descent stage. If they are not functioning

	properly, then a landing would have to be aborted, since it would be impossible to separate the ascent stage from the descent stage, therefore preventing a liftoff from the lunar surface.
8	By now, the LM is 40,000 feet above the lunar surface and is oriented so that Armstrong and Aldrin are now face up from the lunar surface. The LM is still experiencing some communications problems that interrupts data flow to Mission Control. As the LM continues its descent, the computer issues a 1202 program alarm at 33,500 feet above the lunar surface.
7	Armstrong and Aldrin ask Mission Control for help in determining the meaning of the 1202 program alarm. After conferring with flight controllers, Armstrong and Aldrin are assured that they are still go for powered descent and landing. Then there is another 1202 program alarm and again, Mission Control assures them they are go for landing.
6	Armstrong realizes they're too far down range, which means there will be problems on final approach.
5	The LM is now at 16,000 feet. The LM begins to orient itself to a more upright position, with the lunar surface now becoming visible in the lower part of the LM windows.
4	The LM is now at High Gate which is about 7,000 feet, descending at 125 feet-per-second, and approximately 4.5 nautical miles from the landing site. The Braking Phase of the landing ends, and the Approach Phase begins.

	The computer now rotates the LM to a full upright position and Armstrong and Aldrin now have visual on the lunar surface.
	The LM is now at 5,000 feet and is descending at a rate of 100 feet per second.
	Capcom again reassures them that they are still go for landing. They are now at 3,000 feet and descending at a rate of 70 feet per second.
	While descending through 3,000 feet above the lunar surface, the computer now issues a 1201 program alarm. After conferring with flight controllers, Mission Control again reassures Armstrong and Aldrin that they are still go for landing.
	The LM continues on its descent and is now 2,000 feet, descending at a rate of 50 feet per second.
3	The computer now issues another 1201 program alarm and are told they are still go for landing.
	At about 600 feet above the lunar surface, Armstrong assumes manual control of the LM.
	The LM is now at Low Gate which is 500 feet above the lunar surface, and is in the Landing Phase.
	Armstrong asks for another LPD angle.
2	The LM is now 300 feet above the lunar surface and is descending at 3 feet per second.

	Armstrong is continuing to fly manually and is looking for a place to land.
1	The LM is now 100 feet above the lunar surface, descending at a rate of 3 feet per second, and moving forward at 9 feet per second. A red light illuminates to tell them that they have about 5% fuel remaining. A Bingo call is to be made by Mission Control, 94 seconds after the fuel quantity light illuminates. When this Bingo call is made, Armstrong must decide whether or not he can make a safe landing within 20 seconds. The LM is now at 75 feet and Aldrin reassures Armstrong that their approach is good. They are now 60 seconds away from the Bingo call. An abort 20 seconds before landing would be very risky, so when they reach this point, they are committed to the landing. Below 30 feet, Aldrin makes the call that the LM is picking up dust. The LM is now 30 seconds away from landing and Armstrong is now worried about his fuel. The LM is now below 30 feet and Armstrong has selected his landing site.
Touchdown On The Lunar Surface	Aldrin calls "Contact Light." This means that one of the three landing probes attached to the bottom of the landing pads, has made contact with the lunar surface. At this point, Armstrong was supposed to shut down the engine and the LM would fall gently to the surface. But instead, he hesitates in shutting the engine down.

	3 seconds after contact, Armstrong then calls for shut down of the engine, and the LM gently settles the remaining few feet to the lunar surface. After the shutdown checklist is completed, Armstrong transmits his first statement from the lunar surface to Mission Control: "Houston... uh, Tranquility Base here. The Eagle has landed."

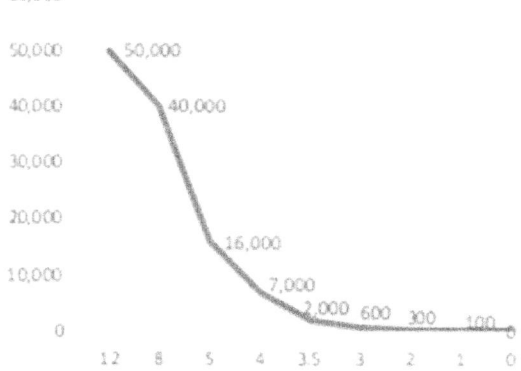

The LM Liftoff

The Apollo 11 LM used the descent stage as a platform for launch. The ascent engine produced 3,500 pounds of thrust for its liftoff and insertion into lunar orbit.

Note: This book will not analyze the alleged astronauts time spent on the lunar surface. That is a matter for another chapter for a later book. Instead, this book focusses on the alleged performance of both the LM and CM.

Along with the LM ascent engine, two other systems were required for a safe ascent and insertion into lunar orbit, the PGNS and the RCS thrusters. The AGS was to be used for guidance, navigation, and control should there be a failure of the PGNS.

There were two phases to the LM ascent; vertical rise and orbit insertion. The vertical rise was for moving clear of any surrounding terrain, and the orbit insertion was of course for achieving the required lunar orbit for the eventual rendezvous and docking with the CM. If the LM engine had failed during the last 30 seconds of the ascent, the RCS thrusters were to be used to complete the ascent to lunar orbit.

As is to be expected, NASA reports that the LM ascent to lunar orbit was perfect.

Apollo 11 Lunar Landing And Liftoff

The Reality

NASA never disappoints when it comes to dramatics in its fictional narrative. However, it is this very dramatic narrative that highlights some of the more unbelievable aspects of the LM landing. In this section, we'll take a look at some of those dramatics and show how NASA is actually telling the world that no manned mission landed on the lunar surface.

As has been mention in Part I of this series, flight testing of the hardware for the Apollo Moon program, was minimal at best. And although there were numerous and seemingly adequate static testing done on some aspects of the Apollo spacecraft, there was no comparable amount of testing done in actual flight conditions, an example of which we've seen with the F-1 engines and the Saturn V. Testing in actual flight conditions is where you validate the static testing data and/or where you find the real problems that can occur because of forces not encountered in static testing. NASA and its contractors knew this rule very well, as is shown here in NASA's own quote:

> The problem resulted from excessive pilot controller sensitivity, which had not manifested itself during any of the numerous simulators carried out during the design and evaluation of the LLRV. It appeared only during critical flight-test maneuvers requiring high levels of pilot workload and concentration, such as takeoffs and landings, particularly during first flights. Since these situations are rarely evaluated during routine development simulators, the problem never occurred until first-flight conditions caused it to surface.[6]

This quote is in reference to the problems that were discovered during the first three flights of the LLRV. As the quote clearly states, there are problems that can only be detected during tests in actual flight conditions. This is the reason that there should be a comparable amount of testing in actual flight conditions, which was not done the LM testing. According to NASA, there were two fully functional LMs that were tested, both of which were manned, one in LEO, and the other in lunar orbit with a descent to within 50,000 feet of the lunar surface. Given the magnitude of these manned missions and the many risks involved, there should have been at least several unmanned lunar landings with the LM before an actual manned lunar landing was even attempted. This is the least that NASA could have done.

Aviation has examples of manned aircraft being tested and flown by pilots for the first time. However, this is built on decades of knowledge in a known environment. But not so with the lunar environment, where the slightest miscalculation would have ended in disaster. This is why there should have been numerous unmanned missions before manned missions were certified, which was well within NASA's capability at the time.

Note: Proponents of the Apollo Moon missions cite tight schedules and lack of funding for the minimal flight testing completed. There may be occasions when tight schedules preclude the need for rigorous testing, but that is usually done in emergency situations, for example, war or catastrophes and usually at great risk to those involved. There was no national emergency which required the Apollo Moon program to be expedited. However, the stringent timelines led to poor quality control, minimal flight-testing standards, gaps in astronaut training and the eventual destruction of documentation and technology for what was called, a significant historical event. The argument too has been put forward that each flight test of an Apollo mission, meant the destruction of the equipment, requiring enormous funding to build more equipment for flight testing. This is an appalling excuse, as it puts cost before safety for the astronauts involved.

Analysis Of The LM Descent To Landing

We'll now discuss portions of the 12-minute descent, to show some peculiarities that should have ended in an abort.

o   ***12 Minutes***

Just as the LM begins its descent, there is a loss of communications between the LM and Mission Control. One would assume that the computer software would have been effective in pointing the S-band antenna to regain communications. But instead, we're told that Aldrin had resorted to manually slewing the S-band antenna, a method that would likely have been inaccurate during the LM's descent, as well as a distraction from his other responsibilities which involved monitoring the LM's systems.

Communication problems happened again during the descent, and again Aldrin tried to manually point the S-Band antenna. Incredibly, this was never practiced during simulations.

o   ***10 Minutes***

The LM is now oriented so the astronauts are facing towards the lunar surface. The reason for this is because of areas which have mass concentrations of gravity (MASCONS). These areas could have affected the descent profile.

This can lead to a very dangerous situation since it wasn't possible to program these MASCONS into the LM's computer. Further, NASA had little understanding of what and where these mass concentrations of gravity were. Therefore, the computer would have been unable to read its true altitude if they were to have encountered one of these areas.

To compensate for this, it is claimed that Armstrong had practiced for this scenario before the mission, by getting together with an engineer to work out a solution. This involved using the LPD grid on the LM window for tracking during the early part of their descent, which is why the LM was oriented so its windows were facing the lunar surface. So, we're told that Armstrong was actually using visual references from approximately 45,000 feet to monitor their approach, which amounts to nothing more than a best guess.

Aldrin then switches on the rendezvous radar to track the CM, should an abort be necessary while the electronic components in the radar and computer were kept in phase. But a design flaw caused the electronic components in the radar and computer, to occasionally go out of phase. The radar was switched on at the exact time the electronic components were out of phase. This action would have led to a series of program alarms, which would have required the astronauts to abort the landing.

It's interesting to note, that the visual method Armstrong used for their initial descent, was never used again by any of the other alleged Apollo Moon landings.

- *9 Minutes*

Although satisfied with the altitude rate, Armstrong notices that at their present position, the LM will land 3 miles past it's landing site. Armstrong then rolls the LM over, so its windows are now facing away from the lunar surface. But then he notices that the roll rate is too slow, which prevented the landing radar (which is on the bottom of the LM descent stage) from locking onto the lunar surface. The landing radar finally locks on, but 2000 feet lower than expected.

At just over 3 minutes into the descent, the LM is nowhere near the precision that would have been needed to safely land the LM. And the MASCONS were still a concern, since the radar wouldn't have given them any warning. They would only know they had encountered MASCONS, when they were already in them, which would then be displayed by the radar in the form of a lower-than-expected altitude, that could have been disastrous depending on their altitude at the time.

Note: The LM radar used the Doppler Effect, which compresses or stretches radio waves, moving toward or away from the antenna. With the LM landing radar, the waves would measure the distance between the antenna and the lunar surface. A good example to compare this to, would be a car horn getting louder as it approaches and lower as it moves away.

o *8 Minutes*

This is when the first program alarm happened and there would be several more before they landed. These alarms indicated an executive overload, meaning the LM computer could not complete all of the tasks it was supposed to. The computer was designed to prioritize the tasks that were important. And incredibly, neither Armstrong nor Aldrin had any idea of what these program alarms meant, which is why they asked for help from Mission Control. If this had been a real mission, and given that they were experiencing communication problems, an abort would have been initiated, considering the impossibility of any rescue attempt if anything had gone wrong.

- o *3 Minutes*

After yet another program alarm, Armstrong switched to manual control to steer the LM himself for the last 600 feet. However, manual did not mean the use of cables or hydraulics. This was a fly-by-wire computer system and when Armstrong made inputs on the controls, this commanded the computer to send signals to position the engine nozzle and thrusters. Yet, there had already been a set of program alarms indicating an executive overload of the computer, so the computer would have to determine which actions to prioritize. In a real manned mission such as this, manual landing would never have been attempted.

Given that this was the first LM to descend through 50,000 feet over the lunar surface and that these program alarms had supposedly caught everyone by surprise, and that this computer's limitations had already been established, a real scenario of this kind would have dictated a rational decision, meaning an abort should have been initiated.

Yet instead, Armstrong is now actively looking for a place to land while facing all these hurdles:

- An overloaded computer that had never been tested before in similar flight conditions below 50,000 feet

- Manually flying the first ever vehicle to use a fully integrated fly-by-wire system

- And moving forward at about 40 miles per hour, trying to avoid a crater while maneuvering over boulders, which was never even planned for nor practiced in the simulator for the latter part of the landing phase

2 Minutes

According to the pre-mission timeline, the LM should have landed by now. And to add to the numerous problems encountered in the last several minutes of its descent, the landing radar now becomes unreliable. This means they were not getting proper altitude information.

o *1 Minute*

To further add to their problems, Aldrin reports that they were picking up dust. This makes it impossible to see features on the lunar surface which obscured Armstrong's view of the landing area. But of course, they continued anyway.

After the censors at the end of the LM landing gear made contact with the surface, Armstrong fails to follow procedure by shutting the engine down. This could easily have led to a harder than planned landing, exceeding the structural limitations of a vehicle constructed of walls equivalent to the thickness of three layers of kitchen foil.

This minute-by-minute analysis reads like a dramatic Hollywood script. Presumably, this was designed to make the astronauts into heroes, distracting away from the technical impossibility of what was supposed to have been the first ever manned lunar landing.

It has been argued too, that the whistleblowers within NASA had intentionally left clues to try and expose the hoax, as authors Mary Bennett and David Percy have articulated in their book, *'Dark Moon: Apollo And The Whistle-blowers.'* And we've seen more examples of whistleblowers leaving clues, sometimes in the form of quotes.

In addition, to an already fictional story, we have this from Grumman engineer Tom Kelly regarding the LM landing gear:

> We had conflicting advice from the lunar scientists. They were telling us all kinds of strange things. If only we were allowed some knowledge of the moon's surface. The landing gear in particular would have been smaller and simpler.[7]

This is a strange thing to say, considering that NASA has released a full analysis of the LM landings. So, either Tom Kelly was misinformed as to the details necessary in overseeing the design of the LM, or NASA's analysis of the LM landings is nothing more than fiction. NASA admits to running computer simulations on all of the alleged Apollo missions. Therefore, it's obvious that Tom Kelly is more than hinting that not only were there serious gaps in the flow of data to contractors, but that these 'perfect missions' were nothing more than computer simulated printouts.

Intentional Errors

Aerospace Engineer Xavier Pascal has done extensive studies of the Apollo Moon missions. In one of his published works, he analyzes the Apollo 11 LM descent. His mathematical and meticulous approach has not been satisfactorily challenged, if at all, much like that of other researchers on this subject.

Pascal made some interesting observations about the vertical and horizontal speed of the LM's descent to the lunar surface in a published article. Through his analysis, he has determined that the LM engine did not have sufficient power to slow down the descent. And since the Moon moves counter-clockwise in its orbit around the Earth, and rotates counter-clockwise on its axis, the LM had to be stationary in relation to the lunar surface; there can be no lateral speed either way.

> If the indicated speed was absolute, as with the previous speeds, it would mean the lunar surface and the LM would move synchronously with each other, and so it would mean that the LM was stationary relative to the lunar surface. Moreover, the LM must be absolutely stationary to the lunar surface when it landed. Otherwise, if it moved laterally, it would surely tip over when coming into contact with the lunar surface.[8]

As Pascal points out in his article, the LM had a horizontal speed of 15 feet per second, which is about 10 miles per hour. But at this speed, the LM was 13.123 feet above the lunar surface and had a descent speed of 3.280 feet per second. This meant that the LM would have made contact with the lunar surface in 4 seconds and would not have had the time to slow the LM to zero in relation to the surface. Therefore, the LM would have landed on the lunar surface with a forward speed of approximately 10 miles per hour.

Pascal is being kind when he says the LM would have tipped over had it landed at this forward speed. But the reality is, by landing with a forward speed of 10 miles per hour and given the flimsy design of the LM, it would have exceeded its structural limits and the damage would have been catastrophic.

Another problem Pascal discusses is the issue of the probes located at the end of three landing pads on the LM. Once the probes contacted the lunar surface, the engine was to be shut down since it was too dangerous for thrust being produced, given that the engine nozzle was so close to the lunar surface. However, there is a design flaw in this procedure.

The procedure left 1.7 seconds for the engine to shut off, before the LM touched down. But as Pascal explains, there was a reaction time between when the astronauts saw the probe warning light and when the engine was shut down, which narrowed that 1.7 second time frame. Further, when the stop button was pressed, the engine did not immediately shut down. The stop button needed to come back to its original position before the signal was sent to shut down the engine. To add to this, Neil Armstrong delayed shutting down the engine. In reality, this would have been catastrophic, which would have meant the loss of the LM and crew.

It's obvious that intentional errors were built into the design of the LM, further supporting the claims by other researchers that some of those directly involved had planted clues to help reveal the hoax.

Note: None of the researchers I've been in contact with, are suggesting that NASA engineers are incompetent. On the contrary, their skills are unique and unmatched by many other professions. However, there is a limit to their skills, and it is these unmatched skills which some engineers used to plant hints within the official reports that all was not as NASA claimed. And sometimes, these engineers involved with the Apollo missions, have proven to be quite direct in their criticism of the Apollo program, examples of which have been cited in this book series.

Analysis Of The LM Liftoff

One main problem with the LM liftoff, was the issue of torque. A similar problem is encountered in single engine propeller driven aircraft. The propeller rotates clockwise from the pilot's position in the aircraft. During takeoff, the down going propeller blade produces what is called asymmetric thrust when it reaches 90 degrees, yawing the aircraft to the left. Further, the propeller causes slipstream, pushing air over the fuselage in a clockwise direction, acting on the left side of the horizontal stabilizer, again causing the aircraft to yaw to the left. To compensate for this, it's necessary for the pilot to input slight right rudder during takeoff and climb. Once out of the climb there is no longer any asymmetric thrust and the pilot coordinates the flight controls for straight and level flight.

The propellent tanks on the LM ascent stage were located at different positions. The oxidizer tank located on the right side of the LM was closer to the ascent engine than the fuel tank on the opposite side. It was designed this way to counter the inevitable torque clockwise as the propellent was depleted in both tanks during LM liftoff.

But unlike the LM descent engine, the ascent engine did not swivel. So, this meant that the RCS lateral thrusters were used to counter the inevitable torque clockwise, due to a decrease in propellent as the LM lifted off from the lunar surface.

However, as Xavier Pascal has determined, the RCS thrusters were not capable of such a task, since each thruster could not be adjusted in the amount of thrust it produced. And further, the LM torque would be constant on ascent, so constant lateral thrust at various thrust levels would be needed. As Pascal points out, with the thrusters, it was all or nothing. This would make it difficult for the lateral thrusters in their original design, to compensate for the varying torque aspects while on climb out from the lunar surface. This fact alone would have caused the LM to enter a troubling erratic pattern on ascent, leading to a situation that would have overloaded the AGC (notwithstanding the fact that this was a fake computer anyway), causing the LM to impact the lunar surface. And if the LM somehow made it to LEO, the chances of it being marooned in lunar orbit were assured, since it would no longer be on its planned lunar orbital track which would have made it impossible to have rendezvoused with the CM.

The Film Footage Of The LM Liftoff

There is no film footage of the Apollo 11 LM liftoff from the lunar surface. However, the last three Apollo missions were filmed during their liftoff from the lunar surface, with the Apollo 17 film having the best quality. This will suffice for our purposes, since all of the Apollo missions used similar procedures during liftoff. The camera was located on the Lunar Rover Vehicle, which was positioned behind the LM and was remotely controlled from Houston by Ed Fendell. We'll discuss information taken from Apollo researchers Xavier Pascal and Julius A. Birch, both of whom studied the Apollo 17 film, now in video format.

Pascal had determined that there were some peculiar anomalies during the initial phases of the LM liftoff from the lunar surface, which can clearly be seen in the footage. As he explains, when a rocket launches from Earth and gains vertical speed, it then starts to slowly move into a horizontal trajectory. As it gains speed in this trajectory, the part of the rocket facing towards the sky creates centrifugal force which counters Earth's gravity. But if the rocket moves too abruptly to a horizontal trajectory it will not have enough speed to create the centrifugal force to counter Earth's gravity, which will inevitably impact the surface.

As the rocket increases in speed it slowly continues its horizontal trajectory creating more centrifugal force. This continues to LEO which by then is in a state of equilibrium of all four forces, that is Earth's gravity, centrifugal force, no drag, and no need for engine thrust in the vacuum of space. Newtonian physics now takes over and the rocket maintains its forward momentum in LEO, as long as Newton's first law is not disturbed.

The same physics is applied to the LM on liftoff from the lunar surface. The LM would need to slowly pitch, while picking up speed for the centrifugal force necessary to counter the Moon's gravity when it achieves lunar orbit. But as Pascal's analysis shows, this is not what happened. Instead, the LM abruptly pitches over taking on a more horizontal trajectory. The video then shows the LM descend which would have been normal, since there wasn't enough speed to produce the centrifugal force necessary to counter the Moon's gravity. So, at this point the LM should have impacted the lunar surface but of course according to the official version, this did not happen. Instead, by some mysterious force, the LM abruptly stops and continues on its ascent. And this mysterious force wasn't from the engine, since there was no ability to adjust thrust. And since there wasn't enough centrifugal force, that too can be ruled out.

The LM then strangely makes sinusoidal moves, similar to sine waves on a graph. Proponents say this is due to the way the camera was controlled from Earth and the 2.5 second delay in the signal. But as Pascal explains, this strange sinusoidal movement takes place near the bottom of the video screen, so surely Ed Fendell would have been skilled in adjusting the camera to center the image. It wouldn't have been too difficult to position the camera to center the image, once he noticed movement by the LM away from the center of the frame. So, it's a mystery as to why this sinusoidal movement is happening. And further, the amplitude of a sine wave usually starts out quite small. But in the Apollo 17 video we see the LM sine wave or sinusoidal movement start out fairly large, which makes one wonder just how much the amplitude would have increased in a real situation. This would have had devasting consequences for the LM.

Then there is the flight path of the LM when it reached lunar orbit. The LM landed with its front facing west. (When looking up at the Moon from Earth, reverse east and west. So, the Moon's west, is our east). The reasons for this, is so the astronauts would not be directly in the Sun when descending the ladder, and to limit the maneuvering of the LM after liftoff. The CM orbits clockwise around the Moon, that is, in a westerly direction. Therefore, the LM would need to liftoff facing west. So, its flight path would be from east to west, that is, from right to left when seen from Earth.

After liftoff, the LM would have needed to gradually track south, then onto a westerly course for its rendezvous with the CM. But instead, the LM abruptly turns south, so much so, that the flight path is now perpendicular to the flight path of the CM. Since the LM ascent engine could not swivel, the RCS thrusters would have had to be used to adjust the flight path back to a westerly direction. However, at this point, the LM speed of approximately 3,200 nautical miles per hour would have required much more propellent to correct the LM's course. And the thrusters used its own propellent source which meant that this propellant was limited. And if the LM was able to correct its course, the limited amount of propellent would have been depleted, preventing any use of the thrusters necessary for the docking maneuver with the CM. So here we have yet another recipe for disaster.

Another revealing point is the data acquisition camera (DAC). The DAC was positioned on the right LM window and was used, among other things, for filming the LM landing and liftoff. However, the remote camera on the lunar surface used to film the LM liftoff, does not match the DAC from inside the LM. Proponents explain this discrepancy saying the camera on the lunar surface was being constantly repositioned to compensate for the time delay in the signal to and from the Moon, similar to the excuse put forward to explain the strange performance of the LM after liftoff. But while the outside camera shows the abrupt maneuver, the DAC camera does not. The LM's performance on liftoff should match at any point in the video, regardless of any movement of the lunar surface camera and clearly, they do not.

All of what we've discussed so far with the LM liftoff, takes place in about 30 seconds. Yet, the launch to lunar orbit is about seven minutes. So, given the erratic maneuvering of the LM after just 30 seconds into its launch, one wonders just how amplified these erratic maneuvers would have gotten after only one minute, let alone seven.

This leads to the inevitable conclusion that the Apollo 17 video was faked and by inference, so was the Apollo 17 liftoff.

Researcher Julius A. Birch did his own analysis of the Apollo 17 video, and came to similar conclusions. And further, he meticulously analyzed the video to determine what was really going on with the LM liftoff. By taking this information and using a scaled version of the LM, he was able to duplicate exactly what took place in the video.

Here is Julius A. Birch's conclusion:

> From the analysis of the Vertical Rise Phase, and using the reported Apollo 11/17 pitch adjustments we have constructed, what we call, the nominal ascent trajectory (we) found that it considerably overshoots the trajectory from the broadcast. This motivated us to investigate two alternatives:
>
> The first was the "space-rocket," which featured a Reactive Control System (RCS) that has considerably higher turn rates than the Apollo RCS. One such 59^0-trajectory fitted the latter part of the broadcast, but failed in the following aspects: (i), it did not reproduce the transition between the Vertical Rise and the early Orbit Insertion; (ii), flying along such trajectory could not be performed with the Apollo guidance logic; and (iii), its pitch adjustments seriously disagreed with the ones actually reported.
>
> The second was the "roller coaster," featuring a scaled-down scene in which a model of the LM AS was moving along tracks that mimicked the ascent trajectory. We were able to reconstruct tracks (their curvature or pitch), motion along which reproduced the broadcast (almost too) perfectly. This suggested that the approach is capable of explaining even the minute variations of motion in the broadcast.
>
> From the failure of space rocket trajectories in describing the Apollo 17 broadcast we conclude that

the broadcast does not feature the LM AS lifting off the lunar surface.

Conversely, from the success of the roller coaster in description of the broadcast we therefore conclude that the broadcast shows an ascent that has been staged in a specialized film studio on Earth.[9]

It's obvious that the roller coaster scenario with a scaled-up version of the LM is what was really filmed, while Fendell's real purpose was to sell the narrative. And as Birch points out, Fendell's actions with the camera (or whoever actually filmed the LM liftoff) show that he seemed surprised with the LM's sometimes erratic ascent in the first 30 seconds after liftoff. And surely, Fendell would have reviewed the computer simulation data for all six Apollo LM liftoffs from the lunar surface, which he would have used to anticipate the trajectory during the ascent. And since the fake Apollo 17 LM liftoff did not conform to the simulation data of the other missions, Fendell's instinct would have been to continue by adjusting the camera to keep the LM in the center frame, hoping that it could be salvaged and used to further the narrative.

But the question then becomes, why didn't NASA re-record the LM ascent to get it right? This is a fair question, which has an easy answer. As we've seen in this book and others, whistleblowers and/or NASA and contractor engineers, deliberately dropped hints, and at times, were quite direct and harsh in their assessment of the Apollo program, for example, the poor lack of quality control. Further, it's obvious that NASA anticipated that most people wouldn't have noticed since they would have understandably been caught up in such an historical moment. And further still, NASA knew most people would neither have the time, the inclination, nor the skills to analyze the footage. But what NASA could not have anticipated decades into the future, is the software technology on a laptop computer that is now available in almost every household, which can be used to analyze the Apollo photos and film record. This really is a case of history being written by the victors, only to be revealed by outside objective sources, exposing the Apollo Moon Missions as an enormous lie perpetrated on an unsuspecting public.

We didn't need film evidence to determine that the Apollo 11 or Apollo 17 LM liftoff from the lunar surface was faked. But it certainly made it much easier to make that determination.

Note: All the information in this section regarding Xavier Pascal's work is from these two articles:

https://www.angelfire.com/moon2/xpascal/MoonHoax/LunarModuleAscent/LunarModuleAscent.HTM

https://www.angelfire.com/moon2/xpascal/MoonHoax/ApolloPropulsion/ApolloPropulsion.HTM

Missing LM Documents

Apollo mission proponents justify the missing or destroyed documents by saying the technology that was used is now antiquated. That is partly true, but documents should be kept until that technology has been built and improved on over the years and decades. And unlike the Aviation Industry, this did not happen with the Aerospace Industry, e.g., the technology used in the Apollo program, specifically for manned lunar landings. Others point out that even though decades old technology is still being used in the Aerospace Industry, for example, the Soyuz spacecraft, modern technology has been incorporated into its design. The same reasoning can be applied to the DC-3, which went into commercial use in 1936, but it's still based on 1930s technology.

The technology used in manned space missions is still decades old, even with enhancements, for example computer software. However, the Aviation Industry has gone from single engine propeller driven aircraft to multiple jet engine aircraft, while the Aerospace Industry is still stuck in what is akin to the propeller driven aircraft era. Therefore, it is imperative for the Aerospace Industry to maintain meticulous documents for access to this antiquated technology for future generations to build on, when this industry is ready to move forward.

A lot of very important documents directly related to the Apollo missions were destroyed without any regard for future manned missions to space, which is highly suspicious to those who believe that the Apollo missions achieved its goals, but perfectly understandable to those who now know these missions were faked.

Two Businessmen And A Fake Lunar Module

As the United States prepared to celebrate its bicentennial year in 1976, two Japanese businessmen visited Long Island's Cradle of Aviation Museum at Mitch Field and met with the director William Kaiser. However, what these two businessmen ended up doing, was far more interesting than what they had originally planned, inadvertent as it was.

The businessmen wanted to borrow a LM to display at a space exhibit in Japan, showing the accomplishments of space missions. The idea was to have a building specifically built for the LM, have two actors play the part of the astronauts, with both of them inside the LM while it slowly descended from the ceiling to land on a simulated lunar surface. Once the LM landed, the astronauts would come out and climb down the LM ladder, walk around on the simulated lunar surface, then climb back up and into the LM and liftoff with just the LM ascent stage. And this was to be done eight times a day for several months. But as Kaiser diplomatically explained, the LM wouldn't even have been able to withstand one of these re-enactments.

To be in the same room when this impromptu meeting took place would have been priceless. To think about what these two businessmen wanted to do and what this would have revealed to the public, with NASA trying to explain why the flimsy design of the LM was not able to withstand even one re-enactment, was just not going to happen. So instead, Kaiser suggested they contact Grumman Corporation which built the LM. After the request by the businessmen, Kaiser was barely able to contain his laughter. However, these two businessmen surely would have had the last laugh, if they had inadvertently exposed to the world the real purpose of the LM, which was to do exactly what these businessmen themselves planned on doing.

Figure 4.5 – The Author Standing Beside the Lunar Module
Source: Author

When it was explained to them that the LM was expensive and that it could not be displayed for such a re-enactment, Grumman decided to build a replica or mockup of the LM. To do this, they needed the design plans for the LM, which shouldn't have been a problem for a company that originally built it. One would assume that Grumman had kept meticulous records filed away for future reference.

Well, not so fast…

Grumman employee Joel Taft:

> All the LM design drawings were stored on one of the warehouses, and we needed some. Because our funds in space were being cut so sharply, they had just been

thrown in boxes. Most of the boxes did not match their inventory sheets, and there were four thousand boxes of drawings. Many were to be thrown away – they were throwing away history – but I managed to find drawings of all the outer features of the vehicle. We ended up calling this last of the LMs 'LM-71/2,' because we used drawings of LM-1 and LM-15.[10]

Once again, we have an example of NASA and its contractors using a lack of funding as an excuse for not keeping detailed records.

Grumman Aircraft Engineering Corporation was founded in 1929. In 1969, its name was changed to Grumman Aerospace Corporation. They produce military and civilian aircraft. So why would Grumman need funding to file away LM documents? Whether or not NASA provided funding, surely Grumman would have wanted to maintain meticulous documentation of the vehicle they designed and built, which was supposedly used in what has been described as the most significant scientific accomplishment of the 20th century. And no doubt they would have had their own resources to do it.

Yet, their LM design plans were thrown in boxes to be discarded to the garbage heap. The proponents will argue that there are still tens of thousands of documents for anyone to access. But this is misleading, since most of the documents that have been destroyed are core documents which would have been needed to build on, leading to future technology for manned lunar spacecraft missions and beyond.

We've just seen another example of core document being discarded and/or destroyed in the quote above, where Joe Taft said they managed to find enough drawings for the outer features of the LM. Enough drawings? Did he mean schematics? And when he said enough drawings, he actually meant the record was incomplete.

There is no excuse for the shoddy record keeping of documentation related to the Apollo program. It's clear, that the real purpose of the destruction of these documents was to prevent any other scientific institution, manufacturer, or even another country from trying to duplicate the Apollo program, and then finding out that this technology never worked in the first place. There just isn't any other explanation. And as mentioned in this series, missing documents are an ongoing issue when it relates to the Apollo program.

In the next chapter, we'll discuss the methods used by spacecraft for re-entry into Earth's atmosphere that led to the methods used in the Apollo space program, and we'll show how perilous a CM re-entry would have been. Further, we'll discuss the passengers and crew onboard two airline flights, who claimed to have witnessed two Apollo CM re-entries.

Chapter Four – Endnotes

[1] National Aeronautics and Space Administration (NASA), World Spaceflight News, Gene J. Matranga, C. Wayne Ottinger, Calvin R. Jarvis, D. Christian Gelzer, *Apollo and America's Moon Landing Program: Unconventional, Contrary, and Ugly: The Lunar Landing Research Vehicle (NASA SP-2004-4535)*, p. 12

[2] Ibid., p. 15.

[3] Ibid., p. 49.

[4] Ibid., p. 63.

[5] Joshua Stoff, *IMAGES OF AMERICA: BUILDING MOONSHIPS: THE GRUMMAN LUNAR MODULE*, p. 76.

[6] Op Cit., Matranga, Ottinger, Jarvis, Gelzer, p.96.

[7] Charles R. Pellegrino and Joshua Stoff, *CHARIOTS FOR APOLLO: THE UNTOLD STORY BEHIND THE RACE TO THE MOON*, p. 65.

[8] Xavier Pascal, Lunar Module Descent and Errors: Intentional Errors (Article) - Apollo Investigation. Lunar Module Descent and Landing: Intentional Errors Introduced into the Record. AULIS Online – Different Thinking

[9] Julius A. Birch PhD, The Apollo 17 Anomalous Ascent Trajectory - Apollo Investigation, The Apollo 17 Anomalous Ascent Trajectory. Julius A. Birch PhD. AULIS Online – Different Thinking

[10] Op Cit., Pellegrino, Stoff, p. 267

Chapter Five

Re-entry Into Earth's Atmosphere, The Final Phase

Another and equally important area for manned space missions, is re-entry into Earth's atmosphere. This would include a sophisticated computer for missions returning from a lunar trajectory. Even before the first Mercury missions, NASA knew that any manned mission to the Moon and back would require an autonomous computer. That meant an autonomous computer capable of all maneuvers without any input from the astronauts, especially on re-entry into Earth's atmosphere.

David A. Mindell

> Before Gemini or even Mercury missions flew, and before President Kennedy's decision to send Americans to the Moon, Robert Chilton began looking at the human role in a lunar flight. Meeting the requirements for a moon mission would be hugely more difficult and complex than for simple orbital strolls: hitting a lunar entry corridor required accurate navigation; maps of the moon had crude precision compared to those of Earth; lunar reentry speeds far exceeded those from orbit; and people had to withstand much longer missions and perform at peak capacity up to the end.
>
> Because a spacecraft returning from the moon would reenter the atmosphere from a trans-earth trajectory at

a much higher speed than Mercury or Gemini spacecraft had, it would need to target a narrow reentry corridor, which called for accurate guidance operating autonomously on board.[1]

To put the CM re-entry into perspective, researcher Marcus Allen uses this analogy:

> It would be the equivalent to someone dropping a small marble from the top of the Empire State Building (about 1,300 ft high), and me holding a 3-inch-wide container at the bottom and catching it - 9 times in a row.

In aviation, it is an established fact that there are two critical phases of flight:

- o Takeoffs &
- o Landings.

In the aerospace industry, there are three critical phases of a mission:

- ➢ Launch
- ➢ Re-entry into Earth's atmosphere
- ➢ Splashdown in either the Atlantic or Pacific Oceans.

However, with the Apollo missions, there was an added critical phase and that was NASA's claim of manned landings and liftoffs from the lunar surface. We've already discussed the dangers of a manned landing and liftoff from the lunar surface. This in reality would have been impossible with 1960s technology. In this chapter we'll discuss the equally dangerous phase of the Apollo missions and the final act in this saga, re-entry into Earth's atmosphere and splashdown into the Pacific Ocean.

Note: As the above quote says, "hitting a lunar entry corridor required accurate navigation" which would have been a necessary component for lunar manned missions. However, we will not discuss the navigation portion of the Apollo missions, since an in-depth analysis of the AGC has already been discussed in Part 1 of this series. This discussion showed that the AGC did not have the capability of maintaining course, meaning that the precise navigation for a lunar entry corridor, would have been impossible.

To better understand re-entry, we'll start with some basic history, theory, and methods used to re-enter Earth's atmosphere, which apply to both unmanned and manned missions.

History Of Spacecraft Re-entry Methods

Although the V-2 rocket was used successfully during WWII (that is, regarding its launch capabilities, since as a weapon it wasn't very effective), it only reached an altitude of between 50 to 60 miles, so there was no need to incorporate a design for re-entry procedures since it was not needed. Re-entry into Earth's atmosphere was only given serious consideration in the early 1950s when the next generation of rockets, the Redstone and Jupiter, reached altitudes that required methods to protect the capsule from extreme temperatures, which would be produced by the speed and angle of the spacecraft on re-entry into Earth's atmosphere.

One of the theories considered for ballistic missiles was to use a method that involved a steep trajectory on re-entry, in which the slender pointed shape of these vehicles produced speeds of up to 15,500 mph. An increase in speed, would cause an increase in air friction and could produce temperatures up to

12,000 degrees Fahrenheit, which is twice that of the surface of the Sun. The boundary layer in front of the vehicle during its trajectory and re-entry created two heat flows:

- One outside of the boundary layer which was defected way from the vehicle.

- And the second, inside the boundary layer that came in contact with the vehicle, which was enough to melt it.

Therefore, an alternative to this method was devised in 1951 by H. Julian Allen, with the blunt re-entry body theory.

The blunt re-entry body theory involved designing a rounded surface on the aft bulkhead of the spacecraft. This method created a stronger boundary layer on re-entry into Earth's atmosphere and deflected most of the heat away from the upper part of the vehicle. The blunt body method was apparently so successful, that it was incorporated into the design of future ballistic missiles and spacecraft including Mercury, Gemini, and Apollo missions. However, engineers returned to the design of the slender pointed shapes for ballistic missiles, when new technology was available to deal with the extreme temperatures on re-entry.

Another benefit from the blunt body method on re-entry is its low ballistic coefficient. Ballistic coefficient is a function of mass, size, and drag coefficient. Vehicles with high ballistic coefficient, which are usually vehicles that are long, slender, and streamlined, enter the upper atmosphere at enormous speeds and do most of their deceleration in the lower atmosphere. But because of the increased thickness of the lower atmosphere, the vehicle becomes very hot for a short period of time, but this short duration still meant the temperatures were extreme. However, with the blunt body method, the vehicle does most of its deceleration in the upper thin atmosphere and although it takes longer to slow down, it generates less heat. The total time of the heat load is essentially the same for both types of vehicles, but the lower temperatures for the blunt body method was more manageable with 1960s technology. But that still meant this technology had to deal with temperatures over 5,000 degrees Fahrenheit. So, a thermal protection system needed to be designed for the blunt body method to work effectively.

The solution to dealing with these temperatures on the blunt body method, was to use the ablative process. The material used in this process is usually made of fiberglass or other natural materials, or it can be a spray-on resin-based coating. During re-entry, the ablative material on the aft bulkhead of the spacecraft that first makes contact with the atmosphere, will take the brunt of the heat forces involved and goes through what is called an endothermic reaction.

> The vaporization of an ablator is an endothermic reaction; i.e., it needs energy input to proceed. A proper ablator will absorb the heat flux incident to its surface and vaporize at a rate proportional to the magnitude of the heat flux. The heat is carried away with the vaporized material, increasing the effectiveness of the thermal protection system. The vaporization leads to a thinning of the ablator, resulting in an upper limit on the amount of heat it can absorb. Perhaps the most unappreciated advantage of ablation is that the coolant (the gas generated by pyrolysis), after accepting all of the heat it is capable of absorbing, is automatically jettisoned.[2]

On re-entry, the atmosphere chips away at the ablator material keeping any heat flux from contacting the main spacecraft structure. This process has to work perfectly to prevent the incineration of the spacecraft, which reinforces the need for an autonomous computer for the precise and complex calculations needed, for the narrow re-entry corridor from a mission returning from the Moon. Any deviation from the planned re-entry trajectory, would require the computer to correct immediately. There is little or no margin for error.

Figure 5.1 – Blunt Body Re-entry Method
Source: NASA

However, there were some problems with this method, the most obvious being that the capsule had to use parachutes to splashdown in the either the Atlantic or Pacific Ocean. But because the capsule lacked the ability for steering to minimize its landing area, many ships over a wide area of water were needed for recovery. The Mercury program used this method and later missions involving the Gemini and Apollo program, had lift to drag ratios incorporated into their design. The new design did create some lift on the capsule which enabled the use of reaction-control thrusters to help in steering the capsule in an effort to narrow its landing area, in theory that is. But eventually it turned out that both Gemini and Apollo capsules still required large areas of ocean with many ships needed for their recovery. There will be more on the parachute landing system below in this chapter.

Figure 5.2 – Splashdown Of Apollo 17
Source: Wikimedia Commons

To better understand the effects of re-entry into Earth's atmosphere from a lunar mission, a program called Flight Investigation of the Re-entry Environment (FIRE), was set up to collect data on spacecraft that re-enter the upper atmosphere at speeds of up to 24,500 mph. This included wind tunnel tests at several Langley facilities. Further, NASA had awarded a 5-million-dollar contract to Republic Aviation in 1962 for two smaller versions of the Apollo CM. Another 2.56-million-dollar contract was awarded to Ling-Temco-Vought to develop what was called, a velocity package. The idea was to launch the spacecraft with an Atlas-D booster rocket to an altitude of 400,000 feet, the same altitude for a returning spacecraft from a lunar mission.

The first Project FIRE flight was on April 14, 1964. The Atlas-D launch vehicle placed the 200-pound spacecraft into a ballistic trajectory along the Eastern Test Range. The Antares fired for 30 seconds, increasing the descent speed to 25,166 mph, and the exterior of the spacecraft reached an estimated 20,000 °F. About 32 minutes after launch, the spacecraft splashed down into the Atlantic Ocean some 5,000 miles downrange, near Ascension Island. The second Project FIRE launch, following a similar trajectory, was on May 22, 1965, and also used an Atlas-D from Cape Canaveral. The spacecraft entered the atmosphere at a speed of 25,400 mph and generated temperatures of about 20,000 °F.[3]

This project led directly to the testing of the thermal heatshield for the Apollo program, which we'll discuss next.

The Apollo Command Module Re-entry Heatshield And Test Missions

The Apollo heatshield materials, construction, and structure are described as follows:

- A brazed PH 14-8 stainless steel honeycomb sheet that was attached to a structural shell.

- A fiberglass-phenolic honeycomb with 400,000 individual cells that was bonded to the brazed structure. Each cell was individually filled with silica fibers and micro-balloons.

- The heat shield weighed 32 pounds per cubic foot.

- The finished product was then attached to the aft bulkhead of the Apollo CM, using 59 bolts to secure it to the main CM structure.

The heatshield was then flight tested on two unmanned Saturn 1B missions:

- ❖ First Flight Test was with mission AS-201 which was launched February 26, 1966, and re-entered from LEO. This mission had lost control on re-entry, which caused the CM to roll. So, it was impossible to know exactly how the heatshield would have performed as planned, even though space historians say it successfully survived re-entry. Therefore, this mission cannot really be designated a success.

- ❖ Second Flight Test was with AS-202, launched August 25, 1966, which was also considered a success. This mission apparently met all its objectives even though it entered the atmosphere at a steeper re-entry than was planned, had experienced greater g-forces, and splashed down 205 nautical miles up range from its planned splashdown point.

Both missions used a method called skip re-entry, or at least AS-202 did as there now seems to be conflicting information as to which method was used, either skip re-entry or direct entry. The re-entry vs. direct entry methods, as well as a discrepancy as to which was used, will be discussed further on in this chapter.

After the first two flight tests involving the CM heatshield, NASA was apparently confident enough to test the heatshield on a Saturn V (given that the first two flight tests involving the heatshields was hardly a success, one wonders where that confidence came from).

- ❖ The first flight test mission with the Saturn V was with Apollo 4, launched November 9, 1967. This mission was to test the worst-case scenario for the heatshield with a shallow re-entry, which would increase the heat load. Temperatures reached over 5,000 degrees Fahrenheit and the mission was considered satisfactory. This was also the first mission to enter the atmosphere at almost 25,000 mph, which was similar in entry speed for an Apollo mission's return from the Moon.

- ❖ The second test mission with the Saturn V was with Apollo 6, launched April 6, 1968. This mission was to test the worst-case scenario with a steep re-entry. But this mission was plagued with problems which were so serious that if a crew had been onboard, they would have had to abort the mission during launch. And according to the telemetry data, the CM had entered the atmosphere at 3,600 ft/sec slower than the previous mission, yet the temperature on the leeward side of the heatshield was higher.

Both flight tests apparently used the skip re-entry method.

NASA listed three reasons as to why Apollo 6 re-entered the atmosphere at a slower speed and had lower temperatures on the heatshield:

o Apollo 6 flew at lower altitudes

o It did not skip out of the atmosphere as high an altitude as the previous mission

o It flew approximately 80 seconds longer to reach its splashdown point

But despite the numerous problems that were experienced with Apollo 6, NASA claims the heatshield performed satisfactorily. However, it is important to note that there were interruptions in telemetry data from the problems experienced, so there isn't a complete picture of what exactly took place on this mission. And as documented in Part 1 when discussing the missing Apollo 11 telemetry tapes, NASA had signed out the telemetry tapes for the Apollo missions in the 1970s from the Washington National Records Center. And around the 40th anniversary of Apollo 11, it was established that the telemetry tapes for all of the Apollo missions were destroyed. Therefore, one should be skeptical as to the validity of any data in hard copy format from these missions, since this data could easily have been taken from computer simulations, which were run for all of the Apollo Moon missions.

Note: For an in-depth discussion on Apollo 6 and the problems that plagued that mission, refer to Part I of this series.

Re-entry, The Official Version

It was from Apollo 6 that NASA went straight to the first manned Apollo mission, which was aboard a Saturn IB, launched six months later with Apollo 7 on October 11, 1968. And just two months later, NASA launched the third Saturn V and the first manned mission of that vehicle with Apollo 8 on December 21, 1968 and then on to the second and third manned missions of the Saturn V with Apollos 10 and 11.

> Apollo 8, the first lunar flyby mission in December 1968, returned with a heat shield that was charred less than that of the Apollo 4 test. The char depth was 0.6 inch at the stagnation point, and 0.4 inch elsewhere. There was, however, a fair amount of impact damage when the capsule splashed down. Apollo 10, another lunar return, entered a flightpath angle of 0.02 of a degree steeper than planned, subjecting the crew to a maximum 6.78 g's. Despite this anomaly, the heat shield performed satisfactorily. Returning from the first lunar landing, Apollo 11 crossed the entry interface at 400,000 feet and at 36,195 ft/sec and -6.488 degrees (versus a planned 36,194 ft/sec and -6.483 degrees). Heat shield performance was listed as nominal.[4]

All of the CMs from a lunar mission were claimed to have re-entered the atmosphere from an altitude of 400,000 feet, and at a speed of just over 25,000 mph. By 40,000 feet the CMs slowed to approximately 300 mph deploying the three main parachutes shortly thereafter.

We'll now discuss the CM parachute system that was used in the final phase of the descent to splashdown in the Pacific Ocean.

Parachutes, The Only Solution

To many of those in and outside of the manned space program, the use of parachutes to safely splashdown in the ocean was seen as a sign of defeat. Further, the astronauts were military pilots who were used to manually flying their aircraft to a safe landing on paved runways. So, not only did the astronauts have to deal with a perceived notion of defeat, they had to also deal with the fact that they had little or no control during the descent to splashdown. This was not the preferred image to what was believed at the time to have been man's greatest technological achievement.

> For the longest time, NASA explored ways to avoid landing its astronaut missions in the sea, which requires the U.S. navy to perform overtaxing water rescues. Furthermore, the astronauts, who were all pilots, found the method objectionable. This was eloquently communicated in 1965 when artist Wen Painter, at NASA's Flight Research Center, drew a powerful cartoon depicting two astronauts sitting in a Gemini capsule bobbing in the water while the Navy steams around in the distance, juxtaposed with a second image of a sleek lifting body landing on a runway with astronauts walking across the tarmac. The caption read: "Don't be rescued at sea; fly back in style." This cartoon captured magnificently what some saw as a key

difference between space-capsule splashdowns at sea and spaceplane landings on a runway. [5]

However, this was the only solution due to the limitations with 1960s technology. Another factor NASA cited for using parachutes, was the possibility of an abort after launch. The reasoning being, since all the Apollo launches took place over the Atlantic Ocean, it made sense for that to be the landing area in the case of an abort. Therefore, the same parachute system could be used in an abort scenario during launch as well as for a returning mission.

According to the Apollo familiarization manual the parachute system is:

- o Activated at 24,000 feet prior to re-entry or in case of an abort, it is initiated 0.4 seconds after launch, where jettison of the launch escape system propelled the CM to a safe altitude.

- o During the abort, the apex cover, which is the forward heat shield, is jettisoned by four gas-pressure thrusters.

- o 1.6 seconds later, the drogue mortar pyrotechnic cartridges are fired.

- o Continuing from either an abort or re-entry, two drogue parachutes are deployed in a reefed condition.

- o 8 seconds later, the reefing lines are severed by reefing line cutters and the drogue parachutes are fully opened.

- o The drogue parachutes stabilize the CM in a blunt-end-forward attitude and provide deceleration.

- o At 10,000 feet, the drogue parachutes are released and three pilot parachute mortars are fired. This ejects the pilot parachutes, which extract and deploy the three main parachutes.

- o The main parachutes open to a reefed position for 8 seconds to further decelerate the CM. The main parachutes are then fully opened (dis-reefed) and the CM descends at a predetermined rate towards the ocean, whether its an abort from launch or re-entry from a mission.

- o If for any reason one main parachute fails, the other two main parachutes will still be able to lower the CM to safety.

- o For both an abort or re-entry, the rate of descent for the CM for the final 5,000 feet to splashdown, was 33 feet per second.

After splashdown:

- o The main parachutes are disconnected.
- o If the CM is inverted after splashdown, a system is activated which inflates three airbags to position the CM in an upright position.
- o The CM is also equipped with a sea dye marker, a flashing beacon light, a VHF recovery beacon transmitter, a VHF receiver, and an H.F. transceiver.

Note: It's a wonder why NASA couldn't have found that little extra space to stow a camera configured with the right lens, to take photos of the stars from the lunar surface. After all, it seemed they had enough space for just about anything else, including a makeshift golf club on Apollo 14, including varying amounts of Moon rocks that were claimed to have been brought back to Earth.

The Apollo landing system is one aspect of the missions that seemed to have worked according to their design, at least from 24,000 feet. However, re-entry cannot so easily be confirmed as to having worked according to its parameters and in fact, when one looks at the record of the numerous sources connected to the Apollo program, a different picture starts to emerge from that of the official record. This, among other aspects of the re-entry method, are discussed next.

Re-entry, The Reality

Both heatshields on the Saturn IB missions were said to have met all of the objectives, and both heatshields on the Saturn V missions were evaluated as having performed, "satisfactorily," despite the fact that AS-201 lost control on re-entry, and the Apollo 6 mission was a near disaster. But NASA engineers did admit that there was still much to learn from the effects of re-entry, and were understandably concerned about any manned mission entering Earth's atmosphere from a lunar trajectory. This of course was an understatement considering that four unmanned flight tests of the heatshield were not enough for the many problems that had yet to be encountered, any one of which could have caused the loss of the vehicle and crew. Yet, NASA claims that these four test missions, led to the flawless performance of the heatshield on all the Apollo manned missions.

In response to the concerns on the unknown effects of re-entry, North American and Avco had over designed and reinforced the heatshield, so the finished product weighed 1,500 pounds, which was 10% of the CM weight. However, missing from other measures that could have been taken to increase the success of a mission's re-entry into Earth's atmosphere, was further unmanned flight testing of the CM heatshield. Minimum flight testing was a running theme during the Apollo program.

As mentioned above, there is little or no margin for error when re-entering Earth's atmosphere. And as discussed in Part 1 of this series, the CM computer was nowhere near as autonomous as NASA claims. And given the lift to drag characteristics of the CM, the proper distribution of weight becomes vitally important once it has entered Earth's atmosphere. Any shift in that weight and the computer would need to compensate right away. This brings us to one of the more sensational claims made by NASA, and that is the estimated 842 pounds of Moon rocks that were supposedly brought back by the Apollo missions. Hence, on average approximately 140 pounds of Moon rock were brought back in each of the six missions that were claimed to have landed on the lunar surface. This is getting close to the average weight of another astronaut, which would have needed to have been calculated for re-entry. However, the official record lists different weights of Moon rocks for each of the Apollo mission, that were supposedly brought back from the lunar surface.

For example:

- o Apollo 11 is claimed to have brought back 47.5 pounds of Moon rocks
- o Apollo 17 is claimed to have bought back 243.6 pounds of Moon rocks.

Although other researchers have determined that these Moon rocks are fake, another equally important question is, just how was it possible for the CM to safely re-enter Earth's atmosphere, without the ability of the computer being able to instantly calculate the necessary adjustments for any shift in weight?

Note: A full analysis of the Moon rocks that debunk NASA's claim that they were supposedly brought back by the Apollo missions, can be found on www.aulis.com and on a series of videos by Jarrah White on his YouTube channel www.moonfaker.com.

As discussed above, lift to drag ratio was designed into the CM. Lift to drag comes into effect once the CM enters the atmosphere. The purpose of this was to give it some lift capability for more stability and control over the descent. This requires that the distribution of weight is properly balanced, much like that of an aircraft. For example, once the passengers and/or cargo are onboard an aircraft, calculations are done to make sure the aircraft has not exceeded its payload limit. Graphs in the aircraft manual are then used to ensure the aircraft is within its weight and balance envelope. The aircraft center of gravity is used as a reference point for this determination. Too much weight forward or aft of the center of gravity will affect the performance of the aircraft, for example, takeoffs and landings as well as fuel consumption during cruise flight. It could even cause aircraft to lose control, depending on what flight maneuvers are made. Many accidents have been attributed to improper distribution of weight alone.

Each aircraft is unique to weight and balance calculations, including aircraft of the same design. For example, the Cessna 172 which is used for most training and sight seeing flights has its own weight and balance information. And it doesn't matter if it's the same model, make or year, for example; the most recent Cessna 172 models would all use the same graphs in its aircraft manual, but each aircraft would have its own basic weight and balance information when using those graphs, before any passengers or baggage is added for weight and balance calculations.

The CM would have been no different. The weight distribution would have had to be within limits and in fact given the circumstances, would needed to have been near perfect. A miscalculation in weight and balance or any shift in weight during re-entry, would have caused the CM to roll. This would have been a very serious situation and would have required immediate corrective action, especially during the early phase of re-entry where the CM could have been destroyed by extreme temperatures, since the main heatshield would have been ineffective due to a constant roll. To prevent this from happening, the onboard computer would needed to have calculated which thrusters to fire and for how long to counter the roll to stabilize the CM on its descent. The calculations by the computer and the actions taken, would have needed to occur in less than a second, which would require a fully autonomous computer. And as we learned in Part 1 of this series, the computer was not as autonomous as needed and in fact, it has been determined to have been a complete fake. And assuming the astronauts had some manual control, there would have been no time to have made calculations to counter any roll and then to take the necessary action. By the time the required action was taken, the CM would certainly have been destroyed. Further, the intense heat turned the atmosphere around the CM into charged plasma during the early phase of re-entry, so it's doubtful the thrusters would have been of much use anyway.

Skip Re-entry Versus Direct Entry

Missions to the Moon and back have a much higher velocity on re-entry into Earth's atmosphere, than missions entering from LEO. Therefore, the preferred method for a returning mission from the Moon, would be the skip re-entry method. When the spacecraft enters the atmosphere, it skips or bounces out of the atmosphere for a few seconds, then enters again. This method helps to slow down the spacecraft when entering the atmosphere and helps to lower or at least stabilize the extreme temperatures. The ablative material on the heatshield protects the main structure of the spacecraft for the duration of the rapid descent through the upper atmosphere.

With the direct entry method, the spacecraft plunges at a high speed of over 25,000 mph and continues its descent without any skip or bounce from the atmosphere. The higher velocity of the spacecraft creates more friction in the upper atmosphere and the spacecraft is at a higher risk of disintegrating as it plunges towards the lower atmosphere. So, one would think that this issue was not only resolved, but the method used would have been agreed upon by everyone involved in the Apollo program, especially the astronauts who supposedly flew the missions. However, that doesn't seem to be the case as we'll discuss next.

To Skip, Or Not To Skip, That Is The Question

As has been discussed above, skip re-entry was documented as being used in the CMs' re-entry during flight tests. Therefore, there should be no confusion or conflict as to the re-entry method chosen for the Apollo missions, since apparently it has been established as fact. But as we've seen with this book series, contradictions permeate the Apollo program and of course we're now seeing this with skip re-entry versus direct re-entry.

Christopher C. Kraft Jr. founded Mission Control and was flight director of the Mercury manned missions, and seven of the Gemini manned missions. He also participated in the design of the Apollo missions and was director of the Johnson Space Flight Center until 1982, in which he oversaw the beginning of the Space Shuttle program.

In a quote by Kraft, he clearly states the re-entry method used for the Apollo program:

> Because the velocity was so high, if you tried to come in directly, the heat-shield requirements would be too great. So, what we did was get them into the atmosphere, skip it out to kill off some of the velocity,

and then bring it back in again. That made the total heat pulse on the heat shield of the spacecraft considerably lower.[6]

This quote clarifies the re-entry method used for the Apollo program, so there should be no misunderstanding. But as we've seen with other examples in the Apollo program, one should always be careful when there appears to be a statement of fact, as we see with this rather terse and angry response from Apollo 15 astronaut Alfred M. Worden:

Chris Kraft is a bad guy. If we could feed him to a bomb, we would.[7]

This quote could surely have been seen as a threat or at least a desire to do physical harm, if the opportunity had availed itself. But of course, the reader should not be surprised at quotes like this, as other Apollo astronauts' quotes have been laced with profanities towards anyone who challenges them on the official narrative, which has been reported on many online sources. Then of course there was the physical assault by Buzz Aldrin on researcher Bart Sibrel. It seems one should keep their distance when one asks a provocative question of these 'national heroes.'

Anyway, Worden now describes the re-entry method as a direct entry. And to confuse the public even more, you have experts who now call the direct entry as, a double dip.

- o Does that mean skip re-entry is a double dip too?
- o Or on direct entry, double dip means the spacecraft briefly skips out of the atmosphere? But isn't that just like skip re-entry?
- o Or, on direct entry, double dip means the spacecraft doesn't quite skip out of the atmosphere, it just sort of briefly gains altitude so doesn't qualify as a skip?

Fifty years later, the saga continues…

It has been reported that only unmanned missions used skip re-entry. However, an unmanned Russian Zond spacecraft, which was designed for two cosmonauts, had successfully used the skip re-entry method on its reappearance from a circumlunar mission in 1968, a month before the Apollo 8 mission. But because there were many problems with the Zond spacecraft, the program was cancelled before any manned missions were approved.

First Lieutenant Emre Kaya of the Turkish Air Force, and graduate student at the US Air Force Institute of Technology (AFIT) Wright Patterson AFB, Ohio, wrote a thesis on skip re-entry to be used for the Orion spacecraft, which is the same basic design as the Apollo CM but a larger version of it.

Kaya says:

> In the Apollo type missions, the return phase had to be initiated in a restricted time window so that the crew module could enter the atmosphere at the preplanned time and be able to land at the planned landing site. Using skip procedures, landing location and time will be more accurate in addition to having the time flexibility for re-entry.
>
> Although total skip entry guidance has been done before for the trajectories of unmanned vehicles, application of this concept is quite new for the manned space missions… Apollo used a 'double dip' entry.[8]

So first, Kaya says that the Apollo missions used the skip re-entry method, then later he adds they used the double dip entry method which further muddies the waters. I'm not saying Kaya set out to deceive the public. But he seems to have realized how sensitive this subject is, when he insinuates that the skip re-entry method wasn't possible for manned missions. So instead of publicly revealing an anomaly, he used a phrase that would camouflage what was really going on by using, double dip. Of course, one can only speculate, but then he goes on to say this:

> The views expressed in this thesis are those of the author and do not reflect the official policy or position of the United States Air Force, Department of Defence, or the U.S. Government.[9]

It seems that Kaya looked at the conflicting data, did his own analysis and saw that the re-entry method would have been impossible for the Apollo missions to use. So instead, he chose to balance the information in favour of both the skip re-entry and direct entry methods with the phrase, double dip. Better to muddy the waters and put forward a solution that can benefit both sides of this discussion, rather than directly contradict the official narrative, which is a possible reason as to why part of this thesis was released to the public:

Mary Bennett:

> One wonders why the AFIT authorities thought it necessary to release a part of his degree work into the public domain. Surely, there were enough NASA studies on that matter already. What this study does do however, is refute Chris Kraft's assertion that the skip entry was the technique used for Apollo. And it is indeed odd that an Apollo flight director should appear to be so blatantly wrong. Taking Kaya's words and Kraft's statement together, could lead one to the inevitable conclusion that the Apollo missions were unmanned. Or that CMs attempted skip re-entries, but were not recorded as such. Something is surely not right with such disregard for the definition and such lack of clarity regarding this Apollo re-entry data. No

wonder the record reeks of confusion and, wittingly or otherwise, obfuscation.[10]

And how convenient that the Apollo mission telemetry tapes have 'disappeared,' leaving no chance of a definitive answer as to whether the CMs used skip re-entry or direct entry.

There were apparently witnesses to three Apollo CM re-entries from four aircraft on route in the same general area, which should have solidified the official narrative. But as we will learn later, it appears that these witnesses were duped into sighting an event that didn't happen. But first, we'll discuss what the witnesses saw according to the official narrative.

Passengers And Crew Onboard Aircraft Witness Apollo CM Re-entries

The Apollo CM re-entry sightings, are as follows:

- Apollo 8: Witnessed by the passengers and crew of Pan Am flight 812 while on route from Fiji to Hawaii.

- Apollo 11: Witnessed by the passengers and crew of a Qantas Boeing 707 flight while on route from Brisbane Australia, to Honolulu Hawaii, and a USAF KC-135 from an altitude of 43,000 feet, which filmed the event taken at 12:20 EDT 24 July, 1969.

- Apollo 13: Witnessed by 60 passengers and crew of an Air New Zealand DC-8 flight from Nandi Fiji, to Auckland Australia.

The sources for the sightings, are as follows:

- Apollo 8, published in the National Geographic on page 624 "A Most Fantastic Voyage", Lt. Sam C. Phillips Vol. 5, May 1969, pp 593-631.

- Apollo 11, published in The West Australian on July 26, 1969, page 12: 'A Bird's Eye View of the Return.' There was a second article published in The Sun Herald titled "82 passengers and 13 crew members on a Boeing 707 saw Apollo 11's re-entry," which was published July 27, 1969. The source for the film was of course the U.S. Air force.

- Apollo 13, published in The Auckland Star article "A champagne re-entry for DC8 flight" April 18, 1970, page 1.

We'll discuss the witnesses to Apollo 11 and Apollo 13, since these two events are documented with the most details.

Passengers And Crew Describe What They Saw

The passengers and crew's descriptions of both Apollo 11 and Apollo 13, are fairly extensive. So, in the interest of brevity, I've chosen the quotes directly describing both Apollo CM re-entries. For a complete description of the passengers and crew experience on both the Boeing 707 and DC-8 flights, you can access the article 'Faked Apollo Atmosphere Re-entry from Space?' published on www.aulis.com.

Captain Frank A. Brown of the Qantas Boeing 707 flight from Brisbane to Honolulu, gave a detailed description of the Apollo 11 re-entry to his passengers and crew. Below are quotes from the captain:

  o There's a little cloud above us but we are going to get a perfect view of Apollo 11

  o We have about two minutes to go, the capsule is about 500 miles from Earth now. It has just crossed the east coast of Australia above Mackay, Queensland.

  o The astronauts are travelling at six miles a second. A staggering speed, isn't it?

- We expect to see an object behind us in just over a minute and a half. It will be brighter than a bright star.
- At that time, it will be something like 500 miles away.

Just before Apollo 11's re-entry became visible, Captain Brown asked the passengers to move to the left side of the plane, to share windows with fellow passengers to witness the event.

Captain Brown continues:

- Here they come on the left, one object brighter than the other. See the two of them, one above the other. One is the command module; the other is the service module. They both weigh six tons.
- They are picking up heat now. The bottom one is leaving an incandescent descent trail. See it flashing. See the trail behind – what a spectacle. You can see the bits flying off. Notice that the top one is almost unchanged while the bottom one is shattering into pieces. The part that is disintegrating is the rocket service module, the top one is the command module.
- It looks to me like a pretty normal re-entry. Mathematically that seems perfectly sound and the timing is perfect. It looks really good to me.
- In my opinion that was the spectacle of a lifetime.

The passengers were then served champagne and given certificates with a reproduction of the medallion, that was supposedly left on the Moon by Neil Armstrong and Buzz Aldrin.

Bob Mosley (Lt. Col., retired) and his crew who took a film of the Apollo 11 re-entry aboard a USAF KC-135 documented what the film showed:

Coming from the West, the non heat-shielded Service Module soon disintegrates into a flaming fire ball, sending burning material in all directions; which turns night into day momentarily. The Command Module, is then seen to continue on, as a diminishing light, in an easterly direction, and a not too distant, highly successful, splash down; Man had been on the moon and returned safely, as per one of the National Objectives set down by President John Kennedy, approximately 7 years earlier.[11]

Several passengers and crew onboard the DC-8 flight from Nandi Fiji to Auckland Australia, gave these descriptions of the Apollo 13 re-entry:

- Flight Attendant Mr. L. W. Smith: It was directly ahead like two headlights, at 5.55 a.m. travelling west to east. Then things began to happen – there was an explosion… a reddish flash… and sparks flew as the modules separated, and things began to disintegrate.

- Captain Ross McWilliams: very spectacular, the sight of a lifetime. It was right in front and above us about 60,000 feet and about 190 miles away. The service module fell away in a flash of bluey-white light. The command module had a long whitish tail, which turned yellow as it neared the sun.

- Air New Zealand crew member Mr. Peter Davidson, who saw the re-entry from the flight deck: It came down like a Roman candle and moved quite quickly from east to west.

- Air New Zealand information service Mr. Ken Hickson: brilliant multicoloured flash, like a sparkler being lit.

- Passenger Miss G. Hemp: A beautiful sight – so staggering I couldn't believe it was happening. It just looked like a comet coming down.

An even more detailed description of the Apollo 13 re-entry is provided by passenger Peter Gabelish onboard the same New Zealand DC-8 flight who made entries in his pocket diary:

- Running about two minutes behind schedule a brilliant fire ball, like a massive bright light appeared over the starboard horizon!
- Travelling horizontally, an incandescent, silver plume of brilliant light, leaving a blazing trail of constant width behind it, arced in from the west at an altitude that didn't appear to be much higher than ours.
- The silver phosphorescent tail it left behind seemed to retain its brilliance as a curved band of luminescent material while the leading body continued at constant velocity across our path.
- I presumed the tail to be the vaporized aluminium and magnesium materials from which the capsules are mostly constructed.
- Every few seconds a bright yellow-orange spark would branch off the main spearhead and arc away on a different trajectory.
- The incredible display continued across our path and arced towards the eastern horizon on our port side. The inferno diminished while still within our sight.
- When it died out, a minute red dot continued on the east bound path, curving out of sight over the horizon.
- I would guess that the whole display lasted three to four minutes.
- We were fortunate that the whole re-entry was seen in total darkness. Several minutes afterwards day began to break and the trail of vaporized metal was visible hanging in the upper atmosphere for the next twenty

minutes or so affording me the chance to photograph it as it hung there.

Peter Gabelish even managed to take a photo of the event. We'll discuss that photo below.

All of the three Apollo missions were seen to have re-entered into Earth's atmosphere during the dark. The darkness illuminated each Apollo CM re-entry, which made for a spectacular light show. Champagne was served to the passengers and crew of the New Zealand DC-8 flight who witnessed the Apollo 13 re-entry.

All this made for some sensational news in the mainstream media and for many, validated the Apollo missions once and for all. And according to passenger Peter Gabelish onboard the DC-8 flight, there was a "professional photographer assigned by a newspaper for the event."

The passengers and most of the crew of these three flights, obviously believed that what they witnessed were the Apollo CMs re-entry into Earth's atmosphere. So, there isn't any deception as per the majority of passengers and crew. But there does appear to be deception on the part of some of the passengers and crew, which will be discussed next.

Taking Apart The Official Witness Narrative

During the Apollo 11 re-entry, NASA must have been more than pleased that Captain Brown just happened to be knowledgeable in spacecraft, and was able to provide so much detail about this event to his passengers and crew. In fact, he was just a little too knowledgeable for it to have been a coincidence.

Here are some key points in Captain Brown's quotes that shows he knew some important details about the Apollo 11 re-entry including:

- How many miles the CM was from Earth at the precise time before re-entry, which he said was about 500 miles.

- The estimated time when the CM would come into view after re-entry into the atmosphere for the passengers and crew to witness.

- On the first sighting of the re-entry, the CM was about 500 miles away from his aircraft.

- There were two objects, Service Module and Command Module and that they were picking up heat during re-entry.

- His observation that it was a "pretty normal re-entry," adding that it seemed mathematically perfect.

These points described by Captain Brown showed he had an incredible amount of technical knowledge of spacecraft re-entry. This technical knowledge was not only relatively unknown to most people at that time, but spacecraft re-entries had never been witnessed before by anyone other than those few personnel closely involved in the military and space program. Further, asking his passengers to move to the left side of the plane was risky to say the least. This surely would have unevenly distributed the weight, affecting the stability the aircraft, which would have required one of the two pilots to compensate to prevent the aircraft from entering a dangerous flight maneuver or stall, or at least keeping a close watch to make sure the autopilot maintained straight and level flight. It is also interesting that Captain Brown was seemingly able to quickly and accurately calculate the precise time and location of re-entry, as well as the distance the CM was in relation to his aircraft. And all of this occurred in the dark and over the Pacific Ocean, in an aircraft fully loaded with passengers and crew. At no time was there any indication of concern for his aircraft and the safety of his passengers and crew, while flying in the vicinity of an alleged spaceship hurtling towards Earth after re-entry.

The question is, just how much technical knowledge would Captain Brown have had about the characteristics of a spacecraft's re-entry into Earth's atmosphere, and more specifically, the precise details for Apollo 11? It could be that Captain Brown had become an expert in his spare time, which is exactly what the official narrative tries to imply. But there are just too many coincidences for this narrative to be taken seriously, including the champagne and certificates that literally sprang out of nowhere.

> Apparently, his side job was some sort of NASA expert. It is probably worth noting that this was an extremely well thought-through event, as champagne and Apollo 11 certificates were ready on board. And also, in his spare time, pilot Brown had constructed a wonderful model of the moon rocket, with which he was caught, completely unprepared, by a photojournalist. Isn't such 'confirmation' rather too much overkill on NASA's part?[11]

However, his description of the CM re-entry would have made sense, if he had been in communication with someone who had provided the technical knowledge about spacecraft and of course the re-entry specifics for Apollo 11, with the captain being supplied a copy of the script should anything go wrong with communications. And as it turns out, this is precisely what happened as was confirmed when the DC-8 captain on the Apollo 13 re-entry, had revealed to his passengers that he was in contact with Mission Control in Houston.

The Qantas Boeing 707 was flying at 39,000 feet and Captain Brown mentioned that there was very little cloud cover, letting the passengers know that the view would be unobstructed. Of course, there isn't usually much cloud cover at that altitude anyway, so a clear view was almost guaranteed. And had there been any cloud cover that could have obstructed the passenger's and crew's view of the re-entry or for that matter, the Boeing 707 had to descend or deviate off course for any number of reasons, you can be sure that there was a back-up plan in place to cover the event. There would have been many aircraft on that route, so another aircraft could easily have been on standby to take over the task of describing the event and if that didn't work out, then the KC-135 or the possibility of other military aircraft in the area, would have been used as witnesses to the re-entry.

It's important to note that during that era, many airline pilots had their flight training in the military, so it would not have been too difficult to find senior civilian airline captains who could be trusted. Military men and women whether active or retired are for the most part, easily convinced to participate in any capacity with the need for secrecy, citing national security. And although NASA was technically a civilian run government agency, the military was very involved in the Apollo missions. The threat of ruining one's career and/or losing one's pension would be most effective at ensuring secrecy and the official narrative is maintained.

Tactics Used For Deception

Most people have heard the claim that amateur radio operators were able to listen in on the Apollo mission communications. I've had many discussions with people regarding this but my main point is, it's one of many tactics used in an attempt to validate these missions. The astronauts on these missions were military pilots, therefore you can be sure that if these missions were real, the military would have used communication frequencies that prevented any amateur radio operator from accessing the communications between astronauts and Mission Control. Furthermore, NASA used GHz frequencies for their transmissions during the alleged Apollo missions while amateur radio operators used MHz frequencies.

I doubt that these amateur radio operators would have had the means to intercept communication signals from approximately 240,000 miles from Earth.

However, communications would have been edited before any of them were released to the public anyway. That includes videos of UFOs by astronauts on the International Space Station. And it's possible that the release of these videos by government agencies, is just more disinformation in an attempt to control the UFO narrative, since there have been many videos from all over the world showing UFOs that cannot be easily explained. And its obvious that the scientific community shies away from any serious investigation of this phenomenon.

Anyway, aside from the tactic of using amateur radio operators, we'll reveal one more tactic that was used in an attempt to deceive the public into believing the Apollo missions were real. But first, we'll discuss the official re-entry data, and the witnesses to these events.

Comparing The Official Re-entry Data, To What The Passengers And Crew Saw

We'll use the Apollo 8 descent profile to its eventual splashdown into the Pacific Ocean, as this data has been documented on graphs. And since all of the CMs followed the same trajectories towards splashdown, we can use the Apollo 8 data for comparisons to the photo of the Apollo 13 re-entry. However, we are specifically interested in the CM descent profile from 90,000 feet at the documented time of 146:53:00. A 3D GoogleEarth image has been made to reflect this part of the descent. The time duration from 90,000 feet to splashdown is approximately three to four minutes, which matches the time duration of what the passengers witnessed with the Apollo 13 re-entry. Therefore, the data for both re-entries should closely match.

Figure 5.3 – Alleged Apollo 13 Re-entry
Source: NASA

Note: A much clearer and colour photo of the Apollo 13 re-entry photo and the 3D GoogleEarth image showing what the passengers and crew should have seen, can be accessed in the article 'Faked Apollo Re-entry from Space?' on www.aulis.com.

Data of the Apollo 8 re-entry is as follows:

- 146:53:00 - CM is at 90,000 feet and descending 2,500 feet per second.

- 146:54:00 - CM is at 50,000 feet and descending 700 feet per second.

- 146:54:47 - CM is at 26,300 feet with drogue deployment, descending 400 feet per second.

- 147:00:42 – CM splashdown.

Note: The Apollo missions were documented in elapsed time from launch to splashdown. For example, 146:53:00 means 146 hours, 53 minutes, and zero seconds.

During the initial re-entry phase, the Apollo 8 CM's trajectory was mostly horizontal with a speed of more than 6,600 feet per second up until 146:52:00. The data above shows that from 146:53:00 the CM was in near free fall from 90,000 feet, with a substantial decrease in forward velocity. But that is not what the passengers describe with Apollo 13. In fact, they describe quite the opposite.

According to passenger Peter Gabelish, the Apollo 13 CM "continued on the east bound path, curving out of sight over the horizon." His statement reflects what all of the passengers and crew witnessed. But given the DC-8's position, the passengers and crew should have witnessed the CM descend further, not along a horizontal path over the horizon. In fact, they should have seen the Apollo 13 CM drogues deployed at 10,000 feet and of course the main parachutes, but that's not what the passengers and crew reported.

The Auckland Star article gives the height of the Apollo 13 trajectory as 75,000 feet at the time the passengers and crew witnessed the event. But that is clearly not what the passengers and crew observed as Gabelish makes clear when he says, "an altitude that didn't appear to be much higher than ours" and in looking at the photo, he appears to be right. And it is fairly easy for people to estimate one's position from another aircraft or object in the skies, which seems innate in most of us. And given the detailed description by Gabelish, it is obvious that he had some very good observation skills. The Auckland Star also mentions in its article that the CM "travelled level with the horizon before it appeared to arch down North Cape." So, the

Apollo 8 data and the Apollo 13 re-entry observations by the passengers and crew, clearly do not match.

There is one more peculiar statement from passenger Peter Gabelish. In his detailed diary of the Apollo 13 re-entry, he says: "The silver phosphorescent tail it left behind seemed to retain its brilliance as a curved band of luminescent material while the leading body continued at constant velocity across our path. I presumed the tail to be the vaporized aluminium and magnesium materials from which the capsules were mostly constructed." As with Captain Brown's description of the Apollo 11 re-entry, Gabelish too appears to have an above average knowledge of spacecraft compared to the general public.

Once again, NASA must have been pleased to have yet another person onboard an aircraft who happened to be knowledgeable in spacecraft design, only this time, the person was a passenger. However, Peter Gabelish may have been a bit overzealous in his description when he stated, "I presumed the tail to be the vaporized aluminium and magnesium materials from which the capsules were mostly constructed" since this is not a realistic description of what should have occurred.

> Also note an error in observation of the capsule trace, made by Peter. **The trace could not actually have consisted of vaporized aluminium and magnesium.** The capsule housing was coated with ablative material. This is a layer of plastic resin, which is heated to a gas which carried the heat away from the CM interior. The capsule was flying with the heat shield facing forward and this part is the most exposed to temperature extremes. The heat shield was made of organic capsule filler. On evaporation and ablation this filler cannot form a white trail. The descent capsule had only reaction control engines. These were low-thrust engines and they operated in pulsed mode and,

therefore, were totally unable to leave a continuous and thick trace in the atmosphere.[12]

The photo of the Apollo 13 re-entry shows a white trail prominently lagging behind the purported CM trajectory, and looks nothing like a spacecraft entry and trajectory. So, if it wasn't the Apollo 13 CM re-entry, just what did the passengers and crew onboard the Boeing 707 and DC-8 flights witness in those early morning dark skies, from approximately 40,000 feet above the Pacific Ocean? That is discussed next.

What The Passengers And Crew Actually Saw

When I looked at the photo of the Apollo 13 re-entry, my first impression was that it seemed more like a vapor trail left by an aircraft. The other impression was that the altitude of the CM trajectory relative to the person who took the photo from the DC-8 flight, seemed rather low compared to what officials were saying. Further, the CM was practically on a flat trajectory which conflicts with the official re-entry data. What the passengers and crew should have seen, was the CM rapidly descending towards the Pacific Ocean, not flying off over the horizon and out of sight.

Therefore, after taking all of the observations into account and factoring in the characteristics of what the Apollo 13 re-entry trajectory should have looked like, it seems that what the passengers and crew actually saw was an aircraft, not a spacecraft.

> What we see in the picture is a contrail left at an altitude of 33-40,000 feet (10-12 kms) by a turbojet engine(s). Also, it is worth noticing in Fig. 3 that this is more like a double trace. A twin-engine jet aircraft? What aircraft exactly? Well, the United States Air Force has to offer a variety of different types of aircraft and cruise missiles that can operate at various altitudes.[13]

Note: Fig 3 referred to in the quote above, is the previously mentioned photo of the Apollo 13 re-entry.

The "double trace" in the photo is another giveaway, as it's difficult to see how the CM could have produced such a contrail. And there are many military aircraft that could have been used in the deception, but obviously they weren't able to closely duplicate the alleged official re-entry data of an Apollo CM. To do so, would have required an aircraft to descend rapidly and deploy parachutes around the same time the passengers and crew witnessed this event. But that was impossible since this would have put the aircraft in danger. A maneuver like this surely would have continued its rapid descent to the Pacific Ocean ending in disaster, and no pilot would have attempted it. So, there was only one way to simulate a re-entry and that was a flat trajectory which conflicts with the official re-entry data. The passengers and most of the crew wouldn't have noticed the difference. Taking into account the build up in the media of these three Apollo missions and then conveniently having civilian and military aircraft in the area to witness the CM re-entries, made these events believable. And there is no doubt that a splashdown in the Pacific Ocean in the dark or close to dawn, would have been risky to say the least. But it did make for a sensational Apollo CM re-entry photo. And further, you'd be right if you were to conclude that these sightings of the CM re-entries were a little too convenient to fit the official narrative, since interestingly, these three Apollo missions were known for their historical significance which made for some sensational news:

- o Apollo 8 for being the first manned mission to circumnavigate the Moon.
- o Apollo 11 for being the first manned mission to land on the Moon.

o Apollo 13 for its drama, which was sensationalized in the media and eventually made into a Hollywood movie.

No other Apollo CM re-entries were witnessed by passengers and crew from any other aircraft and with the exception of Apollo 10, all other Apollo missions re-entered the atmosphere during the day according to the official version. Interestingly enough, there was a witness to an Apollo CM parachuting down to the Pacific Ocean, but this time, the CM was descending from somewhere other than re-entry from space, which is explained below.

The Apollo CM Re-entry Hoax Revealed

During the Apollo CM re-entries, airspace restrictions and an accounting of aircraft were in place for presumably hundreds of miles during the re-entry and trajectory of an Apollo CM. However, one aircraft fell through the cracks and managed to be in a unique position to witness a rather interesting event, which turned out to be an embarrassing one for NASA. This involved a sighting that was never meant to be seen.

Bill Kaysing:

> While appearing on a talk show, an airline pilot phones in and said that he had observed an Apollo capsule being ejected from a large plane at about the time the astronauts were due "back" from the moon. Seven Japanese passengers also observed the incident. The pilot did not give his name for fear of losing his job.[14]

The pilot was flying enroute from Tokyo to San Francisco August 7, 1971. And one could ask just how the pilot knew it was an Apollo CM? Further, how far was he from the incident to be able to see such detail? Well, there are several factors that back up his claim, not to mention the other crew and several passengers onboard his plane. Here are some points to consider:

- In 1960, a qualification program consisted of airdrops of full-scale models of the Mercury capsules. All of them were dropped from a C-130 aircraft from altitudes up to 30,000 feet.
- In 1963, a boilerplate (which is a full-scale mock-up of the CM, using the same dimensions and weight) was used in a series of drop tests from a Douglas C-133 Cargomaster.
- In 2011 and 2012, a series of test drops were conducted using the Orion spacecraft from either a C-17 or C-130.

These drop tests don't necessarily prove what the pilot claims to have seen. But they do prove that dropping a capsule from an aircraft was entirely possible, as it had already been done during the Mercury and Apollo programs. This wouldn't have been common knowledge among the public at that time. Therefore, it was highly unlikely that the pilot and passengers onboard the Tokyo to San Francisco flight would have known about this detail, making it virtually impossible for them to have made up the story. And the aircraft just happened to be flying close to Hawaii on the date and time of the Apollo 15 splashdown.

Figure 5.4 – Mercury Capsule being air-dropped from a Military Plane
Source: NASA

Figure 5.5 – Apollo CM being loaded aboard a Douglas C-133 Cargomaster
Source: www.Aulis.com

For the most part, the media refused to cover the story of the Apollo 15 CM dropped from an aircraft and it basically faded into oblivion. But at least we have the official photo of the Apollo 13 re-entry which showed NASA's attempt at deception. Of course, NASA's mistake was in setting up the passengers and crew of the DC-8 to witness this event, which led to the photo being published in the media, making NASA an inadvertent participant in revealing the deception. But as inadvertent as it was, we thank NASA for providing the opportunity to scrutinize the photo that has helped reveal one of NASA's many deceptive tactics regarding the Apollo missions. And of course, our thanks go to the pilot who phoned in and discussed what he witnessed with the Apollo 15 mission and risked his career in doing so.

In Conclusion

At the end of chapter 2, we determined that the chances of success with the Apollo missions were approximately 54%. This percentage was based on the pre-Apollo missions and the elements that could been encountered beyond LEO. Now we'll continue with adding everything we've learned so far from Part I of this series as well as chapters 3, 4, and 5 of this book to determine a more realistic outcome for the Apollo missions. We'll continue to give NASA the benefit of the doubt by deducting only 5% for each of the following factors:

1. The lack of flight testing of the F-1 engines in actual conditions, which should have at least been comparable to the static testing that was done.

2. The lack of testing in actual flight conditions of the Saturn V before the first manned mission with Apollo 8, which should have at least been comparable to that of the Saturn I and Saturn IB.

3. The decision to use the method of Lunar Orbit Rendezvous, which was resisted by many engineers, given the enormous risks involved.

4. The near disastrous use of the LLRV and LLTV, which was eventually abandoned for training by later Apollo astronauts.

5. The problems encountered with the Apollo 6 CM on re-entry.

6. Their decision not to send unmanned Apollo missions to the Moon and practice lunar landings.

Therefore, given the technology in existence for that era and going by the official record, a best-case scenario for success of the Apollo missions would have been approximately 24%, and that's with giving NASA the benefit of the doubt. However, there is one more factor that needs to be added, and that is logic. It's one thing to write down equations and run computer simulations. But it is another matter entirely to have your latest technological design almost blow-up during launch, which almost happened with Apollo 6, and then neglect to do any further testing in actual conditions of flight to check the repairs that were made. This lack of logic is apparent with other aspects of the Apollo program, some of which we've discussed in this book.

What is most likely the reason for this 'neglect,' is that NASA realized early on in the Apollo program that manned missions to the Moon and back were impossible with existing technologies, especially for that era. This erodes that 24% probability of success, down to what is the real percentage of success for the Apollo Moon missions, which is zero.

Chapter Five - Endnotes

1. David A. Mindell, *Digital Apollo: Human and Machine in Spaceflight*, p. 91.

2. Roger D. Launius and Dennis R. Jenkins, *Coming Home: Reentry and Recovery from Space*, p. 27.

3. Ibid., p. 74.

4. Ibid., p. 78.

5. Ibid., p. 284.

6. Apollo Investigation, Re-Entry Matters by Mary Bennett. A Detailed Investigation into Apollo Command Module Returns. AULIS Online – Different Thinking

7. Ibid.

8. Ibid.

9. Ibid.

10. Ibid.

11. Apollo Investigation, Faked Apollo Atmosphere Re-entry from Space. Alexander Popov PhD and Andrei Bulatov. AULIS Online – Different Thinking

12. Ibid.

13. Ibid.

14. Bill Kaysing, *We Never Went To The Moon*, p. 75.

Chapter – Six

The Odyssey Of It All

The Russians and Apollo 13's Real Journey, The JFK Assassination Connection, Simulation -The Only Way

According to the official narrative, Apollo 13 was launched on April 11, 1970. Shortly after reaching LEO, it began its voyage to the Moon when an incident occurred which ended any attempt to achieve a lunar landing and put the crew at serious risk. However, it continued on route and used the Moon's gravity for its trajectory back to Earth. The rescue mission was apparently successful and they splashed down in the Pacific Ocean.

As we've discussed in Part 1, Apollo 13 was just more fiction for the official narrative. But there is an even more interesting story about Apollo 13, that had all the hallmarks of Cold War intrigue between the United States and the Soviet Union. And what's more, this story is much closer to the truth as to what really took place. It may even indicate that there was a lot more cooperation between the United States and the Soviet Union, in their respective space programs. And quite frankly, there will be people who will refuse to accept such a reality if it clashes with their preconceived notion of what reality should be. However, as everyone's 'truth' depends on their personal point of view and agenda, following where the facts lead is what's important here.

About five months after the April 1970 launch of Apollo 13, TASS (the official Soviet news agency) and the American media published reports asserting that that the Soviets had retrieved an Apollo CM which had been floating in the Bay of Biscay, off the coast of France. More specifically, this was claimed to have been a CM boilerplate with identification number BP-1227. CM boilerplates were used in test missions and for training the astronauts in place of a functional CM. The Russians eventually handed back the CM boilerplate to a United States Coast Guard ship.

It has been speculated that the Soviet Union (now Russia), gained a significant amount of insight into the American space program after finding this CM boilerplate. Although much value could have been obtained from a CM boilerplate, only a fully equipped CM would have provided the insights the Russians seemed to have gained from this event.

Therefore, what follows is an account of the events that strongly indicate that what the Russians really retrieved was a fully-equipped CM. If this were true, it would have put Russia in the driving seat of the manned space program, or at least, given them leverage to use against the American government.

The Russians Capture An Apollo Command Module

The Apollo missions are said to have journeyed to the Moon and back, and splashed downed in the Pacific Ocean. However, in the event of an abort following launch, the Apollo CM's flight path would have required an emergency abort and splashdown in the Atlantic Ocean.

During the Mercury and Gemini launches, NASA had designated five main areas in the Atlantic Ocean should there have been a need for a mission to abort during launch. These abort areas were designated A, B, C, D, and E. These areas were maintained during the Apollo missions with some slight variations. The coordinates for these areas were as follows:

- Area A – 75 degrees north longitude, to 60 degrees north longitude.

- Area B – 60 degrees north longitude, to 45 degrees north longitude.

- Area C – 45 degrees north longitude, to 30 degrees north longitude.

- Areas D and E – 30 degrees north longitude, to 15 degrees north longitude.

So, you don't have to look at a map to try and figure this out, the flight path of an Apollo mission during launch was along the 30-degree line of north latitude or slightly above it, starting in Florida, then on to Bermuda and straight across the Atlantic Ocean to just off the coast of Morocco, North Africa, and beyond. Areas A, B, and C were for automated aborts, and areas D and E would have required the crew to initiate an abort, although for the Apollo launches, I'm sure automated aborts on launch were possible along its flight path for any area over the Atlantic Ocean.

If what the Russians really had was a CM boilerplate, then where did it come from? Was there some sort of mishap during a training exercise that involved an abandoned CM boilerplate in the waters off the coast of Florida? If so, was it reasonably close to the time it was claimed to have been found? And if it drifted across the Atlantic Ocean, would the currents have pushed it to the Bay of Biscay off the coast of France? And what would be the estimated time it would take for a CM boilerplate to drift from Florida to the Bay of Biscay? Some of these questions may never have a definitive answer. But what we can do to try to unravel some of the mysteries is to start with what we do know.

We know that Apollo 13 was launched on April 11, 1970. And we know both the Russian and American media had reported that a CM boilerplate claimed to have been found in the Bay of Biscay, was handed back to the American government five months later, in September, 1970. Since there is no evidence indicating that another CM boilerplate had been lost either prior to the Apollo 13 launch, or leading up to when the Russians officially handed back the CM 'boilerplate' on September 6, 1970, this five-month timeframe gives us something to work with.

Figure 6.1 – CM boiler plate
Source : NASA

Research shows that the Russians and Americans were involved in some very intriguing Cold War tactics regarding their respective space programs. And further, there appeared to be a lot more cooperation between these Cold War enemies over the CM boilerplate than the media cared to admit. This leads to some very intriguing questions:

- ➢ Was this cooperation forced on the Americans after what the Russians really retrieved was an aborted Apollo 13 CM shortly after its launch?

- ➢ Was the CM boilerplate that was reportedly handed back to the American government, used as a cover to hide the fact that this was indeed a functional CM from an Apollo 13 abort during launch?

➢ Was Apollo 13 aborted on purpose to transfer an Apollo CM to the Russians out of sight of the media or for reasons that are of course classified?

➢ Does all of this indicate that both the Americans and the Russians shared classified information on each other's space program?

➢ And could all this mean that both the United States and the Russians had known years before the Apollo missions, that a successful manned lunar landing was impossible?

We'll try to answer some of these questions below, but as previously mentioned the evidence presented in this book indicates that NASA officials knew at the beginning of the Apollo program, that successful manned lunar missions were impossible. But next, we'll discuss the possible connection of a Russian nuclear-powered submarine incident to the launch of Apollo 13.

The Russian Submarine Connection

It has been reported that a Russian K-8 November Class nuclear-powered submarine was lurking in the North Atlantic along the same area where Apollo 13 would have splashed down after an abort during launch. This would indicate that the Russians knew more about the problems encountered in the Apollo program than previously believed, or at least they knew about the instability of the F-1 engines of the Saturn V, and were in the area for the real possibility of an Apollo 13 CM abort during launch. This would have given the submarine commander the information he needed to alert Russian naval forces as to the location of the CM splashdown for retrieval.

And it's reasonable to assume that there would have been a Russian submarine on standby in the North Atlantic for any Apollo mission launch, waiting for the inevitable abort and splashdown of an Apollo CM.

There is a photo of a Russian nuclear-powered K-8 submarine alongside a ship called the Komsomolets Litvy in the Bay of Biscay, the same area that the Russians claimed to have retrieved a CM boilerplate. The photo was taken by an American Orion aircraft on April 10 and was used by the American media to indicate that the submarine was in trouble. But what the photo appears to show is the opposite.

In the article *The April Odyssey and the November Boat* Andrei Bulatov and Alexander Boyko state:

> The US press later inferred that the sub was possibly in trouble, as it was accompanied by two other Soviet ships, one of which, the Komsomolets Litvy, is seen in this photo. The story was that the sub had lost power. Yet this photo shows the sub seemingly under its own propulsion. Even though the press stated that it was in the Bay of Biscay, one small section of sea does not provide confirmation of that fact, and all the photos published in the press make it impossible to evaluate the exact location of the sub. Nor do we know who exactly took this picture – is it from the deck of the other Soviet ship or does the angle of the photo infer an overflying US Orion? It is therefore not clear whether the sub in this photo was the 'covert mission K-8' or a decoy K-8 located in the Bay of Biscay – or elsewhere.[1]

The dates of this submarine 'incident' are interesting:

- April 10 – The Russian submarine is reported to have been in trouble.

- April 11 – The launch of Apollo 13.

- April 12 – The Russian submarine is reported to have sunk.

This alleged submarine incident just happened to coincide with the Apollo 13 launch. And while all of this was going on, the official narrative of Apollo 13 continued and was then sensationalized when the alleged Apollo 13 incident took place while enroute to the Moon on April 13, the day following the Russian submarine incident. This of course eclipsed the Russian submarine incident in the Bay of Biscay, which made it easier for both the United States and the Soviet Union to continue with their Cold War tactics, if indeed that was what really went on.

The official story says that the K-8 submarine had a fire on board and that up to 30 crew members were killed. Yet, this photo appears to show the K-8 submarine moving under its own power, which would seemingly have been impossible given the reported damage. And if 30 crew members were killed, then there would definitely have been dozens more severely injured, and they would have needed to have been taken aboard any ship along side it. What's more, it is the American press that inferred the K-8 submarine was in trouble, while the evidence points the other way. This hints at United States complicity in what now seems to be deception on the part of both of these countries.

Figure 6.2 – K-8 Russian Submarine apparently in the Bay of Biscay
Source: Aulis Online

It was also known at the time that a Soviet naval exercise named Okean 70 was underway during the Apollo 13 launch. But it's not clear whether this K-8 submarine was part of that naval exercise. However, there was yet another Russian nuclear-powered submarine reported to have sunk in the vicinity of the Faroe Islands, northeast of the British Isles. This incident is reported to have happened in the same month as the other submarine incident, but no specific date is provided. But it was reported that this submarine incident near the Faroe Islands had been part of the Russian naval exercise Okean 70. So, now we have a story of two nuclear-powered submarines, both of which carried nuclear weapons and both of which were reported to have sunk in the same month. Just how likely was it for two Russian nuclear-powered submarines to have sunk within the same month? It's possible, but not likely. And why is there no specific date for the submarine incident near the Faroe Islands? There is the American media and BBC reports on April 14, 1970, which may narrow the timeframe of the two incidents to within six days of each other.

There is now some doubt whether there was any Russian submarine incident during the month of April, 1970. And it could very well be that the submarine incident which was part of the Okean 70 naval exercise was in actuality a drill, while the incident in the Bay of Biscay did not happen, at least as was reported in the media. And the Bay of Biscay was not on the flight path of an aborted Apollo mission during launch. Therefore, neither of these two submarines could have been in the vicinity of the aborted Apollo 13 CM when it splashed down. But one thing seems apparent, the evidence strongly indicates that these two submarine incidents were used to distract American military forces at sea and in the air. And it's possible too that a third submarine was used as a marker for the retrieval of the Apollo 13 CM, which likely had splashed down near the Azores Islands.

This would put the Apollo 13 abort during launch in areas D and E. And areas D and E would indicate that there may have been a crew onboard, since they would have been needed to initiate an abort, although as previously mentioned, it is my opinion that NASA would likely have had the ability to initiate an abort from Mission Control over any area of the Atlantic Ocean. And interestingly, there were very few if any ships on standby in areas C, D, and E, since an abort in these areas was considered low.

Note: It's debatable as to whether or not there was a crew onboard Apollo 13. So far, the evidence indicates that there wasn't. And further, there is evidence that other Russian ships were involved in the search and retrieval of Apollo 13 after it's abort, which is too much to go into here. Instead, what I present are the salient points to the retrieval of the Apollo 13 CM after its apparent abort during launch. However, the quotes in this section come from two in-depth articles on the subject, which are sourced at the end of this chapter for the reader to research further.

A Russian submarine incident in the Bay of Biscay the day before the Apollo 13 launch would have lured away any American naval forces and/or reconnaissance aircraft that happened to be in or near areas C, D, and E. And given that the submarine incident in the Bay of Biscay was a distraction, strongly suggests that there was no Apollo CM boilerplate found in this area. This makes more sense, as opposed to a CM boilerplate floating thousands of miles across the Atlantic Ocean, after some sort of mishap on a training mission aboard a ship at sea off the coast of Florida. Therefore, in actuality what the Russians really retrieved was the Apollo 13 CM shortly after its abort during launch.

We'll discuss more on this below, but for now we'll look into how it came about that an American coast guard ship was sent to collect the Apollo CM 'boilerplate'.

Rendezvous With The Russians

Assuming that the Russians decided they had what they needed to know concerning American space capsule technology, they of course decided to officially hand back the CM 'boilerplate' which was being stored at Murmansk, Russia. Therefore, U.S. embassy officials from Moscow were invited to inspect the CM. And just as the decision was made to officially hand over the CM 'boilerplate,' a United States Coast Guard Cutter (USCGC) *Southwind,* which had been four months into its mission, just happened to have been in the general area near Murmansk, Russia. So, the commanding officer of the USCGC *Southwind*, Captain Cassidy, decided to make a port call at Murmansk, or as he put it, "Because we had to stop somewhere and the *Southwind* had sailed under the Russian flag." And just how the *Southwind* happened to be in the general area of Murmansk and was notified of the CM to be picked up, is an interesting story in itself. And you can be sure that it wasn't just a coincidence, as Captain Cassidy would have people believe. Therefore, like anything else with the Apollo Moon missions and related stories, it's necessary to go beyond the news reports to get an idea of what exactly took place. And as we'll learn, for the *Southwind* to have been coincidently in the area or close to it, is just more fiction for the general public.

However, it had been disclosed that the American Embassy in Moscow was contacted two weeks before the official announcement by the Russian government that they had retrieved an Apollo CM 'boilerplate.' And further, evidence shows that Captain Cassidy of the *Southwind*, had known well beforehand of this rendezvous with the Russians in Murmansk, and even had his ship prepared for the official handover of the CM 'boilerplate.'

In the article *The Odyssey of the Lost Apollo CM* Mary Bennett and David S Percy state:

> A scrutiny of the data and photos from the *Southwind* website suggests that even if the commanding officer Captain Cassidy was reported in the press as saying that the stopover was because 'we had to stop somewhere', in fact this handover between the US and the USSR was far less spontaneous than that. The visible clue to the preplanning of this expedition lies in the mode of transport: the Apollo module was returned to the United States in the location normally occupied by the cutter's single 5-inch gun. For this to be possible the gun had to have been removed **prior to the Southwind's departure** from the USA on its June 15 to November 17 1970 Artic East 70 tour.[2]

The *Southwind* made its port call at Murmansk on September 5, 1970, and after the official handover of the CM to the Southwind, the U.S. embassy in Russia reported this:

> The Soviets **did tell us about two weeks ago** [mid August 1970] they had something of ours that **had**

fallen from space and that it was in Murmansk, but they apparently decided without telling us to take the occasion of the *Southwind* visit to give the hardware back.[3] [emphasis added by Bennett & Percy]

This quote not only confirms the United States was given more notice of the CM 'boilerplate' than Captain Cassidy would have us believe; it also gives the impression that the Russians had the CM with designation BP-1227 for only a couple of weeks. But as we'll now show, this is patently untrue. We just established that the *Southwind*'s 5-inch gun was removed, which had to have taken place before its mission on June 15, that was two months before U.S. embassy officials said they were notified of the CM 'boilerplate'. This proves the American government had known of the CM retrieval by the Russians, months before they officially acknowledged it. So, for the U.S. embassy to have released that statement, more than hints at complicity with the Russian government on what really happened to Apollo 13. This goes a long way in proving that the Russians had retrieved the Apollo 13 CM after its abort on launch, and then officially handed it back to the American government five months later in September 1970. But by indicating that the Russians had the CM for only two weeks, fits in with the official narrative that this CM was found floating in the Bay of Biscay. Remember, the U.S. embassy statement says "…they had something of ours…" not "…they retrieved something of ours…" They "had" it, but when did they actually "retrieve" it? To say they "had" the CM, throws the public off as to when they actually "retrieved" it.

There is photographic evidence that shows the *Southwind* without its forward 5-inch gun. Further, there are photos that show the CM 'boilerplate' stored in place of where the 5-inch gun was positioned.

Figure 6.3 – Coast Guard Southwind with its forward five-inch gun
Source: Wikimedia

Figure 6.4 – Coast Guard Southwind without its forward five-inch gun
Source: Aulis Online

Figure 6.5 – CM 'BP -1227' being hoisted aboard the Southwind
Source: Wikimedia

Figure 6.6 – USCGC Southwind with the CM stored above the number 280
Source: Wikimedia

These photos alone show that Captain Cassidy had ample notice, that he was to dock at Murmansk for the official handover of the CM. In other words, this visit to Murmansk was not on a whim as the captain indicated when he said, "Because we had to stop somewhere and the *Southwind* had sailed under the Russian flag." And everything we've discussed so far, indicates that the real mission of the *Southwind* was to officially take back the Apollo 13 CM from the Russians and not a CM boilerplate as had been reported in the media. Further, the method for hoisting the CM onto the *Southwind* indicates that this was not a CM boilerplate, but was in fact a functional CM.

The method used for hoisting a CM boilerplate was different than that used for hoisting a functional CM. Bennett and Percy point out:

> NASA documents stipulate a circumscribed triangle for the lighter boilerplate, **while the full-weight Apollo CM required a robust square base** – as can be seen in the photographs of the Apollo module being loaded onto the Southwind.[4] [emphasis added by Bennett & Percy]

The official statements and media coverage of this event were designed to confuse and frustrate the public. It's a common tactic used by government intelligence agencies in an attempt at obscure the truth. So, in the interest of clarity here is a timeline of the events starting from April 1970 leading up to what we've discussed so far, as well as items not discussed, ending with a very significant resignation from within NASA. Bennett and Percy provide these dates:

> **April 10-12** – The Soviet K-8 November class nuclear submarine saga occurs in the north Atlantic: (Note that the north Atlantic defines all of the Atlantic Ocean above the equator.)

April 11 – Launch of Apollo 13, 19:13 UTC/GMT/14:15 EST.

April 11 – Apollo 13 CM emergency splashdown in the north Atlantic. Module appropriated by the USSR.

April 13 – Pentagon releases press statements to US media on the apparent sinking of the K-8 sub.

April 13 – The official Apollo 13 accident occurs, during its outgoing lunar trajectory.

April 14 – US media publishes K-8 'Pentagon statements.'

May 11-17 – A month after Apollo 13 NASA administrator Thomas Paine meets Soviet Academy of Sciences' Anatoly Blagonavov in New York, USA.

June 15 – The US Coast Guard Cutter *Southwind* leaves on a five-month Artic mission.

July 31 – NASA administrator Thomas Paine writes to Mstislav Keldysh, President of the Soviet Academy of Sciences, discussing the feasibility of a joint space docking program.

September 4 – US Embassy officials from Moscow visit Murmansk to inspect the 'capsule.'

September 5-7 – USCGC *Southwind* in Murmansk, USSR, 'Because we had to stop somewhere and the *Southwind* had sailed under the Russian flag.' said Captain Cassidy.

>**September 6** – The module is loaded aboard the *Southwind* in Murmansk.
>
>**September 7** – The *Southwind* leaves Murmansk for the Kara Sea.
>
>**September 15** – Paine resigns as Administrator at NASA.[5]

I'm sure the reader has noticed three very intriguing events in this timeline concerning NASA Administrator Thomas Paine: his meeting with Anatoly Blagonavov from the Academy of Sciences in New York between May 11-17; his July 31 letter to Mstislav Keldysh, President of the Soviet Academy of Sciences, and his resignation as Administrator at NASA on September 15.

What's even more intriguing is Thomas Paine's meeting with Anatoly Blagonavov and his letter to Mstislav Keldysh both took place within the five months leading up to the return of the CM 'boilerplate.'

This seems to indicate that officials from both sides were negotiating and making plans due to the unexpected or expected abort of Apollo 13 during launch. And of course, the Apollo 13 abort may have been the real reason Thomas Paine resigned, either because of the unexpected abort of Apollo 13 or the possibility that the abort was planned and he wanted no part of it.

There's one more piece of evidence which indicates CM BP-1227 was not a boilerplate. As Bennett and Percy further point out:

>Significantly BP-1227 was different from all the other boilerplates. Normally, the BPs featured three NASA acronyms, one across the hatch, and the other two

around the sides. This particular BP had a single NASA placed far too high up the body of the capsule. The cross bar of the N is incorrect relative to the N used on other boilerplates, and the S does not align correctly.[6]

Figure 6.7 – Photo of boilerplate with markings
Source: Wikimedia

The Real Agenda, Rendezvous In Space

There is some indication that the Americans were covering up what really happened with the Russian K-8 submarine in the Bay of Biscay with their narrative that the submarine was in trouble, when the photo they provided shows quite the opposite. This leads to a possibility of complicity in the whole Apollo 13 story. If so, could that mean Apollo 13 was aborted on purpose for the Russians to retrieve? In other words, was it a way to transfer a functional CM to the Russians for any number of reasons, but without the knowledge of the American and Russian public? It's an intriguing possibility. But as to whether the Apollo 13 abort during launch was due to a malfunction or was deliberate, is difficult to determine.

However, most of the evidence so far seems to indicate the fact that Apollo 13's abort during launch was due to a malfunction. Further, we have evidence that the Russians had retrieved the Apollo 13 CM after it had splashed down in the Atlantic Ocean, and had kept it for five months. This would have led to some very intense behind-the-scenes negotiations between these two nations. This also could have led to a form of - dare I say it - blackmail. The Russians had likely known for years before the Apollo missions that a manned lunar mission was impossible, which meant they knew the Americans had faked their Apollo manned lunar program. But now with the retrieval of the Apollo 13 CM they had material proof of the fakery. So, they did what any perceived enemy would have done and that is, to use it as leverage. And that is exactly what has appeared to have taken place.

The negotiations obviously involved a quid pro quo. This may very well have forced the United States into a formal agreement to participate in a joint venture in space, which was officially called the Apollo-Soyuz Test Project (ASTP). And this could also mean this agreement was just the start of an alliance in their respective space programs that has lasted decades, continuing right up to the present. Once this agreement was made, the Russians formally returned the CM 'boilerplate' to the Americans as reported in the media. And once the story was out, it would have given the Russians permanent leverage over any related negotiations.

In the official press release from the U.S. embassy in Moscow regarding CM BP-1227, the statement had a very interesting phrase in it which said, "they had something of ours that had fallen from space." Therefore, this U.S. embassy statement could have indicated that the Russians were prepared to go public with the fact that they had retrieved the Apollo 13 CM, if the American government reneged on its agreement. And no doubt it seems strange that this statement was released to the public. But governments have often used the media as one of many ways to communicate with each other, and only each side would fully understand its true meaning.

The mere insinuation by another country, let alone Russia, that NASA faked the manned lunar landings, would have put the American government on the defensive. But unlike other countries, the Russians had tangible proof. And if the Russians had gone public with it, revealing the Apollo Moon hoax would have been a public relations disaster for NASA and the American government. Therefore, using leverage like this would have pressured the Americans into fulfilling their part of any agreement for example, the ASTP. And this would have put both the Americans and Russians back on equal footing years and decades after the Apollo missions with their respective manned space programs which would have increased Russian prestige in the international community. In essence, it consigned the Apollo Moon missions to the history books with more than a hint that they were faked, while it put Russia out in front of the whole space program decades later, as is seen with the fact that they have had a successful manned space program. Further, when the Space Shuttle was retired in 2011, the Russians were credited with coming to the rescue when NASA no longer had the capability of launching its astronauts to and from the International Space Station.

So now we come to the rest of the timeline in this story, as documented by Bennett and Percy:

> **October 26-28** – First NASA delegation in Star City USSR, swopping sketches for a docking system that would suit the matching of an Apollo-Soyuz craft. To have 'sketches' ready for consultation (blueprints might be more accurate) means that engineers were working on known differences in the architecture/engineering of each other's capsules **much earlier than October 1970.**

October 28 – NASA and Soviet representatives assemble at the Presidium of the Soviet Academy to sign the "Summary of Results."

November 18-22 – The Baltimore Sun and the US Navy's *Navy Times* publish articles on the *Southwind's* return. These articles refer to the 'historic' Murmansk visit, but ignore the return of the Apollo module.

January 16 1971 – as far as the public were concerned this was the date generally considered as the conception of the ASTP by NASA historians, when Paine was in Moscow dealing with the detail and organizing the return visit of Soviet scientists to NASA which took place six months later on June 20, 1971.[7]

It'll be interesting to research more about the Apollo-Soyuz mission to find out exactly how the training for this mission was done. Rendezvous and docking in LEO is a complicated and complex maneuver for any mission. But here, we have two different spacecraft from two different countries. And although an exchange of blueprints took place and Soviet engineers, scientists, and cosmonauts had travelled to the Kennedy Space Center in February 1975 for training and simulations, computer software simulations were primitive by today's standards. So, it would have been preferable for either of these two countries to have had access to each other's spacecraft and as we've learned in this section, that appears to be exactly what happened.

Apollo 13 Versus Apollo 13

The 'official' Apollo 13 CM is on display at the Kansas Cosmosphere and Space Center in Hutchison, Kansas, and the Apollo 13 CM aka BP-1227 is on display at the Pearl Street entryway of the Van Andel Museum Center, Grand Rapids, Michigan, USA. So, which one is the real Apollo 13 CM? The proponents will point to the scorched area on the Apollo 13 CM heatshield and up towards the surface area near the crew compartment, which they will claim were caused by the effects of re-entry. But this could easily have been prepared on the ground to give the impression of re-entry. And there is no documentation for BP-1227 that details when or even if it was used for training off the coast of Florida, before it was apparently found floating thousands of miles on the other side of the Atlantic Ocean. Researcher Eddie Pugh even filed a Freedom Of Information Act to obtain more information on BP-1227, but to no avail. Therefore, given what we've learned so far, we should be sceptical of any claims by NASA regarding any aspect of the Apollo program.

There is one more intriguing fact about BP-1227, where there is a time capsule sealed inside this CM, which is due to be opened during the U.S. tricentennial celebrations of 2076. Wouldn't it have made sense for officials to have sealed the time capsule in a CM that was supposed to have some meaning? Like maybe the Apollo 11 CM? Or is sealing a time capsule inside a CM boilerplate the whole point? That is, placing a message inside a CM that never even made it to LEO? If so, one wonders if NASA actually has a perverse sense of humour with the message to be unsealed on 2076 with the written words "We faked it." Whatever the reason for sealing this capsule, it is very strange that NASA chose a CM boilerplate with little or no documentation and with little or no historical meaning. However, what we know for sure, is the preponderance of the evidence discussed so far, indicates that the BP-1227 was in fact the Apollo 13 CM. And further, the evidence indicates that the Apollo 13 mission was aborted during its launch.

Next, we'll discuss a subject that has perplexed many researchers for decades, with some now alleging has a connection to the Apollo Moon missions.

The JFK Assassination Connection

Most people do not need an introduction to President John Fitzgerald Kennedy and his tragic assassination. But for those of you who are new to the details of Kennedy and the assassination, we'll do a brief overview. We won't discuss the many aspects of his presidency, since that would take up a whole book in itself. Instead, we'll focus on the events on the day of the assassination and then we will discuss a possible connection to the Apollo Moon missions.

John Fitzgerald Kennedy was the youngest person to be elected President of the United States, and was sworn into office on January 20, 1961. On November 22, 1963, President Kennedy was on an official trip to Dallas, Texas. Air Force One landed at Dallas Love Field airport at 11:30 A.M., and the President's motorcade left at approximately 11:50 A.M. on a route that took them through the streets of downtown Dallas. Sitting in the limousine with President Kennedy and his wife Jacqueline Kennedy, were Texas Governor John Connally and his wife Nellie Connally, along with two Secret Service agents Roy Kellerman and William Greer in the front seats, with Greer as the driver of the car. At about 12:30 P.M., the motorcade turned into an area called Dealey Plaza. As the motorcade moved through this area, 'three' shots were fired from the Texas School Book Depository Building (TSBD) at Kennedy's limousine killing him and severely wounding Governor Connally. The motorcade rushed to Parkland hospital where the doctors tried unsuccessfully to save the life of the stricken President. The assassination itself was caught on several films, most notably a film taken by Abraham Zapruder who was standing to the right of the motorcade as it moved down Elm St. in Dealey Plaza. A couple of hours after the assassination at approximately 2:40 P.M., Vice President Lyndon Baines Johnson was officially sworn in as the next President of the United States onboard Air Force One. His first order as President was for Air Force One to fly back to Washington D.C.

Figure 6.8 – JFK Motorcade on the streets of Dallas moments before he was assassinated
Source: Wikimedia

Figure 6.9 – JFK is reacting to being shot
Source: Wikimedia

Figure 6.10 – Vice-President Johnson being sworn in onboard Air Force as the new President
Source: *Wikimedia*

About forty-five minutes after the assassination, Dallas Police Officer J.D. Tippit was shot and killed allegedly by Lee Harvey Oswald, who was arrested shortly thereafter. Oswald, who was an employee of the TSBD, was charged with killing Tippit and assassinating President Kennedy. Two days later on November 24, Oswald was escorted by two police detectives to the basement of the Dallas Police Headquarters, to a waiting armoured car, which was to take him to the country jail. But despite strict security, Oswald himself was shot by Jack Ruby, a Dallas night club owner. This led to many suspicions of a conspiracy and three weeks later, President Lyndon Johnson rushed to establish a commission to investigate the assassination, led by Chief Justice of the United States Earl Warren, popularly known as the Warren Commission. The Warren Commission formally presented its report to President Johnson on September 24, 1964 and concluded that Lee Harvey Oswald acted alone and that there was no evidence of a conspiracy.

Figure 6.11 – Dallas Police Officer J.D. Tippet
Source: *Wikimedia*

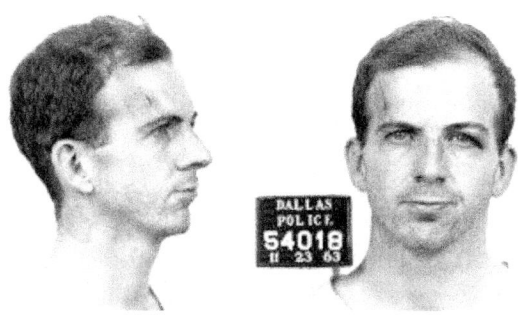

Figure 6.12 - Lee Harvey Oswald
Source: *Wikimedia*

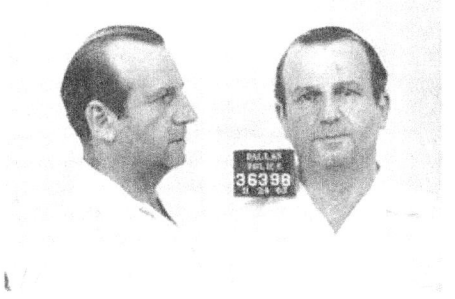

Figure 6.13 - Jack Ruby
Source: *Wikimedia*

Figure 6.14 - Jack Ruby shooting Oswald
Source: *Wikimedia*

Figure 6.15 - Justice Earl Warren, who led the commission which investigated the Kennedy assassination
Source: *Wikimedia*

An Analysis Of The Official Version

President Kennedy was considered by many to have reached an almost rock star like status with his quick wit and charm. So, the shock and depression among the American people and the world was understandable and has lingered for decades. Many have said that America lost its soul on that tragic day.

There have been thousands of books written on JFK in the last several decades, and many of these books have concentrated on the assassination itself. These books were written either in support of the official version or in support of a conspiracy. After reading many of these books myself, I've come to the conclusion that the official version is nothing more than fiction and according to many polls, most people believe the same regarding the events on that day. To believe that Lee Harvey Oswald acted alone in killing the President, defies logic and common sense.

There are several points I'd like to make regarding the events of that day from when Kennedy's motorcade left Dallas Love Field airport, to when he was assassinated just over a half hour later:

- The limousine used for the President was a convertible, and a decision was made to leave off the rooftop. However, Kennedy was entering what was perceived at that time to have been hostile territory, so there have been questions as to why the rooftop of the limousine was not installed, which would have given Kennedy added protection. Further, there has been discussions as to whether Kennedy himself ordered the rooftop to be removed. But given that the main purpose of the Secret Service was the protection of the President, they would have had the final authority on any security aspects of the motorcade, including whether the rooftop of the limousine was used or not.

- Minutes before the shooting, Kennedy's limousine slows down to make a 90^0 right turn from Main St. onto Houston Street. The motorcade travels a short distance then slows down to make about a 120^0 left turn onto

Elm St. The motorcade moves along at approximately 11 miles per hour and just seconds later, shots were fired, hitting Kennedy and Connally. At this point, Kennedy's limousine appears to slow down. There have been many questions as to why these slow turns were allowed and why the limousine travelled at such a slow rate of speed, which made the President even more vulnerable to any assassination attempt. Further, the Secret Service driver should have immediately sped off the at the first sign of trouble, like the sounds of gunshots, yet instead, the driver inexplicably slowed down. The motorcade only sped off when Kennedy was seriously wounded. It just seems that every security protocol was ignored on that day.

- Oswald, who was an employee of the TSBD, allegedly fired three shots from the sixth-floor window. Then just over a minute after the assassination, Oswald is confronted by his TSBD supervisor and a Dallas police officer in the lunchroom on the 2nd floor. It's never been established how Oswald managed to get from the sixth floor to the second floor in just over a minute after the assassination and without being seen by any other employees. Further, witnesses say they saw Oswald leave the TSDB at different times. He then arrived at his rooming house and went directly to his room. The landlady has claimed that shortly after Oswald arrived, a Dallas police car had stopped briefly in front of the house and honked its horn, then sped off. Researchers have speculated that this was a signal for Oswald to leave his house and presumably go to a prearranged meeting place. Oswald immediately leaves the house and shortly thereafter, Dallas police officer J. D. Tippit was shot and killed allegedly by Oswald. However, a witness to the shooting of Officer Tippit gave a description that appears to be someone other than Oswald.

- Oswald then goes to a movie theatre and enters without paying even though he had more than enough money in his pocket. This is strange behaviour for a man accused of assassinating a President and killing a Dallas police officer. Surely if he wanted to hide and then make an escape, he would have had a much better plan in place. But instead, he walks into a movie theatre without paying, which of course attracted attention given the turmoil after the assassination and then sits there until he was arrested. It seems logical to conclude that this was the prearranged meeting place.

- Kennedy's body was illegally taken from Parkland Memorial hospital by the Secret Service and loaded aboard Air Force One. Lyndon Johnson then delays departure of Air Force One, so he can officially be sworn in as President. This is strange behaviour on his part given that no one knew at the time whether or not there was a conspiracy involved, and to delay leaving Dallas could potentially have risked the safety of the new President. In addition, Kennedy's limousine is scrubbed clean which effectively destroyed vital evidence.

- But now events got even stranger. While being paraded in front of reporters by Dallas police officials, Oswald says that he was just a "patsy" and then publicly asks for legal representation. This suggests that he was denied his rights to legal counsel. He is then asked by reporters if he shot the President to which he replies that he didn't shoot anyone and that he had not been charged with that crime. The reporters tell Oswald that in fact he had been charged with killing the President which seemed to have surprised him. Further, there is little or no record of his interrogation by Dallas police officials. And it appears that while all this was going on, Jack Ruby was stalking Oswald in the police station and just two days later, he had somehow managed to get by Dallas police security and shoot Oswald on live television. It has never been explained how Ruby managed to get by such strict police security and get close enough to shoot Oswald.

I had the opportunity to visit Dallas and of course Dealey Plaza some years ago. I noticed immediately how well preserved the site is. It's as if this area has been frozen in history. City officials had decided years before to preserve it as a historical site and rightfully so. The city of Dallas has embraced this area as a symbol of its sadness and a monument to the memory of President Kennedy. Dallas officials have even allowed re-enactments of the assassination itself in the ongoing research to determine what really happened on that tragic day. The other thing I noticed was the fact that Dealey Plaza was the perfect place to ambush a President, with multiple shooters positioned in that area. We'll discuss more on that below.

Figure 6.16 – Dealey Plaza where the assassination took place
Source: Wikimedia

There are many theories as to who was involved in the assassination of JFK. Here are some of the prevalent theories:

- Lee Harvey Oswald acted alone in assassinating President Kennedy and that there was no evidence of a conspiracy, as was determined by the Warren Commission.
- Oswald was an agent for either the Federal Bureau of Investigations (FBI) and/or the Central Intelligence Agency (CIA) and had infiltrated a group of conspirators, but somehow was set up as the pasty, which Oswald himself later claimed in a press conference at Dallas police headquarters.

- The CIA was involved along with Cuban exiles over the disastrous attempt to invade an area called the Bay of Pigs in Cuba in early 1961. The idea for the invasion, was to start an uprising and end Russian influence in that country. But Cuban exiles would have needed the support of some very powerful people. This support seems to have involved the CIA, which had its own reasons for wanting Kennedy removed, since it was rumoured, that Kennedy threatened to destroy the CIA for trying to manipulate him into using the military to invade Cuba.

- The military was involved along with the FBI and CIA in a coup d'état presumably over his Cuba, Vietnam, and Russia policy. Some researchers have claimed that the person who carries the nuclear launch codes, was apparently separated from Kennedy before his motorcade left Dallas Love Field airport. If this is true, it would have been a serious breach of national security protocol, as the person assigned to carry the nuclear launch codes must always be in close proximity to the President in case of a nuclear attack from another country. The inference is, Kennedy had already been effectively removed from power before he left Dallas Love Field airport.

- Lyndon Johnson was involved, or at least had foreknowledge of the assassination. There have been books written on his alleged involvement, which is worth further research.

- There were international connections to the assassination, as President Lyndon Johnson had said in an interview after he was no longer in office. But what these connections are, have yet to determined.

- There was an official investigation into the assassination by Jim Garrison who was District Attorney of New Orleans Parish, Louisiana, from 1962 to 1973. Garrison believed that there was a conspiracy involved to assassinate President Kennedy. Garrison had also subpoenaed the Zapruder film. This was the first time any of the public had seen the unedited film. Garrison lost his case in court, which most believe was due to the fact that his case was sabotaged. The Garrison case was brilliantly portrayed by Kevin Costner in the Oliver Stone movie, 'JFK'.

- To add to the confusing details of the assassination, President Jimmy Carter and his administration established the House Select Committee on Assassinations in 1976. It issued a report in 1979 and in part, said four shots were fired at Kennedy's motorcade and that there was probably a conspiracy involved. So, now there are two different official government conclusions of the assassination; Oswald acted alone, or there may have been a conspiracy involved. As of today, there has been no other official federal government investigations into the assassination.

- There is a very intriguing theory that has been written about in the last decade and that is The Golden Triangle. This involved several countries most notably South Vietnam. The theory is, that the U.S. military was needed to protect the opium fields in South Vietnam from any communist threat from North Vietnam. Opium was converted into heroin and then shipped for distribution to the U.S. This was a multi billion-dollar market and some very powerful forces feared Kennedy would withdraw the military from South Vietnam, which would have destroyed that market.

- Another intriguing theory is that Kennedy tried to limit the power of the Federal Reserve Bank. Kennedy had actually ordered the U.S. Treasury to print bank notes, which may have been seen as a threat by the Federal Reserve. And contrary to what many people believe, the Federal Reserve is not a government agency. Instead, it is a privately owned central bank with possible international connections, which prints money to fund the American government. It then charges interest on that money, which has kept the United States enslaved in perpetual debt, which researchers believe the system is designed to do. This has led many to believe that the United States is no longer a Republic, but is in actuality, a corporation. If this theory is true, then it has far reaching implications, which may be what President Johnson meant when he mentioned the possibility that there were international connections to the assassination.

It's very easy to get caught up in the assassination research and the many roads that it can lead to. But one doesn't need to know all the intricate details to realize that a conspiracy was involved. To get close enough to assassinate a President, security has to be compromised and the Zapruder film clearly shows that Kennedy's security was too far away to have given him any protection. Further, the film shows that the Secret Service were slow to act. It is only when the last shot was fired, that Secret Service agent Clint Hills ran from the second car and climbed aboard the trunk of Kennedy's limousine and pushed Jacqueline Kennedy back into her seat. Hills then attempted to protect the stricken President, but of course it was too late.

It does seem likely that Kennedy's security was compromised from the inside, which indicates that some very powerful and connected people were involved. As for the actual shooting, the Warren Commission says that Kennedy was hit by two bullets of the three bullets that were fired by Oswald. However, many researchers have successfully discredited the Warren Commission's version of the shooting itself. That is discussed next.

Assassination Teams

Many of the researchers who have studied the assassination, realized how impossible it would have been for two shots to have caused so many wounds on Kennedy and Connally. The Warren Commission says that the first shot fired had missed the motorcade entirely. Then it says the second bullet hit Kennedy in the right upper portion of his back, exited the front of his neck, travelled on to hit Connally in the upper right side of his back, exited the right side of his chest, entered his right wrist, then exited his right wrist and lodged in his left thigh. This, as most of you know, is called the single bullet theory, and the Warren Commission would have you believe that this one bullet caused all of these seven wounds.

For the single bullet theory to have worked, the bullet would have had to:

- Turn right after exiting Kennedy's neck.

- Pause and turn left to have entered Connally's back.

- After exiting Connally's chest, pause and turn right to have entered his right wrist.

- Once it exited his right wrist, do a 180-degree turn to have lodged in his left thigh.

As District Attorney Jim Garrison's character in the movie JFK says, "That's some bullet!" However, the Warren Commission effectively positioned both Kennedy and Connally, so that the proper trajectory lined up with the sixth-floor window of the TSBD to make the single bullet theory work. Without the single bullet theory, the Warren Commission's report falls apart.

The Warren Commission then says that the third shot from the TSBD hit the right side of Kennedy's head. Yet, in the Zapruder film, the trajectory seems to be the opposite to what the Warren Commission said, as Kennedy's head is clearly propelled backwards and to the left after the shot is fired, which fits more with a shot coming from the right front of the limousine, not from behind and to the right. It's difficult to determine the actual trajectory of the frontal shot, since it has since been revealed that frames in the Zapruder film have been removed. No doubt this was done in an effort to hide the real trajectory of the shots. But their options for removing some of the frames were limited, as they clearly had no choice but to leave in the frames showing at least one shot from the front. And from what I've read over the years, Kennedy's head actually moves forward first after the headshot, then is propelled backwards, indicating he was shot from behind and front. This leads one to the conclusion that there were multiple shots from multiple directions.

With the positioning of both Kennedy and Connally to fit the single bullet theory, and the removal of frames near the headshot to hide multiple trajectories of shots, the matter was closed. And any dissent was effectively discredited with a CIA program designed to label anyone who questioned the official version, a 'conspiracy theorist.' Then came the 1960s illusion of the counter culture and the rest as they say, is history. But then the real search for the truth had begun, thanks to some very determined researchers. And that search has effectively revealed the Warren Commission for what it really is, fiction.

There are many credible books that analyse the ballistics of the shooting, which effectively destroy the Warren Commission's conclusion. And contrary to what the Warren Commission says, the Zapruder film has professional hit teams written all over it. Therefore, here is a more realistic enactment of the shooting that day, based in part on Oliver Stone's movie JFK and my own research:

- At 12:15 P.M., fifteen minutes before Kennedy's motorcade arrives, a person has an epileptic seizure on the streets of Dealey Plaza. This distracts the police, allowing the **first assassination team** to move into place on the sixth-floor window in the TSBD, which is on the northwest corner of Houston Street and Elm Street. This position gives the assassins an overall view of Dealey Plaza. Interestingly, there is no record of anyone having an epileptic seizure that day, and the floors in the TSBD were being refurbished that week, so workmen were in and out of the building making it easy for the first assassination team to blend in and move into place.

- The **second assassination team** moves into position in the Dal-Tex building which is on the northeast corner of Houston Street and Elm Street. This team is on the first or second floor, giving them a low shot trajectory.

- The **third assassination team** moves into position behind the picket fence on the Grassy Knoll. This gives them a clear unobstructed view of Kennedy's motorcade as it moves down Elm Street.

- At approximately 12:30 P.M., Kennedy's motorcade turns right onto Houston Street and moves towards the TSBD and the **first assassination team**, which is positioned on the sixth-floor corner window. The assassination team has a clear shot, yet they never take it.

- Kennedy's motorcade then slows down to make the 120-degree left turn onto Elm Street. It then moves slowly down Elm Street, which puts Kennedy between three assassination teams in a triangulation of shots.

    1. The **first shot** is fired from the TSBD, but misses the motorcade entirely. Kennedy hears this shot and momentarily pauses waving to the crowd.

    2. The **second shot** is fired from the Grassy Knoll and hits Kennedy in the throat, which causes his arms to flex up to his throat area.

    3. The **third shot** is fired from the TSBD, which hits Kennedy in the upper right side of his back, pushing him down and forward. Kennedy now slumps to his left.

4. The **fourth shot** is fired from the Dal-Tex building, missing Kennedy and hitting Connally in the back. Connally was heard to yell out, "They're going to kill us all!"

5. The **fifth shot** is fired from the Dal-Tex building, which hits a curb on the road to the left and front of the motorcade. Concrete debris from this curb hits bystander James Tague on his right cheek. His injury was minor.

6. At this point, Kennedy's limousine appears to have slowed down. This is when the **sixth shot** is fired, most likely from the Dal-Tex building, hitting Kennedy in the right back portion of his head.

7. The **seventh shot** is fired from the Grassy Knoll almost simultaneously with the previous shot. This shot hits Kennedy in the right front area of his head which violently pushes him back and to the left. He then slumps forward. It is when this shot is fired, that the motorcade speeds out of the area.

So far, we've learned of seven shots in all that were fired at the motorcade from three different locations. And some of the shots were fired simultaneously, making it impossible for witnesses to be precise as to the number of shots fired. And the fact that some of the frames from the Zapruder film are missing, further adds to the difficulty in determining the number of shots fired, which may even be more than what we've established.

Figure 6.17 – The sequence of shots as Kennedy's motorcade drove down Elm Street in Dealey Plaza
Source: Wikimedia

The assassination teams would have carefully planned the shooting once the Dallas trip was announced. Therefore, they would have had plenty of time to pick out the most strategic areas in any of the motorcade routes during the Dallas trip. This would have involved mapping out the area and taking numerous photos. And once the area was chosen for the assassination, the assassination teams would have practiced the actual shooting in a replicated zone in a secure location. By the time they had studied the area, every escape route would have been planned and almost every problem anticipated for. There would have been contingencies in place, with a decision to go or abort. Everything would have been timed to coincide with the motorcade once it entered Dealey Plaza. The area itself would have been augmented to slow the motorcade down. This was done by adding two turns, which restricted the motorcade's speed to 11 miles per hour.

Each of the three assassination teams would have had three or more people, that is, one shooter, one for keeping people clear of the vicinity near the shooter, which would explain individuals carrying fake Secret Service identification, and one to communicate with a central command post. In all, there would have been about 10 to 15 people involved in the actual shooting, including those coordinating the hit from a central command post. And there just happened to be a van parked near the northeast corner of Houston Street and Elm Street, which some believe was the command post for the assassination. After the shooting, the assassination teams made their escape during all the chaos and likely stayed at a safehouse for several days.

When it came to assassinating a President, professional hit teams were recruited and everything had to be planned right down to the last detail. But often, not everything goes according to plan, which may have involved killing Oswald on or near the scene of the assassination immediately thereafter, which obviously didn't happen. As Oswald himself said later while in police custody, "I'm just a patsy." Immediately after the assassination, Oswald realized he was set up and made his escape from the TSBD. He may have contacted someone, who instructed him to go to his rooming house and wait for a signal. Once there, he was signalled by a Dallas patrol car to leave the house. It was after this that Oswald allegedly shot Police Officer J.D. Tippit. The shooting of Tippit may have had more to do with setting up Oswald, to once and for all solidify the case against him in the public mind, especially since the assassination itself didn't appear to go according to plan. Oswald then ends up in a movie theatre presumably to meet a contact, which would explain his behaviour in not paying the movie fee. Oswald was obviously in a state of panic knowing the conspirators had realized their plan had gone awry. And killing Oswald two days later, paved the road for researchers to piece together some of the major aspects of the assassination.

But the lingering question has been, who ordered the assassination and why? Of course, we don't know for sure, but there are some intriguing clues. It has been said that Kennedy had acquired more enemies as President than was normally typical for that era, so there were plenty of powerful people who wanted him out of the way. And this may have included some colourful characters from some colourful secret societies. That, is discussed next.

Those Pesky Freemasons

There is an abundance of Freemasonic symbology connected to the Kennedy assassination and the Apollo Moon missions, which would take an entire chapter to discuss. For our purposes here, we don't need to go into much detail. But the overall subject of Freemasonry and the people involved is worth mentioning, since Kennedy himself was clearly concerned about it. In a speech to the Newspapers Publishers Association at the Waldorf-Astoria hotel in New York City in April 1961, Kennedy had this to say about secret societies:

> The very word 'secrecy' is repugnant in a free and open society, and we are as a people inherently and historically opposed to secret societies, to secret oaths and to secret proceedings. We decided long ago that the dangers of excessive and unwarranted concealment of pertinent facts far outweigh the dangers which are cited to justify it. Even today, there is little value in opposing the threat of a closed society by imitating its arbitrary restrictions. Even today, there is little value in ensuring the survival of our nation if our traditions do not survive it. And there is very grave danger that an announced need for increased security will be seized upon by those anxious to expand its meaning to the very limits of official censorship and concealment. That I do not intend to permit to the extent that it is in my control. And no official of my Administration, whether his rank is high or low, civilian or military, should interpret my words here tonight as an excuse to

censor the news, to stifle dissent, to cover up our mistakes or to withhold from the press and the public the facts they deserve to know.

Many Presidents make promises and appear to be all about change, when in actuality it is nothing more than rhetoric with the business-as-usual agenda, hence the cynicism and distrust that has built up over the decades. But this is a very unique speech by a President which appears to have red flags written all over it. And these red flags include Freemasonry connections with the Apollo astronauts right up to the highest levels of management within NASA, as well as numerous government intelligence agencies, and of course the executive branch of government itself. But we'll limit ourselves primarily to the connections involving NASA and the Apollo Moon missions.

During my research into the Apollo Moon missions, I had begun to suspect a connection to the JFK assassination. But most if not all of the books on the assassination have never mentioned this connection, or at least the ones I've read over the years. However, one author has recently made the connection with his book *ANCIENT ALIENS & JFK: The Race to the Moon and the Kennedy Assassination,* by Mike Bara, published in 2018. The premise of his book is that Kennedy was killed to prevent him from disclosing the existence of alien technology that was in the possession of the secret government, commonly known now as the Deep State. The idea was to keep this technology away from the official government. Bara then draws a direct connection to Freemasons, which lead to some very interesting characters in both NASA and the government that some believe may have been involved in the assassination or at least had set the wheels in motion.

Note: Author Mike Bara has published several books on the theory of ancient alien civilizations on the Moon, which I currently don't subscribe to. However, he does make some interesting connections to some very powerful people within NASA during the Apollo Moon missions in his book, *ANCIENT ALIENS & JFK: The Race to the Moon and the Kennedy Assassination*. These connections don't necessarily prove anything, but they are worth mentioning and it does add intrigue to the conspiracy involved that led to the assassination of President Kennedy.

On the recommendation of Vice President Johnson, who was a 33-degree Scottish Rite Freemason, Kennedy appointed James Webb as Administrator to NASA, himself a fellow 33-degree Scottish Rite Freemason. Webb went on to appoint many fellow Freemasons to positions in management within NASA. However, one wonders why Kennedy would set the wheels in motion for so many Freemasons to be in positions of authority within NASA and presumably in positions of power within the United States government, given his concerns about secret societies and their potential influence on government policy. If his speech on secret societies is to be taken seriously, then it's understandable that he would want to distance himself from any connection to them. But the opposite happened which was a peculiar move on his part. However, Bara offers a possible reason for this:

> Given his distaste for "secret societies, secret oaths and secret proceedings," it is surprising to me that Kennedy allowed this, or that he allowed von Braun to appoint Nazi war criminals like Hurt Debus to run the space center at Cape Canaveral. Either he was forced to accept these appointments as a practical matter simply to get the job done, or he planned to use the secret societies to his advantage. Perhaps a "keep your friends close but your enemies closer" working philosophy. As we have seen, this was a very dangerous game fraught with risks to life and limb.[8]

The subject of Freemasons has come up many times in conspiracy theories, which some interpret as more of a red herring than anything of real importance. But the fact is many of the Apollo astronauts and management of NASA, as well as many politicians then and now are Freemasons or are part of some other secret society. How significant is this? Well, fraternities and sororities are popular in universities and elsewhere, which I've always stayed clear of, much as I stay clear of anything related to secret societies. For me they represent a collective way of thinking that is forced on each member. Independent thought is forbidden, at least within the confines of any particular secret society chapter. But just how influential that collective may be on people in positions of power, is debatable.

- So, were Freemasons involved in the assassination?
- Or was it that some of the people involved in the assassination, just happened to be Freemasons?

From here, I leave it up to the reader to pursue this part of the assassination, but it is an intriguing aspect that can't be entirely discounted.

However, aside from Freemasons, Bara makes some interesting connections to Cold War politics of that era which will be discussed next.

Cold War Politics

Author Mike Bara points out that Kennedy proposed at least three times that both the Americans and Soviets cooperate in their respective space programs. But Kennedy was even more specific about his intentions in his speech to the United Nations General Assembly on September 20, 1963:

> Finally, in a field where the United States and the Soviet Union have a special capacity – in the field of space – there is room for new cooperation, for further

joint efforts in the regulation and exploration of space. I include among these possibilities a joint expedition to the Moon. Space offers no problems of sovereignty; by resolution of this assembly, the members of the United Nations have foresworn any claim to territorial rights in outer space or on celestial bodies, and declared that international law and the United Nations Charter will apply. Why, therefore, should man's first flight to the Moon be a matter of national competition? Why should the United States and the Soviet Union, in preparing for such expeditions, become involved in immense duplications of research, construction and expenditure? Surely, we should explore whether the scientists and astronauts of our two countries – indeed all the world – cannot work together in the conquest of space, sending someday in this decade to the Moon not the representatives of a single nation, but the representatives of all our countries.[9]

I'm sure the reader realizes the significance of this speech. To even suggest cooperation in space with what was perceived to have been its most dangerous enemy, let alone proposing a joint expedition to the Moon, must have sent shockwaves through the corridors of American power. The powers-that-be were still reeling over what they perceived as Kennedy's betrayal over the Bay of Pigs invasion in Cuba and his actions during the Cuban missile crisis. Kennedy's actions with the Russians over Cuba were seen as a failure to end Russian influence in that country. Now Kennedy was proposing to work with their sworn enemy in their respective space programs, an enemy many feel he had already sold out to. And the American public didn't seem too keen on the idea of a joint American/Soviet expedition to the Moon either.

Kennedy then publicly backed away from his joint expedition proposal with the Russians, but strangely just a couple of weeks after his speech to the United Nations, he does the opposite and issues National Security Action Memorandum (NSAM) # 271 to NASA Director James Webb:

> On November 12, 1963, Kennedy was suddenly reinvigorated about it and issued a document known as National Security Action Memorandum #271. The memo, released by the Kennedy Library, was title "Cooperation with the USSR on Outer Space Matters." It instructed NASA Director Webb to personally (and immediately) take the initiative to develop a program of "substantive cooperation" with his Soviet counterparts in accordance with Kennedy's September 20th UN proposal. It also called for an interim report on the progress being made by December 15, 1963, giving Webb a little over a month to get "substantive cooperation" with the Soviets.[10]

Some would say that the perceived notion of selling out the space program in itself could hardly be considered a motivating factor for the removal of a President, especially considering the violent way in which this was done to President Kennedy. But when all the previous factors discussed are added to the mix, a proposed partnership with the Soviets for a joint expedition to the Moon could have been interpreted as an admission to the world that the United States did not have the technology for manned lunar missions, or that no one country could accomplish this on its own, if at all. This proposal could easily have been interpreted as a treasonous act by Kennedy, which may or may not have put the wheels in motion for his assassination. But given what we've learned so far, there should be no doubt that an assassination plan had already been in place before Kennedy publicly announced his proposal for a joint expedition to the Moon with the Russians. All that would have been needed, was to have given the order and then wait for Kennedy to leave the White House for an official domestic Presidential trip, which is exactly what happened with his trip to Dallas, Texas, November 22, 1963, just ten days after

NSAM # 271 to NASA Administrator James Webb. It's also important to put into context the Cold War era of that time. This involved each of these two nations' determination to prove their technological superiority over the other, or at least, to give the impression of superiority.

There was in interesting book on the assassination that was published in the 1970s, which is still relevant and maybe even more so given what we now know. The book is called *NONMENCLATURE OF AN ASSASSINATION CABAL* by an anonymous author who used the name, William Torbitt.

> The agencies involved in this coup are numerous and mysterious. According to the so-called "Torbitt Document" aka NONMENCLATURE OF AN ASSASSINATION CABAL," an anonymous conspiracy book that came out in the 1970s, a large group of agencies and individuals were involved. According to "Torbitt," the killing of President Kennedy was planned and supervised by Division Five of the Federal Bureau of Investigation, a relatively small counterespionage department within the FBI. Division Five has a sub-organization known as the Defence Industrial Security Command (DISC), a group whose very name implies a connection with MJ-12 and the alien presence. According to Torbitt, DISC is an extra-constitutional agency operating illegally inside the US government and was headed by Nazi rocket scientist Dr. Wernher von Braun. DISC acted on behalf of other government agencies like the Defence Intelligence Agency, Atomic Energy Commission and most significantly, NASA. Key figures in assassination conspiracy theories like Clay Shaw, Guy Bannister, David Ferrie, Lee Harvey Oswald, Jack Ruby and others were named as agents for DISC in the period leading up to the assassination.[11]

Majestic 12 or MJ-12, was a committee of scientists, military leaders, and government officials, which was formed in 1947 by President Harry S. Truman. This became known from leaked government documents released in 1984. The committee's purpose was to investigate and recover alien spacecraft and Bara tries to make a connection between MJ-12 and the Kennedy assassination. However, many ufologists consider the MJ-12 documents to have been faked, which is a logical conclusion. These documents could also have been disinformation, which is often used as a common tactic by government intelligence agencies that make it difficult for researchers to determine what is authentic and what is not. However, what is important in Bara's quote above are the names mentioned, all of whom have been discussed in numerous books. And for those who would like a quick reference, all of these names are portrayed in the movie JFK by Oliver Stone except, Wernher von Braun. But the fact that von Braun has been mentioned in connection to the assassination, or at the very least, connected to Division Five of the Federal Bureau of Investigations (FBI), which has been implicated in the assassination, indicates a possible connection to the Apollo Moon missions.

As Bara points out, DISC functions on behalf of other government agencies like the Defence Intelligence Agency. So, none of this means von Braun himself set the wheels in motion for Kennedy's assassination. He just wouldn't have had that level of power. And his involvement with DISC doesn't necessarily implicate upper echelons of management within NASA either. But these connections could lead to factions of the U.S. military, which had a vested interest in making sure the Apollo program was maintained. And Kennedy's proposal to work with the Russians in a joint expedition to the Moon, could have been interpreted as a possible end to the Apollo program, which could not have been allowed by certain factions of the military, with other government intelligence agencies cooperating. This, along with other considerations during the Cold War, made Kennedy a threat to some very powerful people within the military industrial complex. And it was Kennedy's predecessor President Dwight D. Eisenhower, who warned of the dangers of the military industrial complex in his farewell speech to the nation before leaving office.

As the reader may remember from chapter one, we had established a connection between Jack Parsons and Wernher von Braun before World War II. And further, we established the connection between Jack Parsons and the FBI and the real possibility that the FBI was aware of Wernher von Braun years before he was recruited into the United States under Operation Paperclip. And it's interesting that we have now made a connection between Wernher von Braun and the Kennedy assassination, but not necessarily his involvement. And it's worth mentioning that with all this going on, Kennedy had become increasingly concerned about the monetary control the Federal Reserve Bank had on the American economy and presumably domestic and foreign policy. And as previously mentioned, this concern had turned into action when he ordered the United States Treasury to print money, which may have been an attempt to flood the market undermining the influence of the Federal Reserve bank. A lot of researchers believe that this alone would have been interpreted as a serious threat by the Deep State and hence, the need for Kennedy to be removed from office.

However, in addition to the reasons for removing Kennedy from office, there is another element to the assassination, I would like to discuss next.

The Psychological Factor

Many people doubt whether the real power is with the President, and as Kennedy was said to have mentioned, he didn't realize what little power the President had until he assumed the office himself. Some would argue that in terms of his policies, it's reasonable to assume Kennedy did pretty much as he was told. But as we've established, Kennedy seemed to have started steering the country down a path of his own choosing. This may explain the very method used in the assassination itself and the way his assassination was captured in photos and film. This is an important point that I would like to expand on, since it bears witness to what I believe was another intentional part of the assassination, a reason that would explain a lot about the events of that day.

Usually, the mainstream media (MSM) tended to be a lot closer to Kennedy in any of his motorcade routes and was positioned in front of Kennedy's limousine. But as other researchers have mentioned, the MSM was positioned several cars back from Kennedy's limousine on the day of the assassination. However, anyone else was allowed to be within several feet of Kennedy's limousine as his motorcade drove down Elm St. just seconds before shots were fired. And these people were in a unique position to take photos and film of an event, that for all intents and purposes, the MSM had missed. But there is a reason why the MSM was for the most part, shut out of one of the most significant events of the 20th century.

In the 1960s, not all of the MSM were as easily controlled as they are today. Therefore, the conspirators could not have taken the chance of the assassination being filmed and then being leaked out to the public by some elements within the mainstream media. However, the assassination itself was meant to be photographed and filmed since it was necessary for Americans to witness this tragic event. Photos and film have more of an impact than words and those images can resonate for decades and more. But the MSM film cameras were far more able to pick up detail than the average camera available to the public at that time, so the MSM had to be prevented from any direct access to Kennedy's limousine on November 22, 1963. There were still some MSM photographers close to the motorcade in the vicinity of Dealey Plaza, but there wasn't any MSM film crew in position to record the actual assassination.

By allowing spectators to photograph and film the assassination, the conspirators would still have a graphic record of that tragic day. All they needed to do next was to confiscate the cameras and make sure nothing too revealing showed in the images that could have risked exposing the assassination conspiracy. And as it so happened, many cameras were indeed confiscated and some of them were never returned. Further, there were several reports of men showing Secret Service identification near an area called the Grassy Knoll right after the assassination. This is the area to the right and front of Kennedy's motorcade as it travelled down Elm Street from where witnesses say shots were fired. And the Secret Service has said that none of their agents were on the Grassy Knoll that day.

Once the photos and film were scrutinized, they were either returned or disappeared. As for the Zapruder film, it too is alleged to have been edited and some actually believe it was a fabrication. However, the amateur photos and film that were returned were of poor quality and it would be decades before any of the photographic and film record could be enhanced or properly analysed with new technology. Therefore, the conspirators got their photo and film record without exposing those involved. And as they say, the rest is history.

Figure 6.18 – Grassy Knoll, which was to the right and front of Kennedy's motorcade as it moved down Elm Street.
Source: Wikipedia

Figure 6.19 – A frame from the Zapruder film where Kennedy pauses waving to the crowd, after the first shot was fired but missed the motorcade
Source: Wikipedia

Figure 6.20 – Kennedy reacts to being shot. Notice his left wrist flinched up to his face, which matches the Zapruder film
Source: James William Altgens, AP Journalist

So why was it so important to capture this assassination on photos and film, even at enormous risks to the conspirators? It's a good question that requires some further research. However, there are a few points I would like to make.

There are other more sophisticated means of removing a President that didn't include a public execution. One of those ways could easily have been to use Kennedy's numerous health problems. For the most part, Kennedy's severe back problems had been mentioned several times in the MSM during his presidency, but his other health problems were covered up, most notably his Addison disease which required daily doses of corticosteroids. Then there were the numerous alleged affairs that Kennedy had with women before and while he was President, which at the time, was more of an open secret among the MSM. Since then, much of this has been disclosed in many credible books on the subject. So, given the political and media climate of that era, the MSM could have easily been used to reign in any of Kennedy's policies or worse, it would have forced him to resign or at least ruin his chances of a second term as President. Instead, he was brutally killed in broad daylight, in front of many witnesses, including the millions of people who eventually watched and studied the infamous Zapruder film. In short, this was a public execution.

To try and make sense of this, we first need to take a look at how the MSM portrayed the Kennedy presidency. Here are a few examples:

- The young vigorous President with his beautiful and glamorous wife and two children, now leading the charge in the White house.

- His speech to Congress on May 25, 1961 with his proposal for a manned mission to the Moon by the end of the 1960s, putting American prestige out in front.

- The Cuban Missile crisis in October where he was seen by the world to have stood up to Russia, forcing them to withdraw their nuclear missiles from Cuba.

- His refusal to give into corporations, especially his memorable fight with the Steel Industry over prices.

- His famous speech in June of 1963, where he stood next to the Berlin Wall, promoting freedom versus communism.

- Leveraging his office to promote racial equality and calling on all Americans to respect the rights of every individual.

- His commitment to South Vietnam, without involving the United States in a possible war with North Vietnam.

- All of this while his back problems had surfaced in the media, with photos of him occasionally having to resort to using crutches to ease his back pain.

- And then faced with the loss of his newly born son Patrick, who died August 9, 1963.

- Seen by many as a President who balanced American foreign policy with that of human rights.

- Adorned by millions of people not only in the United States, but all over the world.

- Constant coverage of the thousands of people who turned out for each of his motorcade routes.

And then came Dallas on November 22, 1963, where President Kennedy is brutally struck down by assassins' bullets in broad day light, in front of the very people who admired and loved him.

There has never been a tragedy that has had such a profound psychological impact on the American people and the world, as the Kennedy assassination. The MSM photos and film show the enormous shock and mourning of a nation, which still resonates to this day. But there is something else that comes with this psychological impact and that is, the power of suggestion and influence. The American people were in a state of depression and understandably so. And this made people vulnerable to and oblivious to the machinations of government and its policies. One example of this was President Johnson's immediate reversal of Kennedy's Vietnam policy. It was an opportunity to take advantage of the public's state of mind, which would have allowed the upper echelons of power to put forward their own agenda. And that agenda included ending Kennedy's proposal for a joint expedition to the Moon with the Russians and instead, continuing on with the Apollo program. Capitalizing on the Kennedy tragedy made things a lot easier, including faking the Apollo Moon missions and diverting funds to Black Projects. Further, the photographic and film record of the assassination, sent a chilling message to any future politician or President as to what can happen to those who dare to pursue policies of their own making.

The whole Kennedy presidency seems to have had an enormous psychological affect on the American people, which leads one to question as to whether this was by design or just happenstance. And if all this was just happenstance, then there is one more peculiar meeting that took place on the White House lawn that is worth mentioning.

In July of 1963, a group of young men called the Boys Nation had been invited to the White House. One of the members of this group was Bill Clinton. By chance, future President Bill Clinton and the rest of the young men had met President Kennedy.

Figure 6.21 – President Kennedy and Bill Clinton shaking hands
Source: Wikipedia

A President shaking hands with a future President would naturally be seen as coincidental. However, there may be more to this tale regarding a 'chance' meeting between President Kennedy and future President Clinton, as Bara explains:

> When Clinton was under investigation in 1998 for lying under oath in the Paula Jones/Monica Lewinsky affair, a huge controversy erupted over the existence of a key piece of evidence: Lewinsky's semen-stained blue dress. Rumors of Clinton's true lineage had circulated for years, and prosecutor Ken Star wanted the dress so he could perform DNA tests on the semen and determine once and for all if Clinton was in fact an illegitimate Rockefeller or an illegitimate Kennedy. We don't know the results of those tests, but my money has always been on Kennedy. Clinton's mother, Virginia Dell Cassidy, was a nurse, and there are rumors (which I believe to be true) that she was assigned for a brief period to a resort hospital in Castle Hot Springs, Arizona, which for three months beginning just days after New Years in 1945 hosted a recuperating JFK patient. Kennedy was a course a notorious womanizer, a famous war hero and the son of one of the richest men in the world. It's hard to imagine a more attractive lover for a woman like Virginia. Since Bill Clinton was not born until August 1946, there would have been a continuing affair while she was married to her husband. Interestingly, Cassidy, after she was married for a second time, she settled in a town known as Hot Springs, Arkansas.[12]

In a prese conference in 1992, President Clinton stated that he hadn't seen one shred of evidence to suggest a conspiracy in the JFK assassination. It's a typical statement from a man who is alleged to have been involved in many conspiracies himself, which is a subject for another book.

My point is, researching the Apollo Moon mission hoax can lead down many roads, with many possibilities including the fact that what may appear to be a coincidence, is in fact by design, e.g., the 'chance' encounter between Kennedy and Clinton. But for our purposes here, we'll stay with the connection to the Apollo Moon missions which leads to our final section as to how simulations were used to sell the narrative.

Simulation And The Apollo Missions

Considering that NASA knew as far back as the early 1960s that manned missions to the Moon were impossible with existing technologies, they had many years to work on ways to simulate the missions to give the impression that they fulfilled Kennedy's pledge. And contrary to what some of the Apollo mission proponents say, simulating the missions would definitely have been far less expensive and easier to accomplish than actually sending manned missions to the Moon. This would allow funds to be diverted for classified projects with no accountability.

When I was researching how the Apollo missions were faked, I noticed a lot of work on this aspect had already been done. So, there is plenty of information on several websites most notably, www.aulis.com. And there has even been an entire book written on the subject called *THE APOLLO MOON HOAX: HOW DID THEY DO IT? – A Generation Deceived by NASA*, by Trevor Weaver. The book goes through a lot of the technical aspects of how the missions were simulated, how the photos and film were done, and the many people involved in this deception. The book is worth the read and is available on Amazon. So, there's really no point in going through all of it here. However, there are a couple of points I would like to add regarding the deception, since I haven't seen much discussion on it elsewhere.

In this chapter, we've already discussed some of the deceptions NASA used to try and convince the public that the Apollo missions were authentic. But many people have asked, "How did they fake zero gravity in both the CM and LM, since there is film of the Apollo astronauts floating around presumably in LEO and to the Moon and back?" It's a good question and one that doesn't require an in-depth knowledge of photography or film techniques.

> Even greater was the "zero-g LM." They built its cockpit right into the belly of a jet that could simulate weightlessness by flying parabolas. At the top of a parabola, the plane and its occupants would experience several moments of zero-gravity, much like a stone thrown into the air, which, at the end if its climb, would hang motionless and weightless before it started to fall. During those moments of zero-gravity, astronauts could test the restraint system – safety belts – that had replaced the LM's seats. The plane could also fly inverted parabolas, thus simulating the five-gravities that might be experienced during decelerations and descent from lunar orbit.[13]

There is no doubt that since NASA built a replicate of the LM into the floor of an aircraft to simulate zero gravity, then the same was done for the CM. And these simulations lasted approximately 30 seconds each time the aircraft entered the required parabola maneuver. Each of these 30 seconds could easily have been filmed and then edited together. And further, the American military had some of the largest film studios in the world that were used to produce their own documentaries and propaganda films.

Wikipedia:

> **Lookout Mountain Air Force Station (LMAFS)** is a Formerly Used Defense Site which today is a private residence of actor Jared Leto in the Laurel Canyon neighborhood of Los Angeles, California. The USAF military installation produced motion pictures and still photographs for the United States Department of Defense and the Atomic Energy Commission (AEC) from 1947–1969.
>
> The 100,000 sq ft (9,300m) facility was built on 2.5 acres in 1941 as a World War II air defense center to coordinate Los Angeles area radar installations. When the studio was established in 1947, its purpose was kept secret. The studio consisted of one large sound stage, a film laboratory, two screening rooms, four editing rooms, an animation and still photo department, sound mixing studio, and numerous climate controlled film vaults. Using the latest equipment, the studio could process both 35mm and 16mm color motion picture film as well as black and white and color still photographs. It was declared Los Angeles Historic-Cultural Monument number 1098 in 2015.

Thousands of propaganda films were produced which are still classified to this day. So, it's reasonable to assume that film techniques which are still classified, were used in recording aspects of the Apollo Missions in a studio. And after 'Lookout Mountain Air Force Station' was closed in 1969, its facilities were relocated to Norton Air Force Base in San Bernardino County, California. Therefore, given NASA's close relationship with the military during the Apollo program, the facilities for each planned Apollo mission were there for NASA to use.

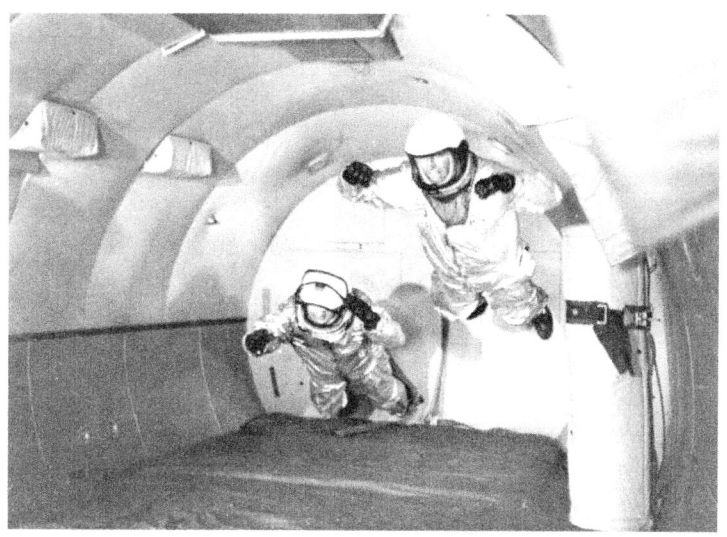

Figure 6.22 – Simulated Zero Gravity in an Aircraft
Source: Wikimedia

It would be near impossible to tell the difference whether the weightless scenes in the CM or LM were filmed in an aircraft or space. And it helped that the simulators were designed with as much detail as possible.

> The LM simulator at the Grumman Aircraft Company facility in Bethpage, Long Island, where the Lunar Module was built, used actual flight equipment to the maximum extent possible. NASA had the LM simulators in Houston and at Cape Canaveral whose main task was training astronauts. These had cockpits that were authentic to the last detail and magnificent out-the-window displays good enough to train for landing in a particular spot on the Moon.[14]

Another question that is usually asked is, "How did four hundred thousand people working on the Apollo program, keep a secret?" As Apollo Moon hoax researcher Marcus Allen has said, "They didn't. It's called, compartmentalization." It's not like all these scientists and technicians were working under one roof and were privy to top-level meetings within NASA. Instead, many of these scientists and technicians worked for several key NASA contractors as well as an estimated twenty thousand subcontractors throughout the country. None of them had access to top level management meetings and all of them worked on a need-to-know basis.

Only a few upper management personnel would have known the true nature of the Apollo missions. And further, NASA had sent unmanned missions to circumnavigate the Moon, for the purposes of training technicians in Mission Control. These unmanned missions along with the numerous Apollo simulations were recorded, which could easily have been used later to give the impression of an actual Apollo mission. The point is, NASA had many options at its disposal. And it's interesting that the only people allowed to communicate with the Apollo astronauts from Mission Control, were other Apollo astronauts. Their official title was capsule communicator or spacecraft communicator, more commonly known as CAPCOM. Therefore, there was a hierarchy of personnel on every level designed to control the flow of information.

Most people believed that what they were seeing was real, myself included. We were caught up in the thrill and excitement of what we we're told was man's greatest scientific achievement and a huge step forward for mankind. Once the simulations were shown to the public, we saw what we wanted to see. It's classic manipulation.

However, all anyone has to do is to look at the numerous problems that were encountered in the Apollo program, some of which are documented and discussed in Part I and Part II of this series, as well as the lack of anything presently resembling a thriving manned space program, and they begin to see the deception for themselves. And when they step back from the details and look at the bigger picture, the deception becomes even more obvious.

This leads one to wonder just what the real purpose of the Saturn V launches were all about. One possibility may have been to launch a space station, which NASA did in 1973 with Skylab. That means the twelve launches leading up to Skylab were unmanned test missions and it's possible they eventually got close to some consistency in the performance of the F-1 engines. But once Skylab was launched to LEO, it was determined that it had sustained damage, probably due to the launch itself. Whether this was specifically due to recurring problems with the F-1 engines, has been difficult to conclusively prove, since NASA destroyed all of the estimated 140,000 reels of telemetry tapes. But the evidence so far, points in that direction. And it's interesting to note, that there hasn't been another launch of a Saturn V after Skylab.

Incidentally, Skylab fell out of LEO in 1979 and disintegrated on re-entry into Earth's atmosphere. It seems a very symbolic way to end the Apollo program era.

Chapter Six - Endnotes

1. Andrei Bulatov and Alexander Boyko, *The April Odyssey and the November Boat*, article Aulis Online, November 2016 www.aulis.com/april_november.htm

2. Mary Bennett and David Percy, *The Odyssey of the Lost Apollo CM*, article Aulis Online, November 2016 www.aulis.com/odyssey_apollo.htm

3. Ibid.

4. Ibid.

5. Ibid.

6. Ibid.

7. Ibid.

8. Mike Bara, ANCIENT ALIENS & JFK: *The Race to the Moon and the Kennedy Assassination*, p. 77.

9. Ibid., p. 62.

10. Ibid., p.64.

11. Ibid., p. 99.

12. Ibid., p. 149.

13. Charles R. Pellegrino and Joshua Stoff, *CHARIOTS FOR APOLLO: THE UNTOLD STORY BEHIND THE RACE TO THE MOON*, p. 73.

14. Don Eyles, *SUNBURST AND LUMINARY: AN APOLLO MEMOIR*, P. 87.

Conclusion

As we have established, NASA's testing standards for the Apollo Moon missions were nowhere near the standards established in any other industry, especially aviation, an industry in which NASA should have modeled its design and testing standards after. And 'testing standards' is a relative term, meaning each industry establishes its own standards by trial and error. That approached in aviation led to rigorous testing standards of its aircraft, which has greatly increased its safety record over the decades. The same approach should be applied to the aerospace industry. As we've discussed in chapter 2, NASA shouldn't be expected to follow the exact same testing standards used in the aviation industry when it comes to testing in actual flight conditions. To test each rocket for hundreds of hours in actual flight conditions, is impractical and far too costly. However, NASA didn't even follow its own testing standards during the Apollo program.

NASA actually started down the road of setting up its own testing standards with the Saturn I and Saturn IB, but then strangely abolished that standard when it involved the Saturn V. Established testing standards would have increased the chances of success with the Apollo Missions. But this approach would likely have meant decades of research and development before any attempt could have been made to land a manned mission on the Moon. But as this didn't fit into NASA's tight schedule, funding, and official narrative, NASA adopted a hit and miss approach in the design and engineering of these technologies during the Apollo program.

The proponents of the Apollo missions often justify the minimal flight-testing standards in the Apollo program, by citing the Space Shuttle program since the first launch also involved the first crew. The Apollo program had at best only a few years' experience of manned missions to LEO to refer to, in order to research and develop the technology needed for a manned lunar landing mission. However, the solid fueled rocket boosters used on the Space Shuttle had decades of proven success, and the main engines had its origins going back to the 1960s before their design and development later in the 1970s, leading up to the first Space Shuttle launch in 1981. So, by the time the first Space Shuttle was launched, NASA had acquired more experience and had a slightly higher probability of success with its hit and miss approach.

Although the first Space Shuttle mission was rated a success, this was still a serious breach in safety protocols, by any industry standards. And as it turned out, there were concerns at Mission Control about possible damage to the Space Shuttle after its first launch, which gives further credibility to those who argued for an unmanned mission to test the systems before any crew was allowed onboard. Surely, there were those within NASA who considered the possibility of losing the first Space Shuttle and its crew.

Further, comparisons have been made between the flight safety record of the aviation industry to that of the Space Shuttle program. Out of the 135 Space Shuttle missions over a 30-year period, two of the vehicles were lost. But the proponents are quick to point out, that still means a 98.50 % success rate. However, this is not a fair comparison. When you factor in the number of aircraft taking off and landing every minute, involving many different aircraft designed and built by different manufacturers which are flown in many countries around the world, there is bound to be a higher incident rate.

With the Space Shuttle program there were six orbiters, two of which were destroyed and the others which were flown over many years with long intervals in between each mission. For example, the Space Shuttle Endeavor flew a total of 25 missions over 19 years, which means there were several months to prepare each vehicle for its next mission. One could easily argue that there shouldn't have been such a catastrophic failure of one Space Shuttle, let alone two.

Note: Both the Apollo program and Space Shuttle program used minimum flight test standards. But even a cursory look at both programs shows that one doesn't justify the other.

Aside from the static testing that was done during the Apollo program which did appear to be adequate, the minimal flight-testing standards raises serious questions as to why NASA would risk the safety of astronauts and more importantly, why the astronauts themselves participated, given that NASA didn't even follow its own flight-testing standards. Rather, the astronauts participated in simulations and not actual missions, hence there was no need for any concern regarding NASA's minimal flight-testing standards. They knew the technology was not there for manned lunar landings, and it helped that the astronauts were military personnel, which made it easier to control the flow of information.

To counter the minimum flight-testing standards, the proponents say that most of the Apollo astronauts were military test pilots and that they were accustomed to testing new aircraft without any previous unmanned flights. This of course was a necessary component, given that automated technology for unmanned aircraft in the early and mid-20th

century was still being developed. But by the 1960s, there were decades of data and experience with aircraft, so the testing of new aircraft with pilots onboard was an acceptable calculated risk. But as already mentioned, there was at best only a few years of manned spacecraft missions to LEO, making the requirement for rigorous testing standards even more imperative, especially given the unfamiliar environment outside of Earth's magnetic field in which these missions were to take place. And by the time of the Mercury, Gemini, and Apollo missions, NASA's contractors had become proficient in automation in the aerospace industry, so unmanned missions were possible which was done with all the variations of the Saturn rocket including the Saturn I, and Saturn IB. In total, there were 14 unmanned launches leading up to the first manned mission of the Saturn IB with Apollo 7.

Now compare the Saturn I and Saturn IB to the Saturn V. Although components of the Saturn V were included in the previous launches of the Saturn rocket, the first stage of the Saturn V which contained the F-1 engines, the most powerful engines ever built before and after the Apollo missions, had only two flights in actual conditions for a total of four minutes in duration. It is from here, that NASA went straight to the first manned launch of the Saturn V with Apollo 8, or so NASA claims.

The proponents argue that from Apollo 8 on, the rest of the Saturn V launches were near perfect and their evidence for that is NASA's official record. The same rationale is also used to explain the near perfect landings of the LM.

Another rather interesting suggestion made by some, was to do an analysis of the voice transmissions of the Apollo astronauts. Their reasoning for this, is that varying stress levels in their communications would indicate that they really did land on the Moon. However, anyone who has practiced in flight simulators, knows the stress brought on by practicing procedures. This is common among pilots in their flight training.

As for my own experience in flight simulators, I would feel my stress level go up with all the physical manifestations to go with it. I used to like practicing precision approaches for my instrument rating in which any type of weather or scenario can be programmed into the simulator by the flight instructor, so you never knew what to expect. And some of these flight simulators are so sophisticated, you would almost forget that it was just a simulator. All these factors allow the pilot to experience a scenario akin to the real thing. Therefore, it would be near impossible to differentiate between astronauts' stress levels, either at the controls of a simulator or in an actual spacecraft, making any analysis of the Apollo astronauts' communications a moot point.

Thanks to many researchers over the last couple of decades, more information is now being revealed. This alone, makes it worth the effort.

The victors write *their* truth. However, you have the power to question that truth.

Use it wisely.

Appendix A

Marcus Allen

The Apollo Moon Landings 1969-1972. Fact or Fiction?

Marcus Allen is the UK publisher of Nexus Magazine, which he introduced to the UK in 1994. Nexus is the world's leading alternative news magazine, covering Health, Future Science, Hidden History, The Unexplained, and UFOs. Nexus originated in Australia, and is now sold in over 100 countries including the USA and Canada.

Marcus has established himself as a passionate and most would say an expert in the pursuit of the unexplained, while promoting scientific based alternative health care methods on a full-time basis. And included in his pursuit, is the Apollo Moon landing hoax which is just one of the many 'taboo' subjects he has researched in the last twenty-five years, which of course, will be the focus of his work presented here. Marcus has raised questions about NASA's claim of landing men on the Moon, which have yet to be satisfactorily answered.

Marcus Allen has appeared on many TV shows during the past 25 years to discuss the Apollo Moon Landing controversy including BBC TV, Channel 4, Channel 5, Sky News, and Sci Fi and Discovery Channels. He has also appeared on Russian, Israeli, German, French, and Swiss TV stations as well as being interviewed on numerous national and local radio shows in the UK, and in the USA on Coast-to-Coast AM and HBO Vice News and most recently, the Conspiracy Show with Richard Syrett in Canada. He has given many public presentations throughout Britain and Europe as well as one in Kathmandu, Nepal, challenging the 'official' narrative of men landing on the Moon over 50 years ago.

I first became aware of Marcus's work while researching my book on the Apollo Moon missions. I was immediately impressed by his wealth of knowledge and skill on photography, which he has used very effectively in exposing the many anomalies in the photo and film record of the Apollo Moon missions. What are impressive too, are his observational skills in noticing these many anomalies in the photographic record years before the average computer software became sophisticated enough to do so.

I had the opportunity to meet Marcus for dinner on a stopover in Britain in 2019. We talked for over five hours, yet it seemed like five minutes. I was impressed by his wealth of knowledge on many topics including the Apollo Moon mission hoax.

Figure A1: Marcus and the author in December, 2019
Source: Author

Marcus continues in his pursuit of the truth, no matter where that may lead. But given his ongoing and revealing research, his information may be upsetting to many peoples' belief in what was accepted as truth for all these decades. Marcus' work can be easily found on Google and YouTube search.

We'll let Marcus end this section, with his own words:

> Man has landed on the Moon! We have seen it on TV, looked at the photographs, listened to the interviews and read the books. So, how can it not be true?
>
> We all want it to be true. Landing a man on the Moon is said to have been the greatest scientific achievement of the 20th century. The Apollo Moon landing in July 1969 has been voted the top TV moment of the 20th century. That would be true if it had all happened the way we have been shown. But did it? Or has NASA yet again lived up to its other name - Never A Straight Answer?
>
> The Apollo Moon Landings took place 50 years ago. The world has now moved on to other matters, and the emotion of the event has dimmed. Now it is being examined in meticulous detail. There are many anomalies in the photographs and the films. There are many unanswered questions as to how humans could survive the very real dangers of the hard vacuum of space and the levels of radiation experienced just a few hundred miles above the Earth's surface. For example:
>
> * How were the acknowledged dangers of radiation in space overcome, when no protection was built in to the Apollo spacecraft, the spacesuits, nor the Hasselblad cameras used on the Moon?
>
> * The Lunar Landers sat on the Moon's surface for up to 72 hours in direct sunlight, the temperature of which, on the Moon, is higher than the boiling point of water (100 deg C/212 deg F). How did the astronauts keep cool? Air conditioning does not work in a vacuum.

* How were all those 'iconic' photographs taken on the Lunar surface? The astronauts used cameras which had no viewfinder, no exposure meter, no means of knowing if a picture had been taken, as well as just manual control of the focussing, aperture setting, and shutter speed rings. The Apollo astronauts were operating their Hasselblad 500EL cameras while wearing full spacesuits, with what were, in effect, heavy duty gardening gloves on their hands. Under such severe restrictions how did they produce such professional results?

* It is well known that photographic film, as used on all Apollo missions, becomes brittle, damaged and the emulsion 'out-gases' in a hard vacuum, such as exists on the Moon.

NASA is the only source for all the evidence of man's landing on the Moon. Much of it is so questionable I contend that it could not have happened the way we have been led to believe it did: At worst the Apollo Moon missions were fabricated, at best we have been seriously misled as to man's ability to survive more than a few hundred miles above earth's surface. Could this be the reason that only now, there are any plans to 'return' astronauts to the Moon?

Appendix B

Robert Williams

Robert Williams is a studio engineer and Master Electrician, and has done some excellent research on the Apollo Moon hoax, which he posts in video format on his YouTube channel, Apollo Detectives. Williams has graciously offered to add production value to my videos, which are also posted on his YouTube channel. And now, he has applied his amazing skills to another aspect of the Apollo Moon missions to determine how photos would turn out, using film in the vacuum of space.

What many people don't realize, is that there is a difference in vacuum levels from the boundary layer of space and beyond. The term applied to these vacuum levels in space is called Torr, named after Evangelista Torricelli (1608-1647). He was an Italian physicist who had invented the barometer in 1644. Torr has an effect on material in a vacuum called outgassing, which may include film. Outgassing is when gas is released from materials in a vacuum, which can be problematic for spacecraft.

This raises some interesting questions as to the effect vacuum would have on film, and whether it was possible to have produced all those pristine photos from the alleged Apollo Moon missions, more specifically, the photos allegedly taken from the lunar surface.

It's important to remember that cameras used film for taking photos back in the 1960s. The first digital camera was invented later in 1975 by Kodak engineer Steve Sasson. Therefore, since film would have been used on the Apollo Moon missions, it may have been subject to outgassing in the vacuum of space, which would likely have had an effect on the photos, especially the photos NASA claimed were taken on the lunar surface. Cameras used in unmanned missions were usually sealed inside their own protective shielding. However, the cameras allegedly used in the Apollo Moon missions did not have any protective shielding, which would have subjected the film to the elements of space.

As altitude increases, pressure per square inch decreases. For example, at 10 miles above see level, the pressure has already decreased from 14.7 pounds per square inch (psi) to 1 psi. That in itself wouldn't be a problem for film, but as altitude increases past 62 miles, which is the boundary layer between Earth's atmosphere and space, the elements of the atmosphere as well as psi, drop off dramatically. To put this into perspective, LEO is Torr 10^{-6}. The lunar surface is Torr 10^{-12}. At Torr 10^{-12}, metals 'cold weld' together, water boils immediately, and liquids 'outgas.'

Williams set out to test the film in a vacuum chamber, to determine if there would have been a problem with the use of film in the vacuum of space. He conducted controlled tests while researcher Scott Henderson monitored the procedures. These included exposing black and while film to a ½ second burst of microwave radiation at 2 GEG, which is the frequency of which the microwave magneton functions. This caused the film to fog. Next, he determined that there was no apparent fogging on colour film, but there were changes in hue. These tests were done at Torr 10^{-3}, which is equivalent to 60 miles above sea level. It wasn't possible to test the film at Torr 10^{-12} given the limitations in the equipment. However, the effects of film on Torr 10^{-3}, gives a very good indication as to what the effects of film in a lunar environment would be.

Figure B1: Vacuum chamber used in the tests
Source: Aulis.com

Williams discussed the effects on film with visual effects expert Tim Trimble, and it was determined that these changes were not necessarily due to the vacuum itself, but due to cycling in and out of the vacuum chamber.

> It is therefore concluded that all the film stowed on board of the LM should have produced the same or similar fogging effect as has been demonstrated in these experiments. And that the multiple exists and entries of the later Apollo missions would mean that such effects should be even more in evidence of their resulting imagery. [1]

Figure B2: The controlled film is on the right. The film on the left was exposed to a vacuum which has lost its sheen and has a brownish hue
Source: Aulis.com

The film would have been exposed to:

- First, a pressurized environment in the LM
- Then the environment on the lunar surface
- And then back again in the pressurized environment in the LM.

This meant that there should have been effects on both the film and photos and as the photographic record shows, there was none.

Williams published his work in a 16-page article with contributions from Marcus Allen and Scott Henderson. In the article, they detail the film and equipment used, as well as the dates and times the tests were conducted. Further, they produced several colour photos that show the effects on film in a vacuum. It was not possible to reproduce the colour photos here, due to the format used in this book. However, the source of this article is listed in the endnotes for anyone to check for themselves. But so far, the evidence indicates that the photos allegedly taken from the lunar surface during the Apollo Moon missions, were actually taken in a studio.

Robert Williams' entire work is posted on his website, www.apollomoonhoax.net.

Appendix B - Endnotes

[1] https://www.aulis.com/vacuum.htm

Appendix C

TJ Hegland

As mentioned in chapter 2, the size of the Earth in photos allegedly taken from the lunar surface appears small when compared to the size of the Moon as seen from Earth. There hasn't been much discussion on this until recently, when an astute author T J Hegland made some interesting observations about the photos of the Earth.

> Earth is 7,927 miles in diameter. The Moon is 2,160 miles in diameter. The Earth is therefore 3.67 times bigger than the Moon, and yet in a lot of NASA pictures, the Earth is shown to be the same size as the Moon looks from Earth, <u>or less.</u>
>
> Imagine this: There are approximately 240,000 miles between the Earth and the Moon. For ease in making my point, imagine that you are standing in space at a point 240,000 miles from both the Earth and the Moon which are <u>side by side</u> - Would they appear to be the same size? If not, why doesn't the Earth appear larger from the Moon than the Moon appears from the Earth? The NASA pictures have a problem because whoever processed the pictures of the Earth and the Moon together didn't think of what I just pointed out… The resulting pictures appear to be 'Photoshopped' and hurt NASA's credibility leading one to ask if we went to the Moon.[1]

Figure C1: AS17-134-20384
Source: NASA

As the photo above shows, the Earth is not only smaller than it should be, it appears even smaller than the Moon does when viewed from Earth. As Hegland points out, when you factor in the respective sizes of both the Earth and Moon, you begin to realize that something is amiss here.

This next photo was allegedly taken from the Apollo 17 mission. Look at the position of the Earth in the top centre of the photo.

Figure C2: AS17-137-20910
Source: NASA

Since the Earth, Moon and the Sun are in the same solar system horizontal plane, the Sun cannot be higher, i.e., above, the Earth shining down on it... So why does the shadow on the Earth show a 45^0 angle?

This suggests the Sun is up and to the left of Earth, why not a few stars, too?

So, the right side of the boulder is in the dark (if the Sun was off to the left). Refer back to the lunar chart of landing sites above – what part of the Moon was Apollo 17 sitting on? Upper right face... at 30^0. And if the Earth is actually almost directly overhead, why is the Earth (in the picture) way off over the horizon? If the astronaut is standing on the Moon, wouldn't the Earth be larger and almost directly on <u>overhead</u>?

So, if Apollo 17 landed $30°$ above the equator (see chart), why is the shadow on the Earth at a $45°$ angle? In other words, Earth should be overhead, facing the Moon, and just a slight distance above the center/equator of the Moon, and should not result in a $45°$ angle to the shadow cast by the Sun. This looks like Photoshop. [2]

Note: The above quote says that the Apollo 17 LM was at 30 degrees above the lunar equator, when in actuality, the official record says 20 degrees. I contacted the author for clarification, and he confirmed there was a typo and that it should read 20 degrees. At any rate, this minor mistake hasn't altered his overall point.

In the quote above, Hegland is referring to this chart, which shows the alleged Apollo landing sites:

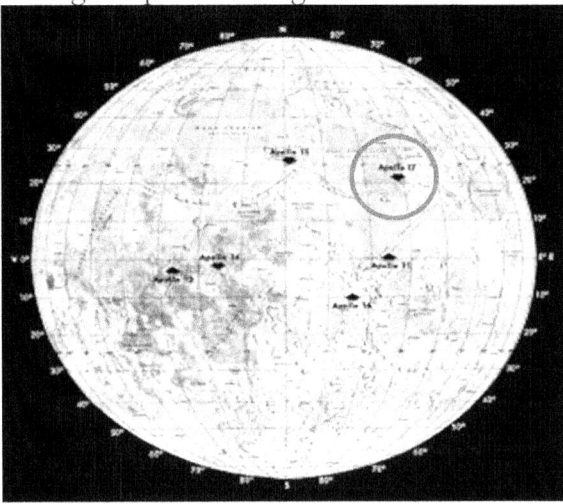

Figure C3: Alleged Apollo 17 landing site
Source: National Air and Space Museum

Notice where Apollo 17 supposedly landed. And since all of the Apollo missions allegedly landed on the side of the Moon facing

the Earth, photos taken from the lunar surface should show the Earth directly overhead of the landing sites.
Instead, the photos show the Earth over to the side.

Either NASA decided that a real depiction of the Earth was too risky, or as Hegland basically says, NASA just didn't think this through. Either way, the Earth appears to have been photoshopped.

T J Hegland discusses these anomalies in more detail in his book, as well as other intriguing and fascinating subjects, which I recommend. His book is listed in the endnotes.

Appendix C - Endnotes

[1] T J Hegland, *Virtual Earth Graduate: Man, Creation, ETs, OPs, Angels, Souls, Holograms, DNA, Serpent Wisdom, Gnosticism, the Interlife, Karma, DejaVu, the Bionet, Simulation, the Control System and more – how they fit our special reality*, p. 550.

[2] Ibid., p. 548

Appendix D

Scott Henderson

In 1969, Scott Henderson was a student in high school who avidly followed the sensational news about the first Apollo Moon landing. Since then, he has been an avid space enthusiast keeping himself up to date on any space related news. However, in later years, Scott began to take a look at some of the books, documentaries, online articles and videos, questioning the validity of the Apollo Moon missions. When Scott retired from his profession as a chef a decade ago, he decided to devote himself full time to researching the Apollo Moon missions. In the process, he's downloaded the entire photo and film record from NASA's website, and has spent over 10,000 hours studying this record. His conclusions are clear: The Apollo Moon mission photo and film record had been fabricated.

Below, I've selected twenty of Scott's photos that he has spent years studying, which is but a sample of his extensive work.

Note: The photos presented here are not of the quality necessary to show the anomalies revealed by Scott Henderson, although in some photos the anomalies should be noticeable. There's only so much detail that can be presented in these types of book formats. However, most of the photos will have its proper identification number, which the reader can use to download from NASA's website. You can also refer to www.aulis.com where most of the analysis of these photos have been published.

AS11-40-5059 In this photo, the arrow points to a car, obviously owned by one of the staff or astronauts. This photo is one of many examples of the whistleblowers involved in the filming, leaking clues to the public of the fakery that went on.

AS15-88-11929 This photo appears to shows a small rock, which is actually a beer can, more specifically, a Canadian beer can. It appears to have a Canadian Labatt label, which is very close in design to the 1970's product. It's interesting too that the LM landing gear was designed and built by Heroux Aerospace of Longueil, Quebec, Canada.

AS17-137-21002 Cars seemed to have been a very popular item while filming the Apollo missions on the Moon set. Here is a corvette convertible. The front end of the vehicle is damaged, the hood is slightly raised, and the windshield is also damaged. The rear of the car is intact, showing the curvature of the rear wheel, with the very distinctive styling of the fenders.

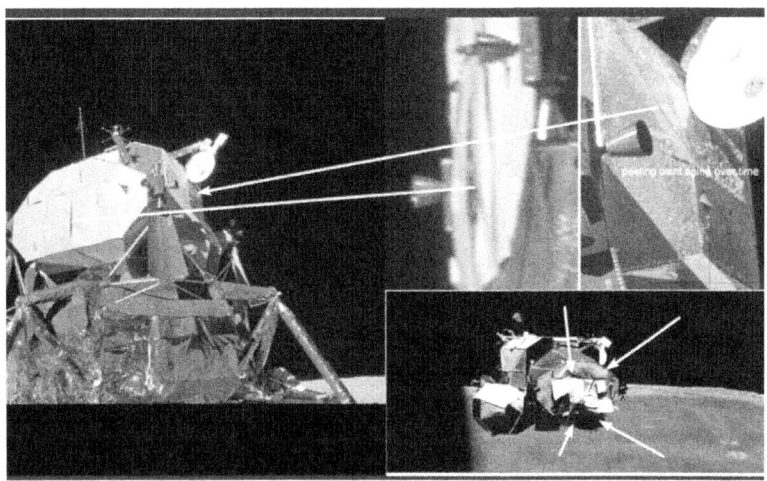

AS16-113-18332 Notice the back of the LM before liftoff from the lunar surface, and then the same area after launch. There is obvious damage to the same area of the LM. NASA does not have any files as to this damage, so it's difficult to ascertain the cause. However, given what appears to be extensive damage, vital equipment behind this panel would also have been damaged, with serious consequences for the LM had this been an actual liftoff.

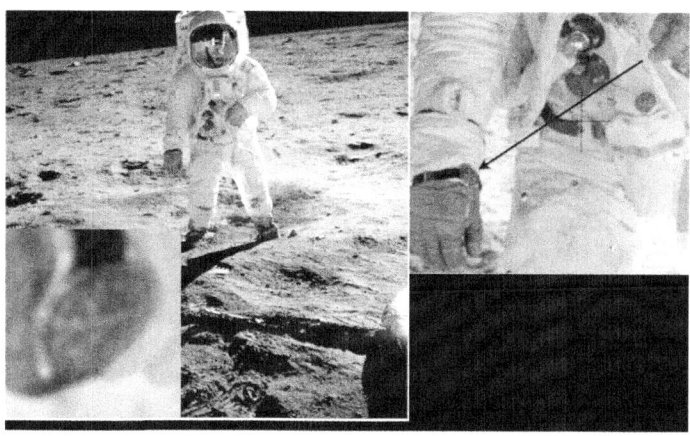

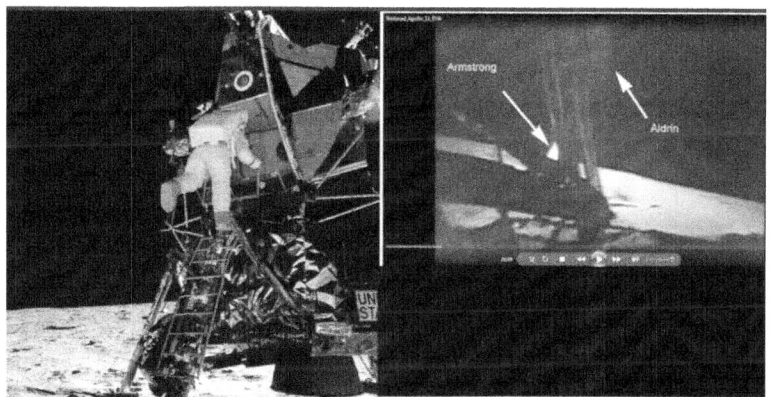

On the left, is a photo of Buzz Aldrin descending the LM ladder. On the right, is Neil Armstrong's position as Aldrin descends. But Armstrong's position on the right conflicts where he should have been to take this photo of Aldrin, so whoever really took the photo, remains a mystery. But one thing that is not a mystery, is this photo was not taken on the lunar surface.

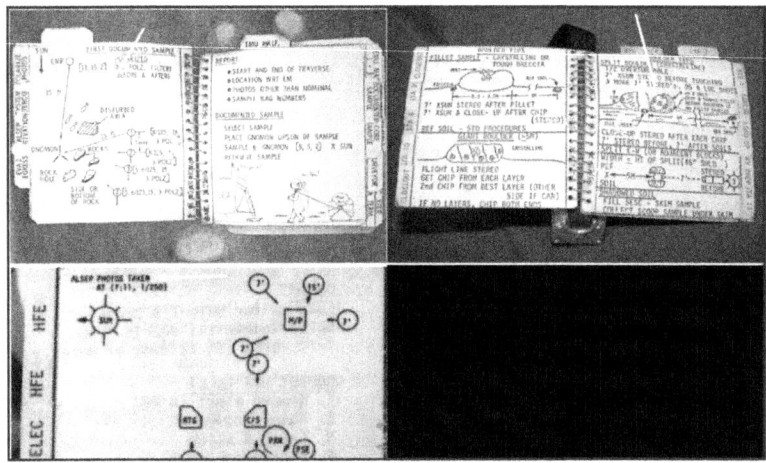

This photo shows the checklists worn on the cuff of each astronaut. It's obvious that these checklists were prepared for each mission, which is peculiar since NASA could not have known minute details of the lunar surface like the size, shape, and locations of the rocks. There are other details like camera settings, position of the Sun, where the footprints would be located, and mineral content of the rocks, which NASA could not have known about.

On the lower left are story boards and cue cards used for filming the scene. Because of the spacesuits, the astronauts could not hear instructions from the film crew and the helmets would restrict their vision. The cuff checklists were not used for the Apollo 11 mission.

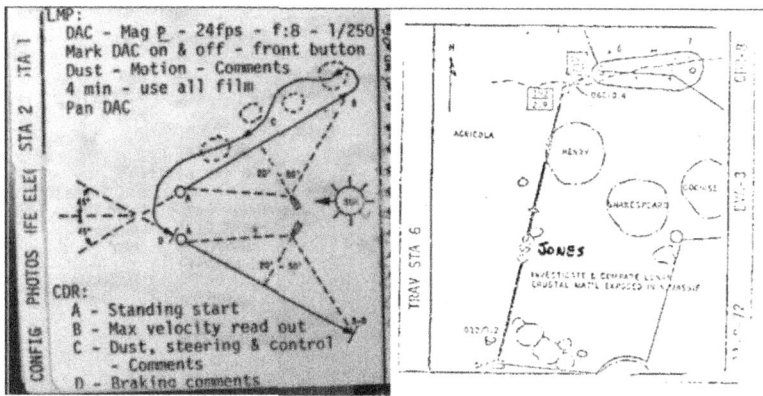

This is the Apollo 17 checklist with more details NASA could not have known about, like the location of craters for the astronauts to drive to and around. The right side of the photo shows the name Jones, who was the onsite inspector for the filming. His location as to where he was standing is clearly marked.

AS-37-5443 This photo is peculiar in that at no time in the mission was the LM in a higher lunar orbit than the CM. So how this photo was taken, is anyone's guess. And the reflection in the CM should show the blackness of space, with some refection from the Earth. But that's not what is shown. Instead, it appears to be some sort of backdrop with three men. Two of them are facing the left, while the other is facing the camera.

AS16-106-17390 and AS17-137-20979 There were supposedly three Moon rovers taken to the Moon. Notice the damage to the fender on both of these Moon rovers. The astronauts placed a map on the fender to prevent the 'Moon dust' from flying up at them. It's quite a coincidence to have the same damage, in the same area, with the same makeshift method of fixing it. This of course is the same rover, that was used for both Apollo 16 and 17.

AS17-134-20383 The arrows in the photo point to moisture on the flag. But moisture will quickly evaporate in the vacuum of space. So, unless one of the astronauts found some means of throwing water on it, the photo was obviously taken in a studio, which *throws water* on NASA's claims.

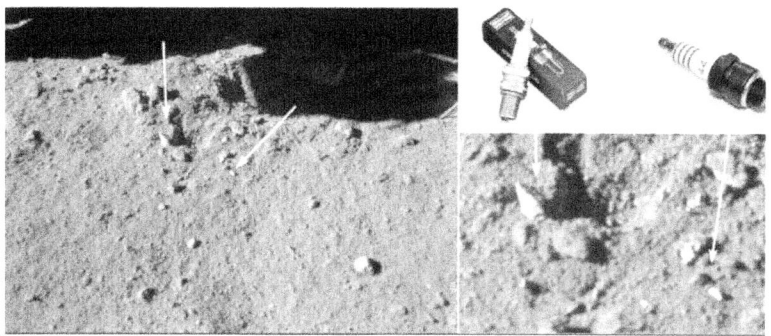

AS15-86-11681 This is the famous Genesis Moon rock, which is now on display. But, there just happened to be two sparkplugs seen inside the rock when it was kicked by one of the astronauts. These sparkplugs were put there on purpose, in an attempt to leave a record of the fakery that went on.

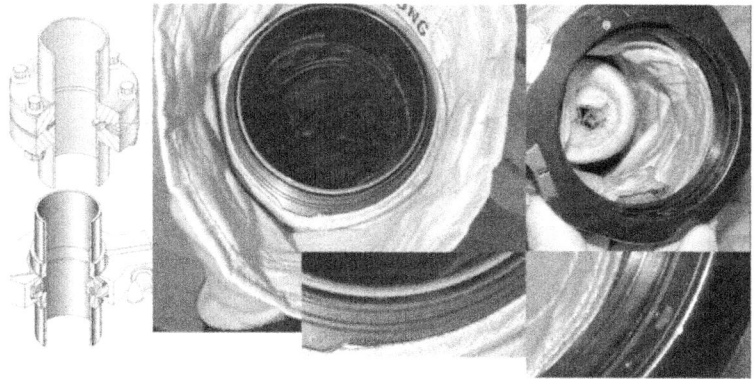

On the left, are examples of seals used to contain a vacuum. For the Apollo Moon missions, seals would have had to be compressed to maintain the astronauts' atmosphere within their spacesuits in the ultra high vacuum on the lunar surface. On the right, is Neil Armstrong's glove. The connection that holds the glove to the spacesuit, is like a door latch that is pushed into the channel. The seal is not compressed between the metal. This connection could not have maintained the pressure within the spacesuit. However, it works well in simulations here on Earth where no pressurization of the spacesuit is necessary.

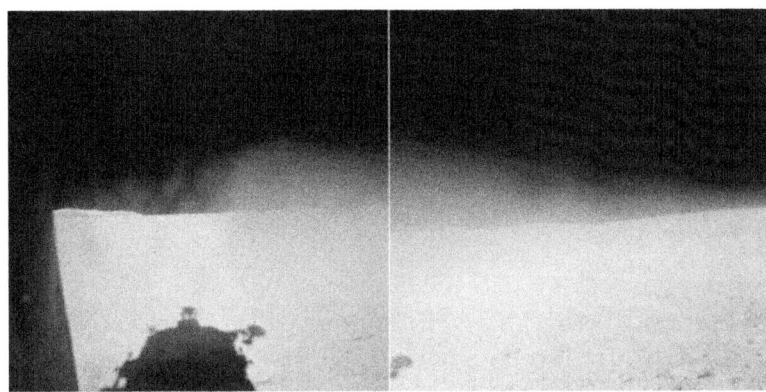

AS16-113-1806 These two photos show what appears to be mist on the Moon. Since there is no wind on the lunar surface, it's obvious the studio work crew kicked up dust, while preparing the scene for the next film shoot. This is another photo that was taken deliberately to show the fakery going on.

AS17-134-2083 In the left photo, Harrison H. Schmitt has picked up some mud on his arm. In the right photo, it has been washed off and the spacesuit is still wet, in which the liquid should have evaporated in lunar conditions long before this photo was taken.

AS11-40-5903 In the left photo, Buzz Aldrin is standing with his foot beside a rock. In the right photo taken twenty-two photos later, the are no longer any footprints beside the same rock. This indicates that the same scene had been reorganized for each photo shoot.

AS11-37-5467 The photo on the right was taken by the Hasselblad camera, and the photo on the left was taken from a video camera. Both of these photos were taken from inside the LM and both show the same scene, yet the flag is in different positions. In the left photo, notice the shadow from the flag is on the left, while in the right photo, the shadow from the flag is on the right. Since both photos were taken from the same position, the flag should be in the same position too and clearly, it's not. And the LM engine had not been fired for liftoff when this photo was taken, as there is no lunar dust being blown around. So, there was no force that moved the flag. The only possibility is either Armstrong or Aldrin climbed back down the ladder to position the flag for a better photo, or the liftoff scene was filmed later. And since there is no record of Armstrong or Aldrin climbing back down the ladder for a second extra vehicular activity, the flag in this scene was repositioned by someone else.

AS15-88-11901   AS16-107-17445   AS17-146-22296   These photos for Apollo 15, 16, and 17 show the rover that was allegedly brought to the Moon. All of the photos show the same oil leak in the rear axle on the left side of the rover. These photos clearly show the same rover being used for all three missions. This is more evidence of fakery since if these missions were real, it would have been impossible to have used the same rover for all three missions.

This is Apollo 17 rover. Notice the different tire tracks. The three Apollo missions that supposedly carried a rover, landed in different areas of the Moon. So, there should only be one set of tire tracks for each mission. Here, we have three tire tracks for one mission. So, either the one rover that was used for all three missions had tire changes, or there was a different vehicle other than the rover responsible for the other tire tracks.

This CM window was damaged or blown out during a pressure test. As is clear in the photo, tape was used to help secure it and a rain guard was installed (which is broken) in an attempt to keep water out. However, notice how the water between the glass is streaking down the window. That's not possible in zero gravity. And further, the glass on the outside would reach temperatures as low as -250 degrees from the window on the outside of the CM. However, there should be no moisture whatsoever, and neither should there be a broken seal, which would have led to decompression of the CM, killing the astronauts almost instantly.

Scott's work is published on www.aulis.com. Further, his work has been produced in video format by Robert Williams which are posted on his YouTube channel, Apollo Detectives.

Appendix E

Phil Kouts, PhD

Phil Kouts has researched different aspects of the Apollo missions. He has a PhD in applied physics and is a research fellow in various universities in the United Kingdom, and has held the position as Research and Development manger in several companies.

One area Kouts has researched, is the photographic record. In one of his published articles, he scrutinizes the only two photos of the Earth allegedly taken from the lunar surface during the Apollo 11 mission, or more to the point, who actually took the photos and how it was done. For example, he details how there was little discussion between Neil Armstrong and Buzz Aldrin while taking the photos, which surely would have been an awe-inspiring sight. Further, he questions just how impossible it would have been for either of the astronauts to have taken the photos, given how Armstrong or Aldrin would have had to position themselves.

Figure E1: AS11-40-5923
Source: NASA

In the photo above, you'll notice the back of the LM, which is almost in centre frame with the Earth off to the right of centre and above it. And the fact that each astronaut's camera was positioned on their chest, would mean either Armstrong or Aldrin would have had to bend backwards up to 55 degrees to have taken this photo. This of course would have been virtually impossible even with one assisting the other.

However, since this was allegedly the first manned landing on the lunar surface, it's reasonable to assume that neither Armstrong nor Aldrin would have taken this photo, given how they would have had to position themselves. Any wrong move could have caused a tear in their spacesuits. That would have spelled disaster and since no one knew for sure what to expect, presumably the safety of the astronauts would have been the first priority. Yet according to the official photographic record, this photo was taken from the lunar surface, but as to which of the two astronauts took it, is not known.

Further, Kouts also scrutinizes the photos taken of the Earth by Mike Collins while allegedly in lunar orbit. But there are many questions about these photos too.

Phil Kouts:

> There is a further series of pictures, AS11-44-66 to 6643, taken, obviously, by Mike Collins after the LM's ascent module allegedly took off from the lunar surface, before its docking with the orbiting Command and Service Module (CSM). In these frames, the Earth is visible in the background when the LM is approaching the CSM. These pictures should have been the definitive evidence of the event. **However, analysis of the timing shows that these pictures do not quite correspond to the expected rotation of Earth. The**

continents should clearly include South America, but they do not.[1]

Kouts also notices some peculiarities with the photos of Earth allegedly taken from the lunar surface on the Apollo 17 mission. Kouts points out that when the photos are enlarged, both the Apollo 11 and Apollo 17 photos that were allegedly taken of Earth from the lunar surface, all show the same position with the Pacific Ocean facing the astronauts which should show Australia too, only for the fact that it is covered by dense clouds. This is strange given that the Apollo 17 mission was in early December, when it was summer over Australia. Therefore, there shouldn't have been so much cloud over Australia, at least during the Apollo 17 mission.

Obviously, these photos weren't taken on either mission. Instead, Kouts believes that if these photos are genuine, then they were taken from the Application Technology Satellite (ATS-1), which was in a geostationary orbit at an altitude of 22,236 miles above the Earth. Its purpose was to provide up to date cloud cover information up until October 16, 1972. And though this satellite was no longer providing photos of Earth during the Apollo 17 mission, similar satellites for example ATS-2 to ATS-4 were producing photos.

Kouts concludes:

> The only view of Earth is over the Pacific Ocean. Despite the Apollo astronauts allegedly having spent about 80 hours on the lunar surface during their EVA's, supposedly over that time seeing virtually all Earth's continents, they didn't take any other views except a few with Australia in the corner. By the start of Apollo flights, NASA developed a capability to take pictures of the full-disk Earth which were entirely suitable for illustrating any flight beyond LEO. It is logical to

assume that photos of Earth taken by the Application Technology Satellites (ATS) were used to simulate those allegedly shot by the Apollo crews.[2]

Phil Kouts' articles have much more detail than what I've presented here, and I encourage everyone to check them out. His work has been published on www.nexusmagazine.com and on www.aulis.com.

Appendix E - Endnotes

[1] Phil Kouts, *Earth Photos from the Moon: Anomalies AFTERWORD to Part One*, November 2014, published on www.aulis.com.

[2] Phil Kouts, Earth Photos from the Moon 3: Inconsistencies: Part Three: Apollo 17.

Appendix F

Emanuel E. Garcia, M.D.

Dr. Emanuel Garcia is a psychiatrist and psychoanalyst by training and practice, and uses his brilliant skills to research the Apollo Moon missions. I came by his work while researching this subject, and I was immediately impressed with his unique approach. In one if his published articles, he analyses some of the strange behaviour of the Apollo astronauts, in particular, the Apollo 11 astronauts shortly after their return from their alleged historic mission to the Moon, which we'll discuss here.

Most, if not all of us researching the Apollo missions remember the moment when Neil Armstrong allegedly first walked on the lunar surface. No matter your age, everyone sensed the historical significance of what had just occurred. It dominated every conversation, and as children, we acted out our new heroes' achievements. It was a moment when we were all united and, it was a moment that would never be quite captured that way again.

As we gain hindsight over the years and decades, we get more clarity. And sometimes that hindsight forces us to re-evaluate our perceived notions of reality, which can often lead to certain truths that some people refuse to accept, no matter how much evidence is presented. This aptly applies to what we once thought was man's greatest scientific accomplishment, the Apollo Moon missions. To find out that you've been lied to by the very people and government you trusted, changes your reality forever. It is an adjustment that some people find difficult to make. But for those seeking enlightenment, it is another path forward.

However, it seems that some of the very people involved in the Apollo Moon hoax, were themselves struggling to make their own adjustments. This is clearly noticeable among the three astronauts in the post Apollo 11 press conference.

Dr. Garcia explains:

> The post flight press conference in its entirety was highly unusual: instead of ebullience, elation or the modesty restrained exuberance of champions after having accomplished one of the most daring and magnificent feats in human history, Armstrong, Aldrin and Collins acted like rather nervously subdued miscreants. It is an item worthy of an essay or perhaps even a book in its own right. [1]

Figure F1: Post Apollo 11 press conference
Source: Aulis.com

For anyone who has watched this press conference, it's not exactly the most riveting description of what was called, man's greatest scientific achievement. Proponents of the Apollo missions often counter this with things like, "If you go to such and such a time in the video, you'll see them smile," "They were worn out and deeply affected by their experience," "They were trained technical professionals and rarely showed any emotion," and on it goes... There was even a moment in the press conference when Michael Collins seems to get nervous and even attempts to correct an answer Neil Armstrong gave in response to a reporter's question, while Buzz Aldrin looked on seemingly perplexed:

> Like the famous dog that didn't bark in Conan Doyle's Sherlock Holmes story *Silver Blaze*, during the Apollo missions stars apparently didn't shine. In a lunar sky that had no distorting atmosphere Neil Armstrong and Buzz Aldrin would have been provided with a dazzling and spectacular display the likes of which no one has ever seen before, a peering into the vast bright twinkling immensity of the universe. <u>At the Apollo 11 flight press conference, the three astronauts were asked specifically about stars by reporter Patrick Moore.</u> The incredulous answer from Michael Collins was: **"I don't remember seeing any."** [2]

Astronauts from onboard the International Space Station have reported seeing an abundance of stars, so both Armstrong and Aldrin should have been able to see stars from the lunar surface. So, astronauts can see stars whether its from LEO, lunar orbit, or the lunar surface. However, Collins apparently saw a need to correct Armstrong, which made for a very tense moment between Armstrong and Collins.

As many of you have observed in the official photographic and film record, there are little or no stars either on photos allegedly taken from the lunar surface, nor on the journey to and from the Moon. There have been several explanations for this, including that the camera lens was not configured to pick up stars. However, the solution to that problem would have been to provide another camera that was configured to pick up the stars. The Apollo 16 mission allegedly took photos of the stars using a Far Ultraviolet Camera. But these photos do not compare to the stars as described by astronauts on other missions. And to spend billions of dollars of taxpayers' money, then neglect to take photos of something that surely would have been a spectacular sight, leaves one wondering how they managed to miss such a golden opportunity.

Then there is the harsh environment of the lunar surface. Yet, the Apollo films show carefree astronauts cavorting on the lunar surface, appearing oblivious to the potential dangers they were literally seconds away from at any moment. One tear in their spacesuits, and the entire mission would have been over instantly. Why any astronaut would take a chance with this type of behaviour on a baren world with a harsh environment, 240,000 miles away, with seemingly no concern for the enormous risks involved on the surface, knowing that rescue was impossible, is as baffling as it is disturbing. However, there's a reason for this strange behaviour:

> These irrational touches, however, were a purposeful part of the mission to persuade, a critical aspect of the most effective propaganda designed to appeal to our deepest irrational urges and allow them to override critical and common-sense thinking. It is a particularly devious method of persuasion that deliberately presents us with patent absurdities, which we willingly swallow hook, line and sinker, making our submission all the more complete.[3]

This goes a long way in explaining some peoples' refusal to look at the Apollo Moon missions objectively. It conflicts with there preconceived notion of reality. To believe otherwise, would force them to re-evaluate an established set of norms.

Dr. Garcia investigates other aspects of the Apollo missions, including the alleged re-entry of the Apollo CM into Earth's atmosphere. His work is available on www.aulis.com.

Appendix F - Endnotes

[1] Emanuel E. Garcia, M.D., *How High the Moon?* Or the *Greatest Deception of Them All*

[2] Ibid.

[3] Emanuel E. Garcia, *Moon Landings: Magnificent and Deviously Contrived Propaganda*

Glossary

AFIT	Air Force Institution of Technology
AGC	Apollo Guidance Computer
AGL	Above Ground Level
AGS	Abort Guidance System
ASTP	Apollo Soyuz Test Project
CALTECH	California Institute of Technology
CAPCOM	Capsule Communicator
CIA	Central Intelligence Agency
CM	Command Module
CSM	Command Service Module
DAC	Data Acquisition Camera
DISC	Defence Industrial Security Command
EOR	Earth Orbit Rendezvous
EVA	Extra Vehicle Activity
FBI	Federal Bureau of Investigation
FIRE	Flight Investigation of the Re-enter Environment
FRC	Flight Research Center
GALCIT	Guggenheim Aeronautical Laboratory at the California Institute of Technology
IERB	Industrial Employment Review Board
ISS	International Space Station
JATO	Jet Associated Take-Off
JPL	Jet Propulsion Laboratory
LEO	Low Earth Orbit
LLRV	Lunar Landing Research Vehicle
LLTV	Lunar Landing Training Vehicle
LM	Lunar Module

LMS	Lunar Module Simulator
LOR	Lunar Orbit Rendezvous
LPD	Landing Point Destination
LRO	Lunar Reconnaissance Orbiter
MASCONS	Mass Concentration of Gravity
MSM	Main Street Media
NACA	National Advisory Committee for Aeronautics
NAS	National Academy of Science
NASA	National Aeronautics and Space Administrator
NSAM	National Security Action Memorandum
OTO	Ordo Templi Orientis
PGNS	Primary Guidance and Navigation System
RCS	Reaction Control System
SPE	Solar Particle Event
TASS	Russian New Agency
TSBD	Texas School Book Depository
USCGC	United States Coastal Guard Cutter
VTOL	Vertical Take-off and Landing Vehicle

Bibliography

Books

Author	Title
Bara, Mike	*ANCIENT ALIENS & JFK: The Race to the Moon and the Kennedy Assassination.* Adventures Unlimited Press, 2018.
Carter, John	*Sex and rockets: THE OCCULT OWRLD OF JACK PARSONS, new edition.* Feral House, March 10, 2005.
Engle, Michael	*LANDING EAGLE: INSIDE THE COCKPIT DURING THE FIRST MOON LANDING.* Telemachus Press, LLC, 2019
Eyles, Don	*SUNBURST AND LUMINARY: AN APOLLO MEMOIR.* Forty Point Press, 2018.
Hall, Eldon C	*JOURNEY TO THE MOON: The History Of The Apollo Guidance Computer.* American Institute of Aeronautics & Astronautics, Inc., 1996
Hansen, James R Platoff, Anne M	*APOLLO: AMERICA'S MOON LANDING PROGRAM: ENCHANTED RENDEZVOUS - John Houboldt and the Genesis of the Lunar-Orbit Rendezvous Concept, and POLITICAL AND TECHNICAL ASPECTS OF PLACING A FLAG ON THE MOON.* Progressive Management Publications, Independently published, January 2013
Hansen, James R.	*FIRST MAN: The Life of NEIL A. ARMSTRONG.* Simon and Shuster Paperbacks, 2018
Harland, David M.	*PAVING THE WAY FOR APOLLO 11.* Springer. Published in association with Praxis Publishing, Chichester, UK, 2009

Hegland, T J	*Virtual Earth Graduate. Man, Creation, ETs, OPs, Angels, Souls, Holograms, DNA, Serpent Wisdom, Gnosticism, the Interlife, Karma, DejaVu, the Bionet, Simulation, the Control System and more – how they fit our special reality*
Launius, Roger D	*APOLLO'S LEGACY: PERSPECTIVES ON THE MOON LANDINGS*
Launius, Roger D Jenkins, Dennis R	*NASA AERONAUTICS BOOK SERIES: COMING HOME: Reentry and Recovery from Space.* CreateSpace Independent Publishing Platform, November 8, 2013.
National Aeronautics and Space Administration (NASA), World Spaceflight News, Gene J. Mantranga, C. Wayne Ottinger, Calvin R. Jarvis, D. Christian Gelzer	*APOLLO and AMERICA'S MOON LANDING PROGRAM: Unconventional, Contrary, and Ugly. The Lunar Landing Research Vehicle (NASA SO-2004-4535).* Progressive Management Publications, Independently published, April 5, 2018.
National Aeronautics and Space Administration, World Spaceflight News, Michael D. Bjorkman, Eric L. Christianson	*APOLLO and AMERICA'S MOON LANDING PROGRAM: Apollo Meteoroid Shielding Design and Analysis at the Manned Spacecraft Center.* Progressive Management Publications, Independently published, January 2013
Pellegrino, Charles R Stoff, Joshua	*CHARROITS OF APOLLO: THE UNTOLD STRORY BEHIND THE RACE TO THE MOON.* Avon Books, INC., 1999
Pendle, Georgre	*STRANGE ANGEL: THE OTHERWORDLY LIFE OF ROCKET SCIENTIST JOHN WHITSIDE PARSONS.* Mariner Books, First edition, February 6, 2006.
Stoff, Joshua	*BUILDING MOONSHIPS: THE GRUMMAN LUNAR MODULE.* Arcadia Publishing, 2004
Thomas, Andy	*CONSPIRACIES: THE FACTS-THE THEORIES-THE EVIDENCE.* Published by Watkins Media Ltd., 2015

U. S. Government, National Aeronautics and Space Administration (NASA), World Spaceflight News (WSN)	*Destination Moon: A History of the Lunar Orbiter Program: NASA Apollo Moon Landing Preparations, Boeing and Kodak Photo System, Problems with the Spacecraft, Great Lunar Exploration Achievements.* Progressive Management Publications, 2018
Wever, Trevor	*THE APOLLO MOON HOAX: HOW DID THEY DO IT? A Generation Deceived by NASA*
Zupp, George A	*APOLLO: AMERICA'S MOON LANDING PROGRAM: Lunar Module Touchdown Dynamics: An Analysis and a Historical Review of the Apollo Program.* Progressive Management Publications, Independently published, January 2013

Bibliography
Internet Sources

Author & Link

Bennett, Mary DM

https://www.aulis.com/re-entrymatters.htm

Bennett, Mary DM and Percy, David S

https://www.aulis.com/odyssey_apollo.htm

Birch, Julius A

https://www.aulis.com/apollo17_ascent.htm

Bulatov, Andrei
and Boyko, Alexander

https://www.aulis.com/april_november.htm

Garcia, Emanuel E., MD

https://www.aulis.com/high_moon.htm

Kouts, Phil, PhD

https://www.aulis.com/moon-earth.htm

Kouts, Phil, PhD

https://www.aulis.com/moon-earth_afterword.htm

Kouts, Phil, PhD
https://www.aulis.com/moon-earth3.htm

Pascal, Xavier
https://www.aulis.com/csm-lm_orbit.htm

Popov, Alexander, PhD and Bulatov, Andrei
https://www.aulis.com/apollo_fake_reentry.htm

Williams, Robert, studio engineer & Master Electrician
https://www.aulis.com/vacuum.htm